THIRD EDITION

GYMNASTICS for WOMEN

Blanche Jessen Drury, Ed.D., R.P.T.
Professor of Physical Education
San Francisco State College

Andrea Bodo Schmid, Ed.D.
Olympic Gold Medalist
Associate Professor of Physical Education
San Francisco State College

Illustrated by
Patricia Thomson, Ph.D.
Associate Professor of Physical Education
Fresno State College

NATIONAL PRESS BOOKS

850 Hansen Way / Palo Alto, California 94304

Contents

Part I   History, Conditioning, Dance

Part II   Modern Rhythmic Gymnastics

Part III Apparatus and Competitive Gymnastics

Part IV   Curriculum, Demonstrations, Meets, Judging

Preface to the First Edition

To move efficiently with grace, dignity, rhythm, and form is perhaps the goal of all physical activity for women. Gymnastics lends itself to the development of a body which responds at will, which moves with rhythmical accuracy, which is effeminate in quality.

It is hoped that with more information about gymnastics, better programs in schools and recreational centers will be developed. Gymnastics is a self-motivating activity, though proper instruction is necessary for safe and correct development of the body.

The purpose of this book is to bring together in one volume the information necessary for a complete gymnastics program. Much of the material has been handed down from teacher to student, particularly the hand apparatus, with little written material available. Likewise, the skills on the apparatus, particularly the balance beam and uneven parallel bars, are as complete as is currently possible.

The authors hope that this information will assist in the development of more girl gymnasts throughout the nation.

June 1964

Blanche Jessen Drury
Andrea Bodo Schmid

Preface to the Third Edition

During the years since 1964, when this book was first published, there has been a tremendous increase in interest in women's gymnastics. As the quantity and quality of gymnastics have developed there have been more and more requests for information.

Many requests have been made to the authors for information on how to execute newer skills which have been invented and combined by gymnasts at all levels. Since the first edition of the text, there have been two Olympics, many national meets and world championships. The greater coverage of these events by the press and television, as well as many new audiovisual materials, has brought a better understanding of this feminine sport. The greater knowledge has in turn upgraded the quality of performance at meets, from the novice to the national and international levels.

With this in mind the authors have attempted to do two things. First, to include many more and many new skills, each one being carefully analyzed and illustrated. Along with the new skills are combinations and sequences to help illustrate the need for continuity and movement flow so necessary in the present gymnastics for women.

Secondly, in response to many requests from teachers and coaches, the authors have listed teaching suggestions for each event. Progression being a most important part in the development of a gymnast, the teaching suggestions will assist the coach and teacher to take the gymnast through the various steps until success is accomplished in the more difficult skills.

To review the specific changes in content, the Introduction and History have been brought up to date. The Warm-up and Conditioning Programs have been revised to be specific for the needs of the gymnast. Corrections and a few additions have been made in some of the skills and drawings in the chapter on Dance for Gymnasts. Also corrections have been made in Part II Rhythmic Gymnastics.

The major additions have been made in Part III Apparatus and Competitive Gymnastics. Each event, balance beam, floor exercise, uneven parallel bars, vaulting, trampoline and tumbling, has been completely revised. A better progression of skills has been organized and numerous new skills have been included. In each of these events, combinations have been included which are fully illustrated.

In Part IV Curriculum, Demonstrations, and Meets, the greatest change has been in Chapter 19. The chapter on the Gymnastic Meet now gives sufficient material so that the novice will have the tools with which to organize a meet, whether it be on the intramural level or higher levels. The content has been split and a separate chapter (Chapter 20) on Judging is included. This gives the new judging techniques which have been developed since the last Olympics and which will be adopted in future meets.

The authors believe this new volume is most complete and should give valuable assistance to the development of gymnastics in this country.

Acknowledgments are in order to the National Press Staff for their cooperation in this revision; and to the many teachers and gymnasts from many classes and clinics who have offered their criticisms and suggestions.

June 1970

Blanche Jessen Drury
Andrea Bodo Schmid

Introduction

Gymnastics is one of the oldest forms of organized physical activity, and today it is being reorganized, revitalized by changes and renewed interest. Gymnastics for women is indeed expressing a new surge of interest in the United States; perhaps because of the renewed interest in physical fitness, but possibly more because of the great changes which have taken place in gymnastics for women. Today, form, poise, grace, and flowing movement are replacing the older concepts of rigidly held positions and strength movements that were frequently copied from the men. There is a birth of new interest in the smaller hand apparatus: the balls, ropes, hoops, wands, and clubs. This interest is founded on the appreciation of the rhythmical assistance that these objects can give to the performer. The inept girl becomes engrossed in the movement of the object and, before she is aware of it, the rhythmical movement has become a part of her body.

Gymnastics holds many values for the performer: The development of courage, the development of a feeling of exultation in the achievement of a skill when finally mastered, the appreciation of beauty in line and movement, the feeling for rhythm in movement, and the appreciation of choreographic design and creativity.

The apparatus for women are used today with an attempt to bring out the beauty of body line, the continuous flow of movement, and the effeminate quality of the performer.

One has but to review the Olympic exercises over the past decade or more to note the great change that has taken place in gymnastics. In floor exercise the whole quality of the compulsory exercise is one of flowing movement, employing many dance steps to bring together the tumbling and special stunts, which must melt into a complete whole. One is conscious of the choreographic design and feminine line and grace which have completely divorced this event from any resemblance of masculine strength. Even the more difficult tumbling stunts must be done with an elegance and with the illusion of effortless strength.

The uneven parallel bars have perhaps seen the greatest change. The movements are almost a continuous flow of swinging, circling, and kipping movements, with only two pauses allowed for preparation for difficult moves. Strength moves have disappeared from this event and one is impressed by the flow of movement from one bar to the other.

The exercise on the balance beam has been shortened over the years to make it more interesting and more dynamic. Though this is primarily an exercise of balance, turns, jumps, leaps, and running steps are interspersed throughout the routine to give it dynamic rhythm. The movements on the beam have been speeded up and only three stops are allowed in the exercise. The gymnast should move fast and only "mark" a static position of balance on hands or feet. There is a trend to use more tumbling moves in the routine. The posture and line of the gymnast is so discernible on the beam, that perfection of line is a must.

As the performance ability has increased in vaulting, the table of values has been raised. With the introduction of such new vaults as the Yamashita, and various twisting vaults, the old straight vaults have been lowered in value. In international competition most of the vaults are now twisting vaults. The turn or twist may be done during the preflight, the afterflight, or in both parts of the flight.

Though competition on the trampoline is not part of the Olympic games, there are many national and international meets on this apparatus. Trampoline is a very popular activity in schools and offers an excellent way to learn control of the body in space. The understanding of the center of gravity of the body, and the feeling of anti-gravity, are best learned on this apparatus.

Tumbling is perhaps the basis of most gymnastics, and should be taught as a foundation for all other events. A basic control of the body is learned, and the gymnast will develop a basic vocabulary and skill for similar movements in all events.

Thus we see that women's gymnastics has grown considerably and great strides have been made in the teaching of gymnastics for girls and women at all levels. Many more regions are organizing for competition, and the development of responsible judges has become a reality. As the sport develops we must always bear in mind, however, that for every one who may go to the Olympics there are thousands of girls who are enjoying the feeling of fitness and the excitement of performing through participating in gymnastics.

Part I   HISTORY, CONDITIONING, DANCE

Chapter 1   A Brief Résumé of Gymnastics for Women in the United States

The historical picture of the woman gymnast is a comical one to the viewer today. We see a girl in a high-collared, low-sleeved garment with ankle-length full skirt, posing rigidly with a wand or dumbbell. Another picture shows a group similarly attired in the gymnasium, rigidly performing exercises with utmost intent and precision.

A look at the first half of the nineteenth century gives us W. B. Fowle, a teacher in Boston who was interested in the gymnastics which had been imported from Germany in 1825, and which system was being introduced in New England for boys. The system included hanging and swinging bars, the use of pulleys, and some arm exercises. Mr. Fowle wrote that he had found women to be much less delicate, feeble, and helpless than had formerly been expressed. (The various early systems and programs are discussed in books included in the Bibliography.)

Although such early experiments with apparatus for girls were apparently very short lived, they gave way to three types of exercise: calisthenics, domestic duties, and dancing. Performance of domestic duties, which may have had some economic value at college of that time, gave way to social training in later years. Dancing has remained a part of the physical education program, and calisthenics, although greatly changed in form and method, remains today.

From 1830 to 1860 the interest in physical education for girls developed around physiology and hygiene. In 1848 a number of political refugees from Germany introduced the gymnastic society called the Turnvereine, and in 1855 they introduced classes for girls. In 1860 Dio Lewis came to Boston and founded his school. His system was composed of light rhythmical exercises using rings, wands, wooden dumbbells; it was designed to develop flexibility, agility, and grace of movement. The school of Dio Lewis was in existence only seven years, but the girls who trained there became the gymnastic teachers in schools and colleges.

In 1881 Dr. Sargent, as Director of the Hemenway Gymnastics at Harvard, stressed a new system of physical education. This system was based on a thorough examination and detailed measurements of the body. Those muscles found to be weak were strengthened by individually prescribed exercises.

In 1889 the Swedish gymnastic school was introduced to the teachers of Boston. This system discarded hand apparatus entirely and instead used marching exercises performed in definite rigid unison.

During the fifty years between 1850 and 1900 the social as well as the physical value of physical training was beginning to be recognized. It was becoming apparent that women were not the weak creatures they were supposed to be and, as a result, physical education for women was becoming a part of the school program.

In the first part of the twentieth century (1900-1929) sports and games became popular and developed into important branches of physical education for girls and women. Dr. Thomas Wood of Teachers College, Columbia University, stated in 1910 that the rigid control and discipline imposed by an instructor in a gymnastic class did not allow for the self-discipline and self-control, nor self-expression, which may be found in the sports program.

This was contrary to the principles set down by William Skarstrom in his book, Gymnastic Teaching, issued in 1921. He believed that definiteness of Swedish gymnastics should train the power of voluntary attention, sharpen the kinesthetic sense, and develop a quick and accurate motor response.

During the years 1924 to 1929 the work of Niels Bukh of Denmark began to replace the Swedish and German systems. The so-called Danish, or non-definite, exercises allowed for more freedom, rhythm, and variety. With interest in greater freedom in exercise came a need for more freedom in costume. There has been a great change from the early gymnasium costume with long sleeves, high collar, and full skirt to the jersey leotard of today.

The need for a freer type of gymnastics became apparent, and the work of Madam Carlquist in the 1939 and 1949 Lingiads of Sweden showed this trend in a new approach to the original principles of Per Henrik Ling, the founder of Swedish gymnastics. Madam Carlquist developed the Sofia girls who toured the United States, and helped to introduce balance movements which are now so popular on the balance beam.

Women first participated in team gymnastics in the Olympic Games in 1928, in Amsterdam. An understanding of this development and the subsequent effect on gymnastics in the schools can best be shown by a comparison of two accounts of gymnastics. The first is a Russian book by B. Velyakov on Soviet Gymnasts;

the second, an American book entitled, The Story of the Olympic Games, 776 B.C. to 1952 A.D., by John Kieran and Arthur Daley. From the detailed accounts of individual women gymnasts discussed in the Russian book, one gathers that the women were really very interested in the development and accomplishments of women in the Olympics; also, that many schools looked to the Olympics as a source of information as well as a goal for their performers. In reading the American account of the Olympics, one gets a different impression; in fact, one has to hunt diligently to find any facts about the early women gymnasts. This, however, was abruptly changed at the 1952 games at Helsinki, when individual events were first held. The Russian girl gymnasts suddenly came up with 60-1/2 points to none for the United States. Ordinarily, this feat would have caught no one's eye; it caught the headlines because it indicated that the Soviet Union was leading America in total points: 137-1/2 to 115, which included women's track and field.

The wonderful coverage of the 1960 Olympics by television brought to the largest audience in the world the latest ideas and very best performers. The lay person was astounded by the beauty of performance of the women gymnasts. Many began to appreciate this newer approach to gymnastics which developed grace, poise, and femininity in the woman performer. With this came an upsurge in the interest in gymnastics—particularly in the schools—and this burst of enthusiasm made an impact on most girls' physical education programs. The systems and methods previously used in developing rhythm and flexibility—such as wands, balls, ropes, clubs, hoops—and which had been discarded as old-fashioned, are now accepted as excellent means for developing freedom and feminine-type movement. Likewise, physical education budgets everywhere began to include requests for a balance beam or uneven parallel bars. In some schools the teachers began to dust off the old vaulting box or horse, while others found old Indian clubs and began to make compositions in music—considered quite original by the newer generation!

We believe there are two possible explanations for this swing of the pendulum toward more gymnastics in the school program:

First, we believe the national interest in developing girl gymnasts capable of Olympic competition begins at the school level. If accomplishment in the Olympic Games helps symbolize the physical well-being of a country, then we must show our abilities and develop women who are capable of vying with the best for honors. Upon this theme the 1963 National Institute on Girls' Sports was held at Norman, Oklahoma, November 4-9. This institute was sponsored jointly by the Women's Board of the U.S. Olympic Development Committee and the Division for Girls' and Women's Sports of the American Association for Health, Physical Education and Recreation. It stressed the need for developing women in gymnastics and track and field. Since then two more National Institutes on Girls' Sports have been devoted partially to gymnastics for the sole purpose of helping physical educators improve their gymnastic programs for girls.

A second reason for the interest in gymnastics may stem from the national stress on fitness. Gymnastics is a natural method for developing the body and one which is perhaps much more satisfying than to do twenty-five push-ups, or fifty sit-ups, or to take a fifty-mile hike.

The 1968 Olympic Games in Mexico City reflected the tremendous growth of the women's gymnastics program in America. The team placed sixth, the best in Olympic competition in two decades. Also in the individual competition, Cathy Rigby placed sixteenth in All-Around, and Linda Metheny placed fourth on the Balance Beam. These are the best individual positions any U.S. girl gymnast has ever achieved. It will be interesting to see how long the pendulum will swing in this direction; only the future can tell.

The preceding is but a brief résumé of gymnastics as a whole; the specific background of each apparatus will be given at the beginning of the respective chapters.

Chapter 2   Warm-up and Conditioning Programs

CONTROL FACTORS

The desire of the gymnast is to have a body that is completely controlled, capable of responding to any demand. Certain factors contribute to this complete control, and these will be discussed in the following paragraphs.

Strength

The gymnast must have developed muscular strength so that she can control her body in innumerable planes of action. Research reveals that girls have very weak shoulder girdles; therefore, a warm-up and conditioning program would certainly have to develop those muscle groups. The force necessary to push off with the feet and spring into the air means that foot and leg muscles must be developed. The control of the trunk means an equal balance between trunk extensors and abdominal muscles. Strength is developed through the "overload principle" and, although weights may not always be used, the weight of the body is frequently sufficient to give this extra demand.

Flexibility

To perform most gymnastic movements, whether on the floor or on apparatus, the shoulder girdle must have complete range of motion, and particularly for dislocate movements. The legs must be capable of stretching into splits. The back must be capable of bending in a walkover. Such flexibility is found naturally in the very young, but it decreases with age. Hence, our conditioning program must include stretches to maintain and to increase the flexibility.

Balance

When using a stationary base, the center of gravity must be determined so that all forces may be balanced. To perform a scale, the tilt of the body forward and the lift of the leg in the rear must be balanced over the gravity point. When the body is moving through space, gravity is still a reality. The relationship of the head to the body and of the arms and legs to the body, the knowledge of the fulcrum point, and the feeling for new body positioning must be developed.

Endurance

Gymnastics makes a great demand upon the physiological processes of the body, on respiration and circulation as well as on the neuromuscular system. To develop endurance, it is necessary to prolong the activity period. The gymnast must have a continuous progression of activities, increasing the energy output and the time of activity. Endurance can be developed through a good program of conditioning exercises which make increasingly greater demands upon the body. Not only do we want to develop stamina, but also a certain emotional control which allows the individual to "throw" herself into the activity with a great amount of dynamic energy.

Coordination

To develop a coordinated movement, the body must call upon all the physiological processes. The movement must be repeated so that patterns of response are established. In gymnastics it is not sufficient to master a single stunt; it must be mastered in relationship to what preceded and what is to follow. Therefore, it is well to organize movements into a series so that the body becomes accustomed to the pattern. Movements are best learned if taught at optimum speed. Generally, it will be easier to learn movements if they are performed at optimum speed since momentum, change of position, gravity, and other related factors are necessary components. A sense of timing comes with repetition of a movement series. This is shown so well when the skilled gymnast does a round-off and a series of flip-flops. Perhaps it is because of the rhythm that is heard, but it is also possible to "feel" the timing of each part in relationship to the others.

The aforementioned components of a well-developed body are the goal of all physical activity. Because of the nature of gymnastics, many of these results can be achieved more quickly than others.

The following exercises are suggested to help the gymnast develop a better controlled body. A warm-up period should precede the gymnastic activities and the exercises listed, as well as various other forms of gymnastics, such as wands, rope stretching, rope climbing, and rhythmic gymnastics, may be used to condition the body for the more difficult movements and apparatus work. Scientifically, we do not know how long the warm-up period should be. This depends upon the situation; i.e., the length of the class period, the ability of the group, the desired objectives. All these factors must be determined by the teacher. It is true, however, that a warm-up period, no matter how short, sets the tone for the class and helps to organize the class activity.

ISOMETRICS*

It has been well established that isometric exercises develop strength very rapidly, though the strength is usually at the particular angle applied. Isometrics have value for gymnasts in developing the shoulder girdle, the abdomen, and the legs. The coach or teacher may want to select certain movements which the gymnast is able to do at home using a doorway or other resistance. It is imperative that the correct positioning and selection of the muscles to be strengthened are understood; also it is important that counteracting stretching accompany the movements to retain the flexibility so necessary in gymnastics.

An example using isometrics is to strengthen the shoulder girdle for dislocation. Have the gymnast sit in tailor or cross-legged position with a partner standing in the rear. The gymnast lifts her arms as if grasping the high bar in the dislocate (Eagle) position, pushing back with great force against the resistance of the partner who does not allow her to move her arms.

WEIGHT TRAINING*

The use of weights follows the physiological principle of overload, i.e., making the muscle work harder than it would normally do, and hence develop strength. Practically any movement may be made more difficult by adding resistance, and again selection is necessary to develop specific muscle groups.

An example in the use of weights might be to practice battements with a weight attached to the ankle. The new snap-on weights are excellent to use for the extremities.

WARM-UP

The type of warm-up should be a lead-up to the apparatus or activity for the day. For example, with the balance beam, floor exercise, or tumbling, more flexibility exercises would be included than if one were starting with uneven parallel bars where the emphasis would be on shoulder girdle and arm strength. If starting with trampoline, very little warm-up would be necessary.

The warm-up should include dance movements to improve form, grace, and posture.

_____

* For more detailed explanation, see Blanche Drury, Posture and Figure Control Through Physical Education, National Press, Chapters XI and XII.

For conditioning exercises the gymnast may use a dance barre, stall bars, or balance beam for support.

CONDITIONING EXERCISES

Exercises for Upper Extremity (Shoulder Girdle and Arm)

1.

S.P. Face lying, hands clasped over the low back, palms turned to the feet.

M. Contract the scapulae adductors and try to draw the elbows closer together; hold the contraction, release; repeat.

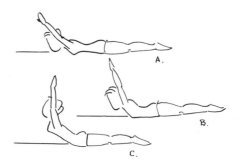

2.

S.P. Face lying, arms stretched over head close to ears.

M. a. Keep elbows extended, lift arms only from the floor, relax; repeat. When capable, progress to b, then to c.
b. Lift arms and head only, relax; repeat.
c. Lift arms, head, and shoulders slightly (do not arch low back).
d. Do all of the above movements using weights. Progress from one pound gradually so that strength is developed without unnecessary strain.
e. Do the same movements using a wand or tied rope (see chapters on wands and ropes).

3.

S.P. Tailor sitting, head in good position, arms horizontal.

_____

S.P. = Starting Position   M. = Movement

M. a. Describe small circles with arms, moving forward, upward, backward, and downward. Describe large circles. Vary between fast small circles and slow large circles.
   b. Do the same movements with weights in hands.

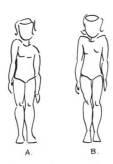

4.

S.P. On hands and knees, back flat.
M.   Fling one arm forcibly upward and backward, simultaneously twisting trunk to same side and looking back; return to starting position; repeat; alternate.

5.

S.P. Standing in good, erect position.
M.   (This series is to develop shoulder flexibility.)
   a. Keep left shoulder and balance of body still, shrug right shoulder (elevate shoulder), then forcibly push downward with "heel" of hand; repeat; alternate.
   b. Shrug (elevate) both shoulders, push down forcibly extending arms with force; repeat.
   c. Keeping left shoulder still, carry right shoulder forward as much as possible; relax; repeat; alternate.
   d. Carry both shoulders forward, allowing elbows to rotate inward and arms to rotate medially.
   e. Keep left shoulder still, carry right shoulder upward and backward (lateral rotation); alternate.
   f. Carry both shoulders upward and backward (get lateral rotation in shoulder joint).
   g. Lift right arm sideways, starting movement with shoulder lift; alternate, keeping the movement going in ripples from one side to the other.

6.

S.P. Tailor sitting, hands at neck. Partner stands in back with knee bracing between the scapulae.
M.   Partner grasps elbows in front and pulls the arms upward and backward, stretching the pectoral muscles.

7.

S.P. Tailor sitting, arms reaching up and back, hands as if grasping the high bar.
M. a. Partner braces knee against back of performer to keep it erect. Holding the performer at the wrists, resist any backward movement. This is a good isometric exercise to strengthen the shoulders for dislocate movements on the unevens.
   b. Try the same exercise using a wand or tied rope to resist as arms are pressed backward.

8. PUSH-UP VARIATIONS

8.1.

S.P. Standing about 3 feet from the wall.
M.   Let the body lean into the wall and push away from the wall with the arms.

8.2.

S.P. Kneeling, body inclined forward, weight on knees and hands.
M.   Bend the arms, bringing the chest to the floor and push up to the original position.

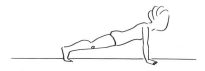

8.3.

S.P. Front leaning rest position, weight on feet and hands, arms straight.
M.   Let the chest drop to the floor as the elbows bend. Push up to the original position.

8.4.

S.P. Front leaning rest position, weight on fore-arms and feet.
M.   Push the body upward, keeping weight on fore-arms, and simultaneously kick one straight leg upward.

8.5.

S.P. Front leaning rest position, weight on hands and feet.
M.   Keeping arms straight and holding the push-up position, swing one arm forward upward and simultaneously swing opposite leg upward.

8.6.

S.P. Back to the bars, feet hooked on the low rung.
M.   Do a push-up with the feet elevated. As strength increases, lift the feet up another rung.

8.7.

S.P. In handstand position against the wall. Spotters standing on either side supporting and holding at the legs.
M.   Bend the arms and push up to the straight arm position. Increase the executions as strength is developed. This is excellent to develop shoulder strength for back extension and springs in tumbling and floor exercise.

9.

S.P. Using stall bars, horizontal bar, or uneven bar. Hanging with back to bars.
M.   a. Passive hanging.
      b. Do a long hang, letting go first with the left hand; replace it, and let go with the right hand.
      c. Chinning. Chin with the hands turned to face the body.
      d. Chin with hands turned away from the body.
      e. Pendulum swing from side to side.
      f. Pendulum swing forward and backward.

Exercises for Lower Extremity

10.

S.P. Long sitting, arms stretched over head by ears.

M. Stretch arms alternately by reaching right, then left, to ceiling; then bounce forward, arms extended. Try to touch toes, keeping knees straight.

      May be done to count of 8, 4, etc.

      Upward stretch releases tension in the low back and helps to stretch the low back and hamstrings on bouncing forward.

11.

S.P. Long sitting, legs spread far apart.

M. Keep legs spread as widely as possible and rolled outward; bend forward over right leg, trying to touch head to knee; return to erect position, bend directly forward between legs (ankles may be grasped to pull trunk forward, but knees point toward ceiling); return to erect position then bend forward over left leg and touch head to knee.

      To stretch hamstrings and low back.

12.

S.P. Long sitting, soles of feet against wall, all of foot touching wall, particularly heels.

M. Keeping knees straight, bounce forward; try to touch forehead to knees.

      To stretch the muscles on the back of calf and thigh, as well as the low back.

13.

S.P. Hurdle sitting. Knees spread, forward leg obliquely to side.

M. Trunk bending forward over extended leg, knee straight; give bounces to bring head to knees.

14.

S.P. Hurdle sitting.

M. Keeping this position, place hands in back of body and fall backward to back-lying position. The bent knee will lift from floor if the fascia is tight. Try to get back to floor and, by vibratory bounces, try to bring the bent knee to the floor. Come to sitting position, stretch legs, relax; alternate.

      To stretch the muscles on top and side of the thigh.

15.

S.P. Hurdle sitting, draw extended leg into other knee so both legs are bent—left in front, right to rear.

M. Grasping left leg in front with left hand on inside of instep, stretch the leg upward and obliquely forward. Right knee may be held with right hand for balance. Return, repeat, alternate.

      To stretch muscles of the thigh.

16.

S.P. Long sitting, legs spread, arms horizontal.

M. Bend to the right with left arm high over head; stretch right arm across front of body. Try to touch posterior portion of right shoulder to right leg, stretching hamstrings and hips.

17.

S.P. Long sitting, legs together and straight, soles of feet against soles of partner's feet.

M. Stretch forward, shaking right hands, then shake left hands, then both hands.
To stretch the hamstrings.

18.

S.P. Long sitting, legs spread, feet against feet or ankles of partner.

M. Grasp partner's hands, bend forward and backward; keep knees straight (may be done to rhyme: Row, row, row your boat...). Try to touch the floor in front and in back, to get a good low back and hamstring stretch.

19.

S.P. Kneeling on one knee, other leg extended forward, trunk bent forward, hands on floor on either side of extended leg.

M. Push the extended leg forward as far as possible. Keep knee straight. Assist by taking some of the weight on the hands. Alternate legs.
To help stretch the hamstring muscles on the back of the legs, preparatory to performing a split.

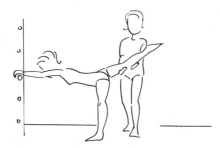

20.

S.P. Standing facing the bars, both hands grasping at waist height.

M. Lift one leg into a scale. Partner stands to one side and pushes the leg upward.

21.

S.P. Back lying, arms reversed T or at sides (passive hamstring stretch).

M. Partner lifts right leg upward, leg rotated laterally. Keeping both legs straight, try to push the lifted leg past the 90-degree angle. For a greater stretch of the gastrocnemius and soleus, push down on the toes.

22.

S.P. Standing, back to barre or to wall.

M. Partner lifts leg forward upward, leg rotated laterally, trying to bring the leg near to the shoulder. This is a good stretch preparatory to splits and kicks or battements.

23.

S.P. Kneeling, knees about 10-12 inches apart, hands at hips.

M. Keeping trunk erect and very still, incline trunk backward; bend at knees only, quadriceps (muscles on front of thigh) and abdominals holding; go backward as far as possible, return to erect position; repeat 6-10 times, increasing range. Stretch out legs to rear (to relax); repeat.

24.

S.P. Sitting on heels in "frog sit."

M. From the sitting position, place hands on the floor in front of the body and lift the hips in the air, taking the weight on top of the instep. Get a stretch throughout the instep to develop a better pointed toe.

25.

S.P. Sprinting (crouch) position, hands on floor, one knee bent, other leg extended to rear.

M. Treading in place, alternately place one leg backwards, then slide the other into place as opposite knee is bent.

26.

S.P. Face lying, toes together, heels rolled outward.

M. Contract the buttocks muscles, roll heels inward, then lift both extended legs so that thighs are about two inches from the floor; relax, let legs roll outward again on floor.
To strengthen the muscles which extend the hip and leg.

27.

S.P. Face lying, knees bent so that legs are relaxed in the air.

M. Contract the buttocks muscles, hold contraction; lift thighs about 2-4 inches from the floor, hold, release.
To strengthen the buttocks muscles.

28.

S.P. Kneeling on all fours, left leg extended backward.

M. Keep knee extended and moving in hip joint only; circle entire leg clockwise. Get a pull in the buttocks and thigh muscles when the leg comes across the back of the body; alternate.

29.

S.P. On all fours, knee scale.

M. Bend the right knee bringing it close to the head, rounding the body. Swing the right leg to rear in a high knee scale, back arched, head up. Repeat several times and alternate sides.

30.

S.P. Side lying; lift top leg about 45 degrees, knee straight.

M. a. Circle leg from hip, moving clockwise and keeping the circle as much as possible to the rear of the body line; relax; repeat; alternate.
To strengthen the thigh muscles.

   b. Place weight on ankle and repeat the movement.

   c. Place weight on ankle and lift leg laterally as high as possible.

31.

S.P. Kneeling, knees about 18 inches apart.

M. Perform a body wave in a kneeling position; i.e., sit back on heels, then push hips forward as the body waves, head coming up last.

32.

S.P. Standing, legs in wide straddle, hands to floor.
M.   a. Walk forward with the hands until the hips touch the floor, body in arched position; push with the hands and come back to the straddle stand.
      b. Place hands in the rear, and go down to a straddle sitting position; with a twist of the torso and pushing of hands, come up to a straddle standing position.

33.

S.P. Facing stall bars, grasp bar at shoulder level, left foot turned outward and parallel with bar, right heel hooked into bar, right leg rotated outward and knee straight; body close to bar.
M.   Hold position, slide down the bar in direction of extended leg to a split, keeping both knees straight and the supporting heel on the floor.
      Good preliminary stretch for a split.

34.

S.P. Facing stall bars, hook one leg into bar directly in front of the body; turn supporting foot outward, hands at shoulder height or lower on stall bars.
M.   a. Keeping both legs straight, bounce trunk forward and try to touch head to knees, stretching the hamstrings.
      b. Holding the same position with feet, lift both arms over head and bend backward as far as possible.

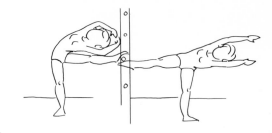

35.

S.P. Standing with side to the bars, hook one leg into the bar at hip height, other leg straight.
M.   Lean the body toward the bars and away from the bars, getting a stretch in the legs and trunk.

36.

S.P. One foot on the third rung, holding the bar with both hands.
M.   Pull away from the bar in a split; alternate foot on the bar.

37.

S.P. Standing facing the bars, one leg extended upward on the bars.
M.   Slide the leg upward as far as possible into a split on the stall bars.

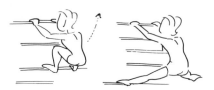

38.

S.P. Standing on third rung, facing the bars.
M.   Jump into a squat position on the third rung; jump to a straddle position on the same rung.

39.

S.P. Standing on the third rung, facing the bars.
M. Jump into a squat position to rung 4, repeat to rungs 5 and 6; jump into a squat position downward.

Exercises for Trunk and Abdominal Region

40.

S.P. Hook lying, arms to sides.
M. a. Lift the hips, lifting the pelvis into the air; lower.
    b. Lift the hips, lifting the pelvis into the air; slowly rotate the pelvic area in a circle.
        To give greater flexibility to the low back and hip areas.
    c. Lift hips and shoulders, taking weight on feet and back of head, pushing hips up as high as possible.

41.

S.P. Back lying.
M. Slowly bend both knees to chest, clasp them tightly and stretch low back fascia. Slowly extend legs, keeping good pelvic tilt; i.e., low back on floor.

42.

S.P. Standing with back to wall; shoulders, head, and buttocks against wall; heels 2 inches away.
M. Retract abdominal muscles (pull them inward), try to touch the low back to the wall.
        To help in getting a correct erect posture.

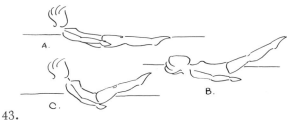

43.

S.P. Back lying, arms at sides or folded on chest.
M. a. Lift head and shoulders about 2 or 3 inches from floor, hold, relax to back lying; repeat.
    b. Lift both legs 2 or 3 inches from mat, hold, relax to back lying (retract abdominals, do not arch low back).
    c. Lift head and legs simultaneously, retracting abdominals and keeping low back flat, relax; repeat.
    d. Lift head and legs and rock from side to side.
    e. Lift head and legs and come to "jackknife" position or "V" seat, balancing on buttocks, upper back and legs in air.

Note. Progress to each section with increased strength in the abdominal muscles.

44.

S.P. Hook lying, hands clasped in front of body, arms extended.
M. Come to oblique sitting position, passing right shoulder on the outside of left knee; relax to back lying; repeat, passing left shoulder on outside of right knee while coming to sitting position.

Note. It may be necessary to start with partner holding feet, or with feet hooked into stall bars or under chair.

45.

S.P. Hook lying, arms in reverse T (arms horizontal, bent at right angles at elbows).
M. Lift both knees to chest, keep shoulders flat on floor, and slowly lower the bent legs (knees together) from side to side. At first, rest between movements; later, go from side to side without rest.

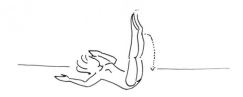

46.

S.P.   Back lying, legs extended to 90 degrees.

M.   Shoulders on floor, slowly lower the extended legs directly sideward, keeping movement going evenly from side to side.

47.

S.P.   Hook sitting, hands bracing body in rear.

M.   Lift both feet from floor, roll to right hip and simultaneously extend both legs close to floor—but not on floor; with legs extended, roll to left hip; come to erect hook sitting position as knees bend. Continue in same direction, keeping movement slow and even. Reverse movement to opposite direction.

Note.   When very strong, perform movement without the support of the hands, and swinging the arms in opposition to legs.

48.

S.P.   Long sitting, hands bracing body to rear.

M.   Lift legs from floor and, with scissor movement, spread and cross legs; alternate leg on top, relax to long sitting; repeat.

Note.   The scissor movement may also be done up and down. It may also be done without support by hands.

49.

S.P.   Back lying, arms horizontal, palms up.

M.   a.   Raise right leg toward ceiling, swing right leg across left trying to touch left hand; return right leg to center toward ceiling, replace right leg; repeat movement or alternate to opposite side.

b.   Keeping legs extended and spread on floor, come to sitting position touching left foot with right hand; return to back lying; sit up, touching right hand to left foot; return to back lying.

c.   Combine <u>a</u> and <u>b</u> movements in a continuous manner.

50.

S.P.   Back lying, hands in fist under hips to hold correct pelvic position.

M.   a.   Raise legs from the mat and describe a clockwise circle with the right foot.

b.   Raise legs from the mat and describe a counter-clockwise circle with the left foot.

c.   Raise legs and do <u>a</u> and <u>b</u> simultaneously.

51.

S.P.   Back lying, hands in fist under hips to hold correct pelvic position.

M.   Describe a figure 8 with both feet circling to the right (clockwise); describe a figure 8 with both legs circling to the left (counter-clockwise); repeat for a series; reverse direction.

52.

S.P.   "Bicycling" position, head on mat, hips pushed upward and held in place by elbows and hands.

M.   a.   Slowly perform bicycling movement of legs; as proficiency is gained, lower the legs and bicycle movement at 45-degree angle.

b.   Bicycling position as above, but with legs widely spread, perform a bicycle movement in this position.

53.

S.P. Neck stand, back lying.

M. From back lying kick legs upward toward the ceiling, taking the weight on the shoulders. Keep legs extended toward the ceiling, balancing on elbows and neck; hold the position, gradually uncurl to back lying— completely relax in back lying.

54.

S.P. Back lying.

M. a. Yoga ploughshear. Lift straight legs upward and let them drop to floor over head. Keep knees straight and get pull in low back.

 b. Return to long sitting position with head to knees; alternate forward and backward positions with easy momentum.

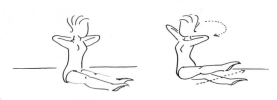

55.

S.P. Long sitting, hands at neck.

M. Twist trunk to the right and simultaneously cross right leg over left; return to starting position. At the beginning, left leg may rest on floor, later lift both legs.

56.

S.P. Kneeling on left knee, right leg extended to side, left arm stretched over head.

M. Bend trunk laterally to extend leg directly to the side, give vibratory bounces; return to erect position; repeat, alternating sides.

57.

S.P. Hook lying, hands on floor, thumbs to ears.

M. a. Taking weight on hands and feet, push body upward in a back bend.

 b. From the back bend position, walk feet to hands to increase the arch.

 c. From a deep back bend as in b rock back and forth toward hands, then toward feet again and push up to standing. (A spotter may stand to one side or between the feet helping to lift at the low back.)

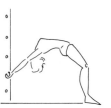

58.

S.P. Standing, back to bar or to wall.

M. Reach over head with hands, gradually walk down the bars or the wall with hands, bending the back into an arch or bridge.

59.

S.P. Hanging from a bar, back to bar.

M. a. Raise both knees to chest; return to original position.

 b. Raise both knees to chest; extend both legs forward, bend knees again, return to original position.

 c. From a long hanging position, immediately lift both legs into a pike position, hold, return to original position (see sketch).

 d. Hanging in pike position, do a scissor movement of the legs.

 e. Lift the legs upward to a pike position, drop them from side to side.

 f. With the legs in pike position, make a circle with both legs.

 g. With the legs in pike position, make a bicycle movement with the legs.

60.

S.P. Back lying on floor, feet hooked under lowest rung.

M. a. Arching upper back and lifting chest first, come to a sitting position. Curl body and return to floor. Partner may hold feet.

b. Try movement without feet being held.

WARM-UP COMBINATIONS

Warm-up movements may be done in sequences with or without music, though most younger students seem to work better with the background of popular music. The following are examples, and each teacher may want to make up her own sequences.

Combination 1

Do each of the following movements as isometrics or with dynamic tension, i.e., hold the extreme of each movement for 10 seconds.

1.1. Standing with feet together, arms stretched over head, arch the body backward as far as possible, keeping legs straight.

1.2. Bend forward and place palms on floor, keeping knees straight.

1.3. Bend left knee and slide right leg backward as in a spring position, but with weight on tip of toes and hands, back arched, head back.

1.4. Slide left leg back, weight on top of toes and hands, back arched, head back.

1.5. Lower hips to floor, and extend ankles. Place hands by shoulders and push the upper back in a high arch, keeping hips on floor.

1.6. Lower to floor and push up to regular push up position.

1.7. Slide feet under body to sitting on heels in frog sit—arms extended on floor.

1.8. Lift hips in air, taking weight on top of instep and on hands.

1.9. Place feet on floor, reach up and back with right hand as left palm remains on floor near left foot. Reach up and back with left hand as right hand is placed near right foot.

1.10. Slowly in 10 counts, do a body wave to standing.

Combination 2

The following sequence of movements may be set to any popular music, preferably with a good even beat or catchy tune. Each one requires 16 measures.

2.1. a. Stretch both arms upward over head—4 measures.

b. Legs straight, touch floor—4 measures.

c. Squat hands on floor, stretch knees keeping hands on floor (do this twice)—4 measures.

d. Hands on floor, kick right leg back into a needle scale, kick left leg back—4 measures.

2.2. Repeat all of part 1—ending with the legs spread.

2.3. Bounce forward touching palms to floor—4 measures. Slowly circle body, arms are extended by ears, make a complete circle from left back to right—4 measures. Repeat bounces—4 measures, and circling right to left—4 measures.

2.4. Développé right—front, side, back, and side—8 measures. Développé left—front, side, back, and side—8 measures.

2.5. Battement right to a lunge—shift weight to back leg and lift right leg in rond de jambe, front to rear—4 measures. Repeat on left side. Repeat again on right and left sides. End in wide stride standing.

2.6 Wide stride standing, arms horizontal, touch right hand to left toe, left hand to right toe, and do a slow arabesque turn to the right and repeat to the opposite side.

2.7. Hitch kick forward, hitch kick backward, repeat forward and backward. Pas de basque forward—taking a small leap on each step. Jeté in a circle and end in a ballet point.

Chapter 3   Dance for Gymnasts

Dance plays an important part in all gymnastic movements, whether it be floor exercise, balance beam, or tumbling. The freedom of the body gained through the dance lends balance, flexibility, timing, poise, strength, coordination, and a certain fluidity in movement that are lacking in those persons who have not been trained in dance. Ballet is particularly suited for the gymnast, because of the precision and line which are taught in each movement.

Modern dance background is also desirable for the understanding of movement in space, the communication of ideas through movement, and the freedom of a well-trained body.

All gymnasts will benefit by studying dance. Following are a few of the more common ballet movements which the gymnast can use effectively, particularly in floor exercise and the balance beam. The writers are cognizant of several different schools of ballet, and have selected skills which will best help the inexperienced performer to develop her body. It is suggested that many of these dance movements be incorporated into the daily conditioning or warm-up portion of any gymnastic class. Most gymnasts need much work on arm movements, and it is hoped that the usual "ports de bras" or training in the correct arm positions will accompany each of the suggested skills. The arms give meaning and emphasis to the head and upper body, and special attention should be given to them in all movements.

BALLET FOR GYMNASTS

In all ballet movements the body should be erect, hips tucked under, and shoulders relaxed. Good posture and form should be stressed in each movement. The following dance steps can be performed to the right or left side, and may be performed in open position (effacé) or crossed position (croisé); they may also be performed forward and backward, and on half-toe.

To start, it may be desirable for the performer to practice many of the steps using a barre. If none is available, use stall bars, or have the students place a hand against the wall or balance beam for balance. Most ballet movements are taught at the barre, and then tried on the floor without support.

Five Fundamental Positions of Feet

The fundamental positions of the feet will help the performer in developing the turned-out position of the foot and leg, which gives good line to the extremity. The fifth position is seldom used in gymnastics.

1. FIRST POSITION   Feet in line, heels together, toes pointed away from each other.

2. SECOND POSITION   Feet in line, heels separated about one step distance, toes pointed away from each other.

3. THIRD POSITION   Feet in line, pressed together, the heel of one foot half covering the other foot, toes pointed away from each other.

4. FOURTH POSITION   One foot forward about the length of one foot. Feet are turned outward, heel of the forward foot in line with the toe of the rear foot.

5. FIFTH POSITION   Feet in line, toes pointed away from each other, heel of one foot pressing flat against the toes of the other foot.

Arm Positions

For the gymnast, the arms should be an important part of the movement, particularly in floor exercise and on the balance beam. Unnecessary movements of the hands and arms are very distracting, whereas fluid movements of the arms from one position to another give line and beauty to the body positions.

Many ballet schools suggest different positions for the arms. The more commonly used arm positions are those suggested by the Sadlers Wells Ballet and, because these seem to fit with gymnastic movements, they are included here.

As preparation, the arms are held in an oval in front of the body, low in front of the thighs, palms facing inward.

6. FIRST POSITION   The arms are raised to a slightly higher position so that the hands are about waist high. The arms are slightly more in front of the body, palms facing inward.

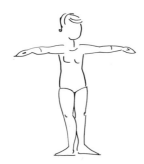

7. SECOND POSITION The arms are extended to the sides, slightly below shoulder level. Arms are not completely extended, but are slightly flexed at the elbow. Palms may face forward, downward, or upward, according to the movement.

8. THIRD POSITION   One arm is raised in an oval over the head, slightly forward from the body to within line of vision; the other arm remains in second position to the side. Either arm may be lifted.

9. FOURTH POSITION One arm is raised in an oval over the head as in third position; the other arm is curved forward in first position. Either arm may be over the head.

10. FIFTH POSITION   Both arms are curved in an oval over the head, slightly forward so that they are within the line of vision; palms are facing downward.

Pliés (Knee Bending)

Pliés should be performed in each of the above five positions, both at the barre and away from it. These positions should be used in practicing the pliés. Pliés may be demi (bending the knees only halfway) or grand (bending the knees as far as possible). In either case the accent should be on the return to the extension. Pliés, or bending of the knees, are important to the take-off of any jump, and elasticity of the muscles will be improved if the bending is done with a feeling of snapping back to position. Slow, sustained deep-knee bends are not desirable since they do not develop this elasticity and, furthermore, they may strain the knee ligaments.

The following commonly used ballet movements are also frequently used in gymnastics for women.

Battements (Kicks)

The battements assist in developing a strong leg and good point and arch. Correct form should be stressed at all times.

11. BATTEMENT TENDU (A BEATING OR KICKING OF THE LEGS)

Fifth position, right foot in forward; slide right foot forward lifting right heel. The leg is rotated outward. Snap it briskly back to fifth position; repeat, alternating legs.

May also be done to the side (see sketch) or to the rear.

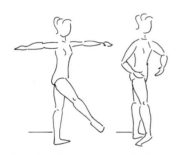

12. BATTEMENT TENDU JETÉ

Similar to battement tendu, but instead of sliding the foot along the floor, the foot is thrown briskly upwards to a point forming an angle somewhat less than 45 degrees with the floor. The knees are straight, the hip rotated outward, the toe pointed. Snap the foot back to fifth position. Care must be taken that in raising the foot the toe is the last to leave the floor and the first to touch in descending.

May be repeated to the side or to the rear.

13. BATTEMENT FONDU

Fifth position, right foot forward. Extend the

right foot forward on the floor, then bring it back placing it on the left ankle (sur le coup-de-pied), right heel in front of the ankle.

May be done to the side and to the rear.

14. BATTEMENT FRAPPÉ

Fifth position, right foot in front. Place right foot at the left ankle (sur le cou-de-pied), then forcefully kick the right foot forward to about 45 degrees. The right ankle is strongly dorsi-flexed (bent) when at the left ankle, and forcefully extended when in the air.

May be done to the side (see sketch) and to the rear.

15. GRAND BATTEMENT

Fifth position, right foot in front.
a. Forward kick. Slide the foot along the floor, then lift it as high as possible in front. Get the feeling of pushing down on the hip joint as the leg is raised. Toe is pointed, leg rotated outward.
b. Sideward kick. Rotate the leg outward so that the knee is toward the ceiling. Again get a lift with a pushing down of the hip joint.
c. Backward kick. Keep the body erect, rotate the leg outward and slide the foot along the floor, then lift it to the rear as you get the feeling of pushing down on the hip.

Note. In all of the battements, the supporting leg should remain straight and should not "give" with the kick.

Rond de Jambe (Circling of Legs)

16. ROND DE JAMBE À TERRE EN DEHORS
(OUTWARD)

(A circling of the foot on the floor forward and
to the rear)
First position. Slide the right foot forward; the leg is rotated outward so the
little toe is on the floor. Draw an imagi-
nary circle with the foot to the side and to
the rear, return to first position. The toes
remain in contact with the floor. Movements should be continuous and smooth.

17. ROND DE JAMBE À TERRE EN DEDANS
(INWARD)

(A circling of the foot from the rear to the side
and forward)
First position. Extend right foot to the rear,
toes on the floor; slide the foot to the side
and to the forward point position, then back
to first position. Movements should be continuous and smooth.

18. ROND DE JAMBE EN L'AIR EN DEHORS

Fifth position, right foot forward. Lift right leg
forward, to the side, and to the rear in a
continuous movement.

19. ROND DE JAMBE EN L'AIR EN DEDANS

(A circling of the leg in the air from the rear
to the forward position)
Fifth position, right foot in the rear. Lift
the right foot as high as possible, carry it
to the side, and forward in a continuous
movement.

Développé

20. DÉVELOPPÉ FORWARD

Fifth position, right foot in front. Raise right
foot to the ankle of left foot (sur le cou-de-
pied), carry it upward until the toe of right
foot touches the inside of left knee (tire-
bouchon). Extend right leg forward, hips
rotated outward, lifting right leg to at least
a 90-degree angle. The supporting leg must
remain straight.

21. DÉVELOPPÉ SIDEWARD

Start in same position as for forward movement, but extend the leg to the side. Again
the leg is rotated outward, with knee toward the ceiling.

22. DÉVELOPPÉ BACKWARD

Start in same position as for forward movement, but extend the leg to the rear. The
leg is rotated outward. It is important to
keep the right knee high as the leg is extended to the rear. Do not let the knee drop
below the original position that it was in
when the foot touched the left knee. Keep
the body as straight as possible.

Note: The développé is excellent for developing
strength and freedom of the hip joint, since
it brings into play all of the thigh muscles.
Movements from the développé position to
an attitude or arabesque (scale) or ballet
point are frequently performed in gymnastics.

Other Beginning Movements

23. ARABESQUE (SCALE)

Start in first or fifth position. Keeping the weight
on the right foot, lift the left leg to the
rear as high as possible, bending the trunk
forward. The arabesque may start from a

kick up or from a développé. It may be done in numerous ways, either in open (effacé) position or closed or crossed (croisé) position. Position of the arms may vary.

24.   ATTITUDE

Fifth position, right foot forward. Lift right foot to the knee of left leg, then lift right thigh to the rear with the knee bent. (This may also be done by a quick lift of right leg to the bent position from a rear fifth position.) If the right foot is lifted, usually the right arm is curved over the head, the left arm to the side (third position). This may be done in open position (effacé) or closed or crossed position (croisé).

25.   BALLET POINT

(Commonly a ballet curtsy.)

Fourth position, right foot forward, weight taken on left foot in the rear in a demi-plié; the right foot slides forward in a point, and the body is bent forward over the right foot. Arms may be in second, fifth, or to the rear.

26.   CROISÉ (ATTITUDE CROISÉ DEVANT)

Fifth position, right foot in front. Lift right leg to a semi-bent position so that the right foot is at about the height of left knee with the leg slightly forward. Arms are in third

position with left arm high. There may be a twist of the body to the right, and may be a rising to the left half-toe (relevé).

Sautés (Jumps)

Sautés are part of allegro or quick movements. They may be divided into the following categories:

From one leg to the other
Starting with both legs and finishing on one.
Starting with one leg and finishing on both.
Starting with both legs and finishing on both.
Consecutive jumps on one leg (a hop).

Sautés or jumps give added lift and the feeling of aerial freedom to floor exercise and balance beam. They are also used in tumbling as preparation movement.

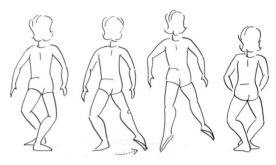

27.   ASSEMBLÉ

Fifth position, right foot behind.
a.   Demi-plié on both feet, thrust right leg into the air about 45 degrees from the floor as you push upward with left leg. Land in a plié with right leg in front; reverse the movement to the left.
b.   This may be done traveling to the rear by starting with the forward foot brushing to the side and closing to the rear.

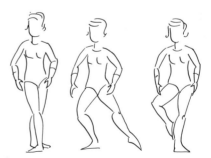

28.   JETÉ

Fifth position, right leg in front. Left leg is thrust to the side as in assemblé to about 45 degrees. The right leg pliés and then pushes off. Land on left foot with the knee bent; right leg is bent and behind the left ankle. To repeat, place the foot in front in fifth position and continue as above. This may be done on either side by reversing the foot position.

29.   JETÉ BALLOTTÉ

Fifth position, right foot forward. With a spring, right foot opens forward as left leg opens from a développé to the rear. Land on both feet. Reverse on left foot by springing to the left foot as the right opens backward.

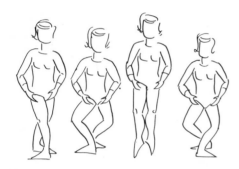

30.   CHANGEMENT DE PIEDS (CHANGING OF THE FEET)

Fifth position, right foot in front. Demi-plié on both legs, pushing vigorously from the floor with both feet and jumping up. Both legs open slightly to the side and the legs are changed in the air, so that in landing the left is in front. The movement should finish with a plié in the landing and then straighten the legs.

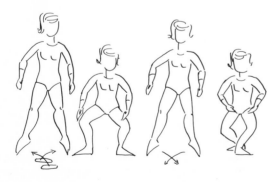

31.   ÉCHAPPÉS

Fifth position, right foot forward. Demi-plié, followed by a spring into the air produced by pushing from the floor equally with both feet. The legs separate when they are in the air, and upon landing they are in second

position in plié. A second spring is made into the air, this time landing in fifth position with the left in front.

32.   BALLONÉ

Fifth position, right foot in front, left shoulder forward. The right foot is at the left ankle (sur le cou-de-pied). Demi-plié on the left leg and at the same time thrust the right foot forward and jump onto the left toward the right direction. End with a plié on the left and the right at the ankle, ready to repeat.

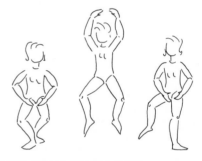

33.   PAS DE CHAT (CAT LEAP)

Fifth position, right foot forward. Demi-plié on both legs. The left leg is quickly lifted sideways with bent knee (croisé position), the right leg following immediately and performing a similar position. There is an instant when both legs are in the air. The landing is made on the left leg and the right leg is brought down into fifth position, the knee remaining bent.

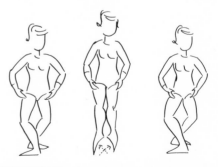

34.   ENTRECHAT

There are numerous variations of the entrechat. Actually, they are jumps into the air with a beating together of the legs. A simple type is described here.

Fifth position, right foot in front. Demi-plié and spring into the air. Both legs open in the air into a narrow second position and quickly close again with a brisk tapping of the calves. In the Entrechat Royale, the right leg remains in front until just before it reaches the floor, and finishes behind in a neat fifth position.

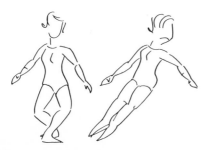

35. BRISÉ

a. Brisé en avant (forward)

Fifth position, left foot in front. Demi-plié on both legs as the right leg is thrown energetically forward to about knee level. The left foot pushes up from the floor and is thrown forward to beat the calf of the right leg while both legs are still in the air, and is then passed quickly forward to land in fifth position with the left foot in front. Both feet land at the same instant, as in an assemblé.

b. Brisé en arrièr (backward)

Fifth position, left foot in front. Demi-plié on both legs, the left foot is thrust to the rear, the right foot pushed from the floor and thrown back to beat the front (shin) of the left leg; it then passes quickly behind to land, both feet together, in fifth position with left in front.

36. CABRIOLE

The cabriole is a jumping step entailing beats. It differs from an entrechat in that the legs do not change place in the beats; instead, the under leg beats the upper leg from beneath, pushing it still higher.

There are a number of ways to do a cabriole; one is suggested, below.

Fifth position, right foot in front. Right leg is thrust into the air, keeping the knee very straight and toes pointed. Demi-plié on left leg; then the left leg is thrust into the air to beat the calf of the right leg. The beat should force the right leg higher into the air, the left leg landing in demi-plié. This may be reversed or done sideways, backwards, and also with bent legs.

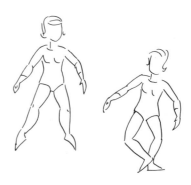

37. SISSONE

There are many variations of the sissone, depending upon direction and facings. Below is a simple type.

Fifth position, right foot in front. Spring into the air pushing from the floor equally with both feet; land on left leg, the right resting on the left ankle (sur le cou-de-pied). This may be done with the other foot, and forward or backward.

38. PAS DE CISEAUX (SCISSOR OR HITCH KICK)

A quick jumping and changing of the feet in the air.

Fifth position, weight on left foot. Kick right leg into the air, followed immediately with the left, then the right again in a scissor movement; land on left. The movement may be done starting with the left foot, or may be performed with kicks to the rear.

In gymnastics, a half-ciseaux is usually used; i.e., kick the right foot forward, followed by the left, and end on the right.

39.   SOUBRESAUT

Fifth position, right foot in front. Plié on both feet and push up from the floor, knees straight and toes pointed to the floor. The feet retain their position, one in front of the other in the air, and the legs must be held so tightly together that there is no light between them. Land in plié on both feet.

Connecting Steps

The following are movements on the floor. They are used as preparation steps for jumps.

40.   CHASSÉ

Fifth position, right foot forward, right shoulder forward. Rise on the half-toes. The right leg slides up the front of left leg to knee level in a kind of développé. It then drops forward in plié in fourth position croisé. From this position both legs are pushed up from the floor to meet, tightly pressed together in fifth in the air with the knees, insteps, and toes held very stretched and straight. To finish, the back leg (left) lands in plié while the right foot immediately drops into fourth position forward, ready to spring up again and repeat the step. The chassé may be done to the rear and facing in various directions.

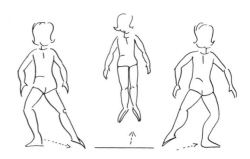

41.   GLISSADE

Fifth position, left foot forward, left shoulder forward. With a gliding or sliding movement move right leg forward, the leg being very slightly lifted off the floor; the left leg must help this movement as it pushes from the floor. The knees must be well stretched when the legs are in the air, and the toes are pointed. During the jump the right leg is separated from the left and drops forward into fourth position, the weight of the body passing to the forward right foot which finishes the jump in plié. The left foot then glides into fourth position across the front of the right. Reverse to the opposite side.

42.   PAS DE BOURRÉE

Fifth position, right foot in front. Keeping a tight fifth position, rise to both toes, and take little steps on the toes diagonally forward to the right. Keep legs close together, knees straight. Alternate the sides and also perform this movement to the rear.

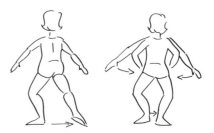

43.   PAS DE BASQUE

Fifth position, right foot forward. Step on right

to the right, taking the weight on the right foot. Brush the left foot through the first position to front of right foot, close right foot in the rear fifth. Alternate sides. May also be done moving to the rear.

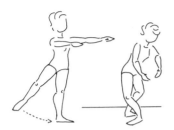

44. BALANCÉ (TO SWAY)

Fifth position, right foot in front, arms in first position. Demi-plié and slide the left foot to the left side and step on it. Simultaneously bend the trunk slightly and tilt the head to the left and swing both arms to the left side. The right foot closes in back of the left and takes the weight for a second, with an immediate shift of the weight back to the left foot as the right foot rests in back of the left ankle. Reverse to the opposite side. This may be done moving sideward, forward, or backward.

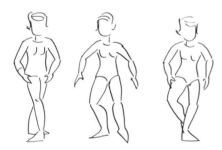

45. COUPÉ

This is a cutting step.

Fifth position, right foot in front. Demi-plié on the front leg. Raise left leg slightly from the floor, toes pointed to the floor. The left foot is then quickly placed on the floor, and the heel of left foot is lowered with sufficient force to displace the right. This is usually done by a slight spring into the air.

Tours (Turns)

Turns assist in the changing of direction, and in giving variety and finesse to an exercise. Many of the previous skills may be done with turns. The more commonly used turns are described.

46. CHAÎNÉS TURNS

Half turns on each step. Start on the right, stepping to the right, turn halfway around. Step on the left and complete the turn. These are usually done on half-toes, although they may be done in plié. If the turns are to be fast, very small steps should be taken to the sides.

The focus of the eyes and movement of the head are very important in avoiding dizziness. In stepping to the right on the right, turn the head to the right and focus on a given spot; hold this focus as long as possible as the step on the left is taken, then turn the head at the last instant. If done in a series, keep the same focus. The arms are usually open in second on the step and come to first on completion of the turn.

47. COUPÉ TURNS

Step on right foot to the right. Draw left foot up to the right ankle and make a complete turn. End with the weight on the left in a demi-plié and continue the turns to the right. Reverse the direction.

48. COUPÉ TURNS WITH JETÉ

Fifth position, weight on left foot. Spring to the right on the right, and draw left foot to the ankle of right foot. Turn on the half-toe of right foot. At completion of the turn, take the weight on the left foot in plie and repeat. Reverse to the opposite side.

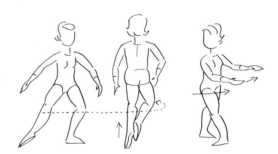

49. PIROUETTE

The pirouette is a rapid spinning of the vertical body on the tiptoe, as though the body were a top. To be precise, the body is not absolutely vertical during the pirouette, but leans very slightly forward. This is an inevitable adjustment in rising on tiptoe from the flat of the foot. The free foot may be held in various positions; i.e., at the ankle, in attitude, in arabesque, or in second, depending upon the type of pirouette. An example of a simple pirouette is described on the next page.

Fourth position, right foot in front, left arm open in second, right arm midway between first and third position, eyes straight ahead. The pirouette commences with a preparatory demi-plié on both feet, the body leaning very slightly forward. The next three motions are done simultaneously:

a. The body is raised to the left half-toe.
b. The right foot is brought firmly to the left ankle.
c. The left arm delivers the rotatory jerk, both hands immediately falling to first position during the spin.

50. BATTEMENT TOURNEY (KICK WITH A TURN)

From a standing position, kick right leg forward in a grand battement. Hold the position of the leg in the air and twist the body to the left, ending in a scale or arabesque with the right leg to the rear. This is usually preceded by a chassé or glissade in order to get the necessary momentum.

It may also be done with a jeté, in which case there is a spring into the air on the left foot as the right leg is kicked forward. This should be practiced on both sides.

51. TOURS JETÉ (JUMPING TURN)

This movement is usually preceded by a chassé or glissade. Kick one leg into the air, and quickly change legs as the body is turned to face the opposite direction. (It is like a scissor kick with a body turn.) If done to the right, glissade forward on the left, swing the right leg from the rear to a forward kick, twist the body to face the op-

posite direction as the left leg is kicked up in back. End in a scale or arabesque with the left leg extended to the rear.

52. ROND DE JAMBE TURN WITH BODY TWIST

Fifth position, right foot forward. Lift right leg in a wide circle forward, sideward, and to the rear. Let the body lean to the right as the arms open from first to second position. As the right foot is in the rear, twist the body and turn to the right, ending in the original position.

This may be performed on either side, and may also be performed with a jeté or jump, or with leg straight or bent.

53. PETIT TEMPE LIÉ EN AVANT (FORWARD)

("Tempe lié" means a smooth movement.)

This is a good sequence for foot and arm positions.

Fifth position, right foot in front. Slide right foot in croisé (across left), arms in low circle in front of body (first position). Hold in a right point for a second, then shift the weight so that the left is pointed to the rear as the right arm continues over head, left to side (third position). Close left foot to right, arms in low circle in front (first position); plié on both knees and, keeping the left knee bent, slide the right foot to the side, arms horizontal (second position), and close the left in front, arms in low circle (first position). Repeat to the left side.

The above movements have been given as separate skills; however, to get the most effective use of dance movements, they should be combined into sequences and thus get the feeling of flow of movement.

MODERN DANCE FOR GYMNASTS

Many movements from modern dance can be effectively used by the gymnast. The concept of contraction and release, which are found in many modern dance movements, lends itself well to correct use of the hips and trunk in getting the feeling of complete contraction and complete release or relaxation. Also, aerial movements or leaps, which are perhaps freer in modern dance than in ballet, may lend strength to a floor exercise sequence.

It is not the purpose of this book to include all of the modern dance skills but, rather, to give a few illustrations so that the reader can see the relationship between modern dance and gymnastics, particularly floor exercise and balance beam. In most school situations, the teachers are more familiar with modern dance than with ballet, yet both types should be taught for adequate development of the gymnast.

1.   CONTRACTIONS

Stand with feet parallel and slightly apart, knees slightly bent. Retract the abdominal wall and simultaneously reach forward with both hands. The back should be rounded to the rear, hips to the rear. Release by bringing the arms to the sides as the hips and trunk return to position.

Note. Freedom of the hips is particularly necessary in such movements as body wave. (See Floor Exercise.)

2.   SWINGING MOVEMENT

The purpose of these movements is to get freedom of the body in a relaxed ballistic type movement.

a.   Simple swing
Stand with feet parallel and slightly apart, arms stretched over head. Swing the arms downward as the legs are bent to a deep squat; continue the arm swing to the rear as the knees straighten. Swing the arms from the rear, through the squat and to a complete extension of the body—arms stretched over head.

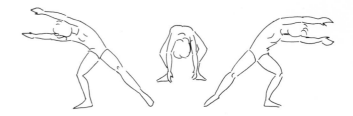

b.   Sideward swing
Stand with the feet wide apart and arms reaching to the right, body twisted to the right. Swing the arms from the right stretched position, across the body as the knees bend to a deep squat and the arms touch the floor. Continue the swing to the left as the legs straighten and reach to the left side.

3.   AERIAL MOVEMENTS

Various forms of leaps are effective to give strength in the feet and legs, and to give the feeling of overcoming gravity. Leaps may vary in all directions, and the following is a very simple example.

With three running steps (left, right, left), spring into the air, spreading the legs in an aerial split. Reverse the split by starting the steps on the opposite side. The position of the legs in the leap may vary; i.e., one may stretch to the rear, and the forward one bend as in a stag leap; or both legs may be bent.

4.   FLOOR STRETCHES

Many of the floor stretches used in modern dance are employed as warm-up movements for gymnastics; these are therefore included in the chapter on Warm-up and Conditioning.

MODERN JAZZ DANCE FOR GYMNASTS

Modern jazz music and movements have been used in competition. However, they must be done in good taste and must fit the personality and performance ability of the gymnast.

FOLK DANCE FOR GYMNASTS

Folk steps and folk music in floor exercise were used to some extent in the recent Olympics. The music selections must be carefully made, and if only parts of the composition are used, ease and correct transitions must be made both in the musical score and in the movements. A complete floor exercise routine in the folk idiom may become repetitious, just as folk music may be repetitious. A selection which gives some feeling of folk music and folk steps may be used without resorting to the ethnic music and ethnic steps.

Part II MODERN RHYTHMIC GYMNASTICS

Chapter 4 Introduction to Modern Rhythmic Gymnastics

By definition, "modern rhythmic gymnastics" means gymnastic movements done in rhythm. This, then, includes exercises done in a rhythmic manner such as floor exercise done rhythmically or to music. It may also include hand apparatus such as balls, ropes, wands, hoops, clubs, ribbons, flags, or scarfs.

The use of balls has become very popular in school programs. Many students can perform in unison, yet each is individually working with a ball. Medau ball movement originated in Europe. Some claim that it started in Germany, others in Sweden. It seems to have become popular in many places simultaneously. Exchange teachers have taught the skill in the United States, and it has now become a popular physical education activity.

Rope jumping has been very popular in Sweden and, although rope jumping of various types has been a part of the activity program of most children, the rhythmic use of individual ropes and rope jumping to music with creative patterns has been developed recently. Schools find this an excellent skill for developing endurance, and large numbers can participate with a minimum cost.

Throughout the years the Turnvereines have used wands and clubs as part of their program. This skill is finding its way back into the physical education program. The pieces of equipment are inexpensive, and they do assist in the development of the shoulder girdle. Hoops have been used effectively in a creative way in Germany and in most of the Scandinavian countries.

Whether it be mass exercises set to music or the use of various hand apparatus, the rhythmic appeal is great with the student; and where large numbers of students must be handled in a limited space, these activities can lend new interest and fun to the physical education program.

Both schools and recreational groups can use rhythmical gymnastics in class situations as well as in special demonstrations. The ingenuity and creativity of the students should be considered; and after they have mastered basic techniques, they should be encouraged to create new movements and to participate in competition.

The hand apparatus mentioned above have been used in team competition for women in the Olympics; ribbons, flags, scarfs, and rhythmic sticks have also been used. The Hungarians first used the ribbons and flags; the Russian girls were the first to use scarfs; and the Germans have frequently used two balls and two rhythmic sticks for team competition.

After the 1956 Olympic Games, team competition in rhythmic gymnastics was eliminated from Olympic competition. However, leaders of women's gymnastics felt that this area of gymnastics was very important and should be developed into a competitive sport of its own. They called this new sport "Modern Gymnastics" and hold world championships in it. The first world championships was held in 1963 in Budapest, Hungary. The world championships include, besides team competition, individual competition in the various events.

Modern gymnastics includes compulsory and optional exercises with hand apparatus, i.e., balls, ropes, etc., and also free floor routine without hand apparatus and without tumbling. The exercise is performed in an area of 12 x 12 m. (39-1/3 x 39-1/3 feet). The gymnast is expected to use the entire area. The exercise shall be executed with accompaniment of music. The gymnast must make use of the entire body and move in harmony with the motion of the hand apparatus. The exercises with hand apparatus (ropes, balls, hoops, Indian clubs, flags, scarfs, ribbons, etc.) must contain movements involving both the right and left hand.

The longer the scarf or ribbon, the greater the skill required to work it. The movements with scarfs and ribbons are light, swinging, and flowing, and are similar to ballet movements. The flag exercises on the advanced level have the same techniques as used with Indian clubs.

As mentioned above, international rules and judging have been established for modern rhythmic gymnastics. This presents another very interesting possibility for schools to develop competition in this aspect of gymnastics, particularly with the present interest in hand apparatus at the secondary level.

Line formation, with ample space between students, is perhaps the easiest class organization for teaching large groups. If the group is small, single or double circle formation lends itself to a more creative design, and because the students can better see each other, they are more likely to perform in unison. Perhaps the easiest teaching method is to demonstrate the skills. After the basic movements have been mastered, the students should be able to follow verbal directions. Music should be used with all hand apparatus, as it lends much to the activity and helps the student to develop a sense of rhythm. Music should be appropriate, although popular music can be used.

Records with music especially selected for the material in this book have been directed by the authors. (Rhythmic Gymnastics, Balls and Ropes 4010-1 and Rhythmic Gymnastics, Clubs and Hoops 4010-2, Hoctor Dance Records, Inc., Waldwick, New Jersey.) These records contain music for performing individual skills and also contain short routines with each of the hand apparatus, which demonstrate how skills may be combined choreographically.

Chapter 5   Balls

The use of a large ball in rhythmic gymnastics for girls has been very popular in European countries for some time. With the exchange of teachers and ideas facilitated by faster means of travel, this activity has been brought to the United States, and has met with great popularity in the physical education programs at all levels.

It is difficult to pinpoint the origin of this type of movement. Some say it started as Medau ball in Germany; others, that it was developed at the Royal Gymnastic Institute of Sweden. Regardless of the source, it has been adopted by most countries, although very little has been written about it in this country.

EQUIPMENT

The size of the gymnastic ball should be 14-19 cm. (5-1/2 - 7-1/2 inches in diameter). For general school use a rubber playground or utility ball is the most economical. These can be purchased in different colors, which make the ball exercises more appealing.

TECHNIQUES

In using the ball as a hand apparatus, it should always rest in the hand. It should not be grasped with the fingers. When tossing the ball the impetus should come from the shoulders and the movement should go from the feet through the whole body with a relaxed bouncy feeling. When catching the ball take it with the fingertips and let the ball slowly roll down into the palm. Again, the whole body should follow the movement and give with the catch. Emphasis should be on a relaxed flowing or swinging-type movement with complete body freedom.

For swinging and rolling movements the ball is held in a wrist grasp; i.e., the wrist is bent at a right angle so that the ball rests between the palm and the forearm.

For some movements the ball may be held in both hands, with the palms in various positions.

MOVEMENTS

The exercises are much easier and more pleasant to perform if done to music. Waltz rhythm or a 6/8 beat is the best to get the relaxed rhythmical swinging movements; however, the music should not be so slow that it loses the life and fun of the movement.

The focus should be on the ball so that the movement of the body follows the ball. Good posture should be emphasized. All of the movements can be done on either side. They will be described for one side; the reader should reverse the movement for the other side. Also, it is hoped that the movements described here will assist in creative movements developed by the reader.

The ball movements are divided into the following skill classifications:

Swinging movements in which the ball remains in the hand.

Rolling movements in which the ball is rolled on the floor or on the body.

Bouncing movements in which the ball is bounced on the floor in various ways.

Tossing movements in which the ball is tossed by one or two hands into the air in various directions.

Movements that are similar to conditioning exercises in which the ball is held in the hand, between the feet, or in some other way, are not considered rhythmical ball exercises.

Swinging Movements

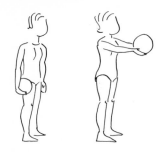

1.   FORWARD SWING

S.P.   Ball in wrist grasp in right hand, arm to the side.

M.   Swing right arm forward to shoulder height, change the ball to the left hand and swing the left hand back. Continue swinging the arms forward and backward.

Variations: a. Do the same movement with a forward stride, shifting the weight forward and backward with the ball.

b.   Do the same movement with a glissade forward.

c.   Make a complete circle with the ball and finish the circle in front of the body.

d.   Make a complete circle as in c, but add a glissade forward.

2.   SWING ACROSS THE BODY

S.P.   Ball in wrist grasp in right hand, arm to the side.

M.   Swing the right arm across the body to the left, change the ball to the left hand and swing it across to the right side. The body should sway from side to side with the ball swing.

Variation: Make a complete circle with the ball, then change to the left hand.

3.   FORWARD CIRCLING

S.P.   Ball in wrist grasp in right hand, arm to the side.

M.   Circle the ball in a complete circle forward, upward, and backward, and forward again. Change to the left hand in front of the body and continue to the left.

Variations: a. Step backward on each circle.

b.   Glissade forward or backward with each circle.

c.   Reverse the direction of the circle.

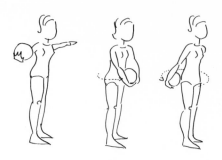

4.   CIRCLING AROUND BODY

S.P.   Ball in wrist grasp in right hand, right arm in side extension.

M.   Swing the ball across in front of the body to the left. Change to the left hand and the left hand carries the ball to the rear and change to the right hand.

Variations: a. Do the same movement while performing a chaînes turn.

b.   Do the same movement, but at the end swing the ball from the right hand over to the left hand in front of the body and reach to the left side with the left hand; repeat to the opposite side.

5.   TRUNK BENDING

S.P.   Standing, ball in wrist grasp in right hand, arm in side extension.

M.   As the trunk is bent forward, sideward left, back and to the right, reach out and make a horizontal circle with the right arm in the same direction. Change hands and reverse the movement.

6.   BODY WAVE

S.P.   Standing, ball in wrist grasp in right hand, arm in side extension.

M.   Body wave as the ball is brought downward and backward and over the head. Change to the left and repeat to the opposite side.

Variations: a. Do a body wave with a step forward and backward.

b.   Ball in both hands in front of body, ball making a circle in front of the body and reaching over the head as the body wave movement is done.

_____

S.P. = Starting Position   M. = Movement

7. WALTZ TURN

S.P. Standing, ball in wrist grasp in right hand, arm in side extension.

M. Step with the right foot, ball is brought down in front in a forward circle. On the second waltz step on the left side, the ball changes to the left hand and is circled backwards.

8. SPIRAL

S.P. Standing in wide stride, ball in wrist grasp in right hand, arm in side extension.

M. a. With ball in wrist grasp, swing the arm across in front of the body to the left, shifting the weight to the left.

b. Bend the right elbow carrying the ball in a circle toward the body under the elbow, turning the palm inward and upward. The ball ends near the right side; shift the weight to the right.

c. From the position in b, carry the ball to the left over the head as the weight is shifted to the left and then bends to the left.

d. Continue the movement circling above the head as the body bends backward. The right arm circles the head and returns to the original position in side extension with the ball in wrist grasp. This should be a continuous spiral movement.

Rolling Movements

9. SIDE FLOOR ROLL

S.P. Standing in wide side stride, ball in wrist grasp in right hand, arm in side extension.

M. With a slight toss, roll the ball along the floor to the left, letting the ball roll up into the left hand as the weight is shifted to the left and the trunk is bent.

Variation: Add a chassé step to the side as the ball is rolled along the floor.

10. V SEAT ROLL

S.P. Long sitting, legs straight, ball in wrist grasp in right hand, arm to side.

M. Lifting the straight legs upward to a V seat and balancing on the buttocks, roll the ball under the legs to the left side; reverse the movement.

11. ROLL AROUND BODY

S.P. Long sitting, legs straight, ball in wrist grasp in right hand, arm to side.

M. Bending the trunk forward, roll ball to the floor around the feet to the left, change the ball to left hand and roll the ball around in back of the body, change to the right hand.

Variation: Start the movement the same as above, but when the ball gets to the left side continue rolling it with left hand as the body goes to a back lying position. Roll the ball over the head and change to right hand. As the ball is brought to the right side of the feet, come to a sitting position.

12. ROLL ON LEGS

S.P. Long sitting, legs straight, the ball in wrist grasp in both hands.

M. Lift the legs tilting the trunk backward and let the ball roll down to the chest. Grasp the ball with both hands, reach up over the head with the ball, and bend forward placing it on the feet again.

13. PRONE LYING

S.P. Prone lying, arms horizontal, ball in wrist grasp in right hand, to right side.

M. Lift the chest as the ball is rolled from right hand under the chest to the left hand. Keep arms horizontal.

14.   TOURS JETÉ WITH ROLL

S.P.   Standing, ball in wrist grasp in right hand, arm
        in side extension.

M.   Roll the ball on the floor from right to left.
        Glissade and tours jeté alongside the ball,
        reach down and let the ball roll into the left
        palm at completion of the movement.

Variation: Do the same movement, but finish the
        tours jeté in a kneeling position, then catch
        the ball as before.

15.   ROLL WITH CHAÎNÉS TURN

S.P.   Standing, ball in wrist grasp in right hand, arm
        in side extension.

M.   Roll the ball on the floor from right to left.
        Chaînés turn to the left and bend forward,
        letting the ball roll into the left hand. With
        the ball in wrist grasp, reach out to the
        left side.

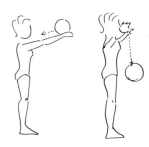

16.   ARM ROLLING

S.P.   Standing, arms stretched in front of body. Both
        arms together and slightly above the hori-
        zontal. Ball held in both palms which are
        upward.

M.   With a very slight upward impetus to the ball,
        turn the palms downward, let the ball roll
        down the arms toward the body. The ball
        will drop between the arms in front of the
        chest. After the ball bounces to the floor,
        catch it with both hands on the rebound.

17.   SHOULDER ROLL

S.P.   Standing, ball in right palm, right arm in side
        extension.

M.   With a very slight toss of the ball upward, and
        quickly turning the palm downward, let the
        ball roll along the right arm to the shoul-
        der. The body is bent slightly to the left.
        Let the ball drop behind the body, then
        twist to the left and catch the ball on the
        rebound with the left hand.

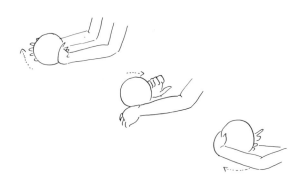

18.   HAND ROLL

S.P.   Standing, both arms curved in front of the body,
        palms facing the body.

M.   The ball is held between the palm of right hand
        which is outside, and the back of left hand.
        Quickly change position of the hands as the
        ball rolls in an outward spinning motion.
        Roll the ball several times and finish with
        a toss in the air.

Variation: Start the same rolling movement from a
        deep squat position to a complete extension
        of the body, ending with feet in fifth posi-
        tion on toes and reaching with the ball over
        head.

Bouncing Movements

19.   BOUNCE WITH ARM SWING

S.P.   Standing, ball held in both hands in front of
        the body.

M.   Bounce the ball in front of the body as the arms
        swing horizontally to the sides and back
        to front position, catching the ball. The
        knees and body "give" with the bounce.

20. BOUNCE WITH KNEE BEND

S.P. Standing, ball in the right palm.
M. Bounce the ball alternately with left and right hands, gradually bending the knees until the bounce is in a deep knee bend position. Return gradually to a standing position, keeping the ball bouncing and alternating hands.

21. BOUNCE ACROSS BODY

S.P. Feet in wide stride, weight on the right foot, ball in right palm extended to the side.
M. With a shift of the weight from the right to the left, bounce the ball in front of the body catching with left hand. Reverse.

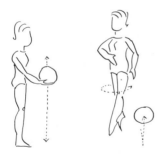

22. BOUNCE AND TURN

S.P. Standing, ball in front of body, held in both hands.
M. Bounce the ball hard with both hands, immediately spin around and catch the ball with both hands on the rebound.

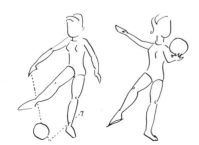

23. BOUNCE UNDER LEG

S.P. Standing, ball in right palm, arm in side extension.

M. Lift right leg and at the same time the right hand bounces the ball diagonally under the leg. The leg swings over the ball. Catch the ball in left hand. Reverse the action with the left leg.
Variation: Starting in the same position, bounce the ball diagonally under the left leg and catch it with the left hand.

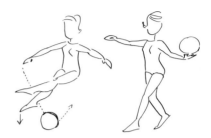

24. BOUNCE WITH SCISSOR KICK

S.P. Standing, ball in right palm, arms in side extension.
M. Bounce the ball diagonally under both legs as they scissor kick; i.e., first lift the right, then the left, jumping over the ball. Catch the ball with left hand. Reverse the movement.

25. BOUNCE WITH GRAPEVINE STEP

S.P. Standing in a wide stride, weight on right foot, ball in right palm, arm in side extension.
M. Step to the left with the left, cross the right over the left, and bounce the ball with the right hand. Catch the ball with the left hand and step to the left, reaching to the left with the ball.
Variation: Step to the left, right crossing over left; bounce ball in front with right hand. Step to side, bounce ball with left hand, step across with the right and bounce with right hand. Step left to side, catch the ball with the left hand and reach to side. This is a continuous movement.

26. CHASSÉ FORWARD

S.P. Chassé position with left foot forward.
M. Chassé and bounce the ball twice with right hand. On the second bounce take the ball in left hand and repeat the chasse to the right.

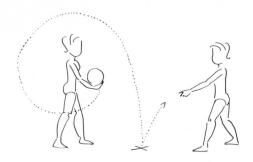

27. PARTNER BOUNCES

S.P. Standing facing a partner, feet in front stride position, ball in both hands in front of the body.

M.   Swing right hand downward and backward in a circle, ball in hand. When the ball is over head, bounce it to partner. The ball should be bounced to the right side, to avoid collision. Practice with one ball, then use two balls, each person doing the movement simultaneously.

Variations: a. A group standing in a circle, facing center. Starting with the ball in both hands, bounce the ball with both hands to the person on the left.

   b. In a circle formation, taking the ball in right hand, make a complete circle with the ball and then bounce it to the left to the next person.

   c. Alternate a toss and a bounce.

   d. Reverse direction.

Tossing Movements

Most of the tossing movements can be done with a forward, backward, or sideward stepping; or with various dance steps.

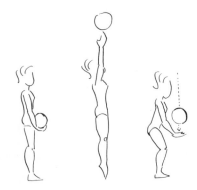

28. TWO-HAND TOSS

S.P. Standing, knees slightly bent, ball held in both hands low in front of the body.

M.   Toss the ball upward, getting a complete exten-

sion throughout the body, rising up to the toes. As the ball descends, try to catch it with the fingertips, and let the body bend slightly as the hands carry the ball down to the starting position.

Variation: Do a changement with the feet as the ball is in the air.

29. ONE-HAND TOSS

S.P. Standing in a forward stride, right foot forward, weight back on left foot as right foot is pointed, ball held in right hand at right side.

M.   Transfer the weight forward as the ball is tossed forward with the right hand. Reach and catch the ball with both hands, and then transfer it to the right hand again. Repeat to the left side.

Variations: a. Perform the same movement, but transfer the ball from right to left hand as the foot position is also changed.

   b. Stand with the feet crossed (croisé); i.e., right across in front of left. Toss the ball with the right hand several times, or change the crossed position and alternate the ball from right to left.

   c. Do the same ball toss walking forward, alternating hands.

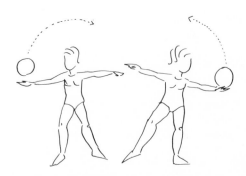

30. OVER-HEAD TOSS

S.P. Standing, feet in wide stride, ball in right hand, arm in side extension.

M.   Toss the ball over the head, catching it with left hand as the weight is shifted from right foot to the left.

      As the skill is mastered, try to end each

movement with a sideward point on the opposite foot, and a reaching to the side with the ball.

31.   FRONT-SWING TOSS

S.P.   Standing, feet in wide stride, ball in right hand, arm in side extension.

M.   Toss the ball from right to left low across in front of the body as the knees bend and the hips are thrust to the left. Catch the ball with left hand, reverse the action to the right. The hands follow the body in a relaxed sideward swinging movement.

32.   FLICK TOSS

S.P.   Standing, feet in comfortable stride position, ball in right hand, arm in semi-side extension.

M.   Flick the wrist and toss the ball upward; i.e., starting with the ball in a wrist grasp in right hand, bend the elbow and wrist in a complete inward and downward circle, and with a flick of the wrist toss the ball upward at the end of the hand circle. Catch it with the same hand or change hands.

Variations: a. Flick the ball with the right hand so that it moves in a circle across to the left. Continue the right arm circling across the body and catch it with right hand. It may also be changed to catch it with left hand.

b.   Make a complete circle with the ball in right hand from the right side, over the head and out to the right side again, then flick the ball upward and catch it with the right.

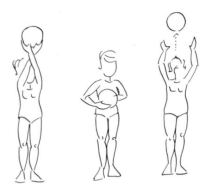

33.   CROSS CATCH

S.P.   Standing, ball in both hands, held low in front of the body.

M.   Toss the ball upward with both hands. Reach up and cross the hands to catch the ball. (Right wrist across left wrist, ball held in both palms.) Bring the hands downward to chest height and, making an outside turn so that the ball is brought in toward the body, toss the ball upward and catch it with both hands.

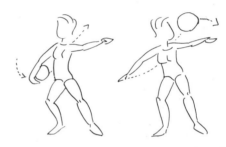

34.   THROW BEHIND SHOULDER AND CATCH

S.P.   Standing, ball in wrist grasp in right hand, arms horizontal.

M.   Bend the trunk to the right, swing ball downward and behind body, tossing it straight upward behind left shoulder. Catch it with left hand. Reverse direction.

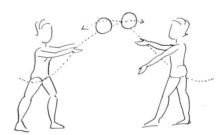

35.   PARTNER TOSSING

S.P.   Standing in front stride, left foot forward, ball in both hands in front of body.

M.   a.   Swing right arm to the rear, shifting the weight to the right foot in the rear.

b.   With an underhand swing, toss the ball to your partner. Balls should be tossed to the right side to avoid collision. Practice with one ball, then with two balls.

DANCE STEPS USING BALLS

1.   RUN AND LEAP

S.P.   Standing, ball in right hand, wrist grasp.
M.   Step left, right, left, and leap on the right as the ball is tossed upward. Catch it with both hands or with one hand.

2.   TOURS JETÉ

S.P.   Standing, weight on right foot, ball in right hand.
M.   Glissade step to the left (step, close, step) to get a lift. Kick right leg forward into the air, and quickly scissor kick the left into the air; end with the weight on the right foot after making a complete turn in the air. Left leg is usually in a scale or arabesque at the finish.

   The ball starts in the right hand, which is swung across the body on the glissade, and the ball is tossed into the air on the scissor kicking movement, both arms reaching upward. It may be caught by both hands, or by the right hand. It should end in the right hand, right arm extended forward as the movement finishes in a scale.

3.   BATTEMENT TOURNEY

S.P.   Standing, weight on right foot, ball in right hand, arm extended sideward.
M.   Glissade step to the left (step left, close, step left). Swing the straight right leg across the left in a high battement (kick). Hold the right leg in the air, and twist the body to face the original position. The ball is swung across the body on the glissade, and is tossed with both hands over the head on the battement tourney, and is caught again in both hands or the right hand. Finish the movement in scale, the right arm holding the ball.

4.   ARABESQUE TURN

S.P.   Standing, weight on right foot, ball in right hand to side extension.
M.   Step on left foot, turning completely around to the left as right leg is lifted in a moderate arabesque. The ball swings from the right hand and finishes with the ball in left hand. To alternate, change the ball to the left side and step turn to the right.

5.   CHASSÉ

S.P.   Standing, weight on right foot, ball in right hand.
M.   Chassé step to the left (open left leg through a développé to the left side, spring with both legs together in the air, step to the left again). Toss the ball over the head during the chassé step and catch it with left hand. Repeat to the right side.

6.   WALTZ

S.P.   Standing, weight on right foot, ball in right hand at the side.
M.   a.   Do a waltz step forward as the ball is tossed upward and caught low by the left hand.
       b.   Do the waltz step backward and toss the ball upward, catching it with the left hand.
       c.   Waltz turn. The ball may be tossed over the head from right to the left hand as the waltz turn is made to the left.
       d.   The ball may be passed around the body during the waltz turn; i.e., start on the right with the ball in the right hand. Waltz turn to the left as the ball crosses low in front of the body, changing from right to left hand during the turn. This may be finished with an impetus to the left side in a reach to the left.

7.   SCHOTTISCHE

S.P.   Standing, ball in right hand.
M.   Schottische step. Start with a left step, right step, left step, and hop on the left, lifting the right knee. The ball is bounced on the right side on the first left step, and then is tossed into the air on the step hop.

BALL EXERCISE TO MUSIC

Music: Chopin Valse, Russell Ballet record 31B, or the exercise may be arranged to fit any waltz.

1.   16 measures. Start standing, ball in right hand wrist grasp.
     a.   Swing right arm across body to left—1 measure.
     b.   Swing right arm back to right horizontal.
     c.   Swing right arm across body to left and toss ball up, catch it with left hand.
          Repeat the above to the left side; repeat all of a.

2. a. (16 measures). Overhead toss of ball as in No. 30; toss right to left, left to right; repeat.
    b. (16 measures). One-hand toss as in No. 29, performed in a side stride; do it four times: r, l, r, l.

3. a. (4 measures). Bounce with grapevine as in No. 25.
    b. Front-swing toss as in No. 31. Repeat 1 and 2 to opposite side.

4. Partners facing, balls in both hands over head. Bend down to crouch position, ball touching floor.
    a. Partners standing, toss as in No. 35 except toss is from both hands, and there is no weight shift.
    b. Partners bouncing as in No. 27a. Repeat d.

5. a. Front-swing toss as in No. 31.
    b. One-hand toss as in No. 29. Repeat 1 and 2.

6. a. Chaînes turn as in No. 4a and b.
    b. Overhead toss as in No. 30. Repeat 1 and 2 to opposite side.

7. a. Two-hand toss as in No. 28, and bounce down from both hands.
    b. Arm rolling as in No. 16.
        Repeat 1 and 2. Do a cross catch as in No. 33, and finish in a squat position.

8. Finish. Group A reaches up in moderate arabesque, ball over head on count 1; down to squat on count 2.
    Group B repeats as A holds squat position.

Formation for exercise

Group A	B	A	B
x	x	x	x
x	x	x	x
partners		partners	

Chapter 6   Clubs

The club is the oldest hand apparatus. Man first used it as a weapon many centuries ago. After a long period of development, it has become a hand apparatus especially used by women. The clubs were first used in gymnastic demonstrations by the Sokol in Czechoslovakia. They were first used in competition in Hungary in 1928. A great deal of skill is required to bring the body movements together with the club movements. The club movements should follow the natural movements of the body.

In the high school physical education program, clubs can be used effectively with large groups in the development of good posture, rhythm, and strength in the arms and shoulder girdle—usually a weak area of the body for girls. Clubs can also be used for school demonstrations. A demonstration in the evening with the clubs lighted is highly spectacular. A wire can be put through the club with a small light on the end which is controlled by the hand. Also, clubs can be painted with phosphorescent paint. For the best effect it is well to start with the lights on so the audience can see the exercise, then turn off the light and get the effect of the lighted clubs. This gives circles of light in darkness and is very beautiful.

EQUIPMENT

The club is generally made of limewood, and usually painted red, brown, and black or may be the polished natural wood. Today, we find many types of clubs, but the dimensions listed below are best for general use.

Club head   1-1/4 inches in diameter
(3-5/8 inches in circumference)

Club neck   3/4 inch
(2-5/8 inches in circumference)

Club body   2-1/8 inches
(6-1/2 to 6-3/4 inches in circumference)

Club length   13 inches

Club weight about 12 ounces

GRIPS AND TECHNIQUES

1. Swinging Movements (regular grip)
The grip for swinging movements is as follows: Hold the club with thumb and middle finger around it with the straight index finger.

the neck, just below the head of the club, supporting it with the straight index finger. The fourth and fifth fingers rest on the head. Swinging movements are done from the shoulder with arm straight.

2. Circling Movements
When circling with the club, hold it on the neck just below the head with thumb, index, and middle fingers forming a loose ring around the neck so that the club can circle freely. Circling of the club is aided by its weight. Circling movements with the club should be done with relaxed wrist and flexed elbow. The circle should be performed in the plane at which the movement is started; i.e., a vertical, horizontal, or lateral circle.

Grips for the circling movements are of two kinds, depending upon the plane of the circle:

a.   Reverse grip
With the hand in supination (palm upward), grasp the club with thumb and middle finger supported by the index finger which is under the club. The third and fourth fingers rest on the head.

b.   Regular grip
The hand is in pronation (palm down), grasping the club as noted in swinging movements.

3. Dropping Movements

Hold the club in a regular grip in right hand which is horizontal to the side. Quickly bend the elbow and drop club onto the forearm of right hand. With this movement the club comes down to ballet first position; swing the club to any other position.

4. Kip and Swing

a. False kip or half kip

Right arm is horizontal to the side, grasping the club in a regular grip (hand in pronation). Kip the club back of the forearm; i.e., drop the club with a push with index finger, holding it with all fingers as the club finishes the movement parallel and in back of the forearm. Then make a downward and inward circle with the arm bending at elbow, bringing the club down in front of the forearm; swing it up and back to original position.

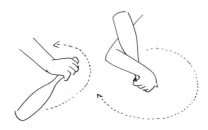

b. Kip

This is the same as the half kip; but after the half kip finish with the club resting on the inside of forearm, and then swing the club in a reverse circle (upward and inward to the body) and swing the club down and out to the original position.

When the basic techniques have been learned, combine the exercises with leg and trunk movement. All movements should be taught on both sides, first on the right and then on the left, and only then should one attempt to perform with both hands, or with two clubs.

In all circling and swinging movements, relax the knees. When the club is down, bend the knees; when the club is up, straighten the knees, so that the club movement is coordinated with the body movement.

5. Learning Circling Movements of the Club

The following sequence of movements will help the performer to learn the circling movements with the club:

a. Start with the arm horizontal, drop the club and let it swing back to the horizontal position.

b. Give a push with the index finger when the club is dropped, and return to the horizontal position.

c. Let the student experiment to learn how much push is necessary to get sufficient momentum to make a complete circle. First make only one circle and, at the end of the circle, support the club again with the index finger.

d. Do two or three circles in a continuous manner.

e. Perform the same movement in back of the forearm (backward circle).

SKILLS PERFORMED WITH ONE CLUB

All of the skills for one club will be described for one side or for one hand. They should be learned with both the right and left hands, and should be mastered separately before the two clubs are used simultaneously.

Swinging Movements

1. FORWARD SWING

S.P. Standing, club in right hand, regular grip, arm at side.

M. Swing the right arm forward to a horizontal position, quickly change the club to the left hand and return the left arm to the left side. Bend the knees on the up-swinging of the arm, and again on the down-swinging of the left arm.

Variations: a. Perform the same movement with a walking step forward, or with a chassé.

b. Perform the same movement with the feet in a forward stride, right foot forward. Swing the body forward to the right foot on the upward swing of the club, and backward on the left foot on the downward swing.

2.   SIDEWARD SWING

S.P. Standing in a wide side-stride position, club in right hand in regular grip.

M.   Swing the club downward across the body to the left hand and transfer the weight from right to left foot. Actually reach to the side at completion of the swing. Reverse to the opposite side.

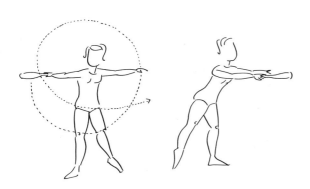

3.   SIDEWARD CIRCLE

S.P. Standing as in No. 2.

M.   Swing the club as in No. 2 sideward swing but, instead of stopping when the club reaches the left side, continue the swing making a complete circle and end out to left side. The weight remains on the right foot during the circling, and transfers to the left leg at completion and side reaching.

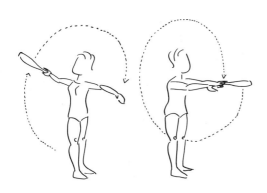

4.   CRAWL ARM CIRCLING

S.P. Standing, feet together, club in right hand at side, in regular grip.

M.   Keeping the arm straight with movement from the shoulder, swing the right arm backward and over the head to a forward horizontal position. Change the club to left

S.P. = Starting Position   M. = Movement

hand and swing the club down and backward over the head to the forward horizontal position, returning the club to right hand.

Variation: This movement may be done with a walking step or a chassé.

5.   REVERSE CRAWL SWING

S.P. Standing, feet together, club in right hand at the side, in regular grip.

M.   Swing the club forward, over head, and backward in a circle, ending in a forward horizontal position. Quickly change the club to left hand and again circle forward, over head, and back to a front horizontal position.

6.   BODY CIRCLE

S.P. Standing in a wide stride, club in right hand in regular grip.

M.   Bending at the waist, circle the club in a semi-horizontal circle over the body from the right across the body to the left and in back around the body, returning to the original standing position. Get as much back bending as possible at the waist. Reverse the movement.

7.   BODY WAVE

S.P. Standing with feet together, arms horizontally in front, club in right hand.

M.   As the body performs a "body wave," swing right hand downward and backward over the head, return to original position with the right arm in a forward horizontal position. While the right arm is circling and the body is performing a body wave, the left hand should remain in the forward horizontal position. Change hands.

Variation: When the club is in right hand, the left foot should be forward. As the club is changed to left hand, step forward with right foot.

8. FORWARD CURL

S.P. Standing, feet together, club in forward horizontal position in right hand, in regular grip.

M. Curl the trunk forward as knees bend and the club is swung downward to hyperextension position. Straighten the knees as the club swings. Return the club to forward position as the knees bend and straighten again.

Variation: Do the same movement with the body in a ballet point position.

Circling Movements

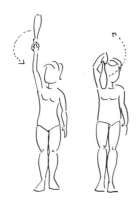

9. CIRCLE IN FRONT OF THE HEAD

S.P. Right arm stretched over head, club in regular grip.

M. Bend the elbow and drop the club outward and downward in front of the head; continue the circle returning to the original position.

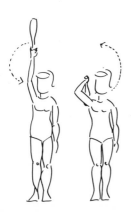

10. CIRCLE IN BACK OF HEAD

S.P. Right arm stretched over head, club in reverse grip.

M. Bend the elbow, drop the club outward and downward in a circle in back of the head, return to original position.

11. COMBINE FRONT AND BACK HEAD CIRCLING

S.P. Right arm stretched over head, club in regular grip.

M. Combine No. 9 and 10, make a circle in front of the head, club in regular grip; and then make a circle in back of the head, reverse grip (palm upward). This is like a continuous figure 8 movement, first in front and then in back of the head.

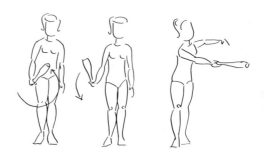

12. CIRCLE IN FRONT OF THE BODY

S.P. Standing, right arm in side extension, club in regular grip.

M. Drop the club making a small inward circle in front of the body, swing the club to the left. Swing the club down in front of the body again and make a small outward circle and end in the original position.

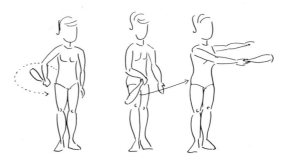

13. CIRCLE IN BACK OF THE BODY

S.P. Right arm in side extension, regular grip.

M. Drop the club and arm to the side, pushing with the index finger; bend the elbow and swing the club upward and outward behind the elbow, making a small circle to the rear. Bring the club in front of the body and swing the club to the left. Change the club to left hand and reverse movement.

14.   FRONT AND BACK CIRCLING AND
SWINGING TO OPPOSITE SIDE

S.P.   Right arm in side extension, regular grip.
M.   Make a circle downward in front of the body,
then make a circle in back of the body.
Elbow should be bent on the circles. Swing
the club to the opposite side in front of
the body.

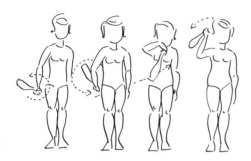

15.   COMBINATION OF FRONT AND BACK
CIRCLING OF BODY AND HEAD

S.P.   Right arm in side extension, regular grip.
M.   Circle the arm downward and inward in front
of the body, then make a circle in back of
the body, keeping the elbow high above the
head as a circle is made in front of the
head and then is dropped in back of the
head to make a rear circle of the head
(see No. 14, 11).

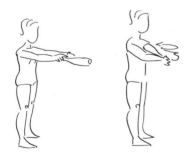

16.   HORIZONTAL CIRCLE INWARD

S.P.   Arms in front horizontal position, palms inward, club in regular grip in right hand.
M.   Left hand remains in position as the club is
pushed with the index finger, making a
horizontal circle with the club above the
right forearm. Starting the circle inward,
change club to left hand and repeat, or
repeat several times on the right.

17.   HORIZONTAL CIRCLE OUTWARD

S.P.   Arms in front horizontal position, club in
reverse grip in right hand. Left arm
remains stationary.
M.   Push with index finger and circle the club in
a horizontal circle outward over the top
of right forearm.

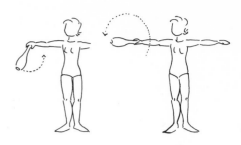

18.   CIRCLING IN FRONT OF ARM

S.P.   Standing, right arm in side extension, regular
grip.
M.   Make a small circle inward toward the body,
slightly bending the elbow; end in regular
grip.

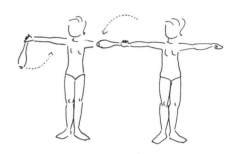

19.   CIRCLING IN BACK OF ARM

S.P.   Standing, right arm in side extension, reverse
grip.
M.   Do a backward circle in back of the forearm,
slightly bending the elbow, and return to
reverse grip.

20.   COMBINATION OF FRONT AND BACK
ARM CIRCLING

S.P.   Standing, right arm in side extension, regular
grip.
M.   Make a small inward circle in front of the
forearm, as in No. 18. Switch the club to
reverse grip and make a small backward
circle in back of the forearm as in No. 19.

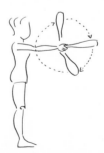

21.   VERTICAL CIRCLE OUTWARD

S.P.   Standing, right arm in front horizontal position,
club in reverse grip.
M.   Make a vertical circle with the club on the
outside of forearm. The elbow bends
slightly.

22.   VERTICAL CIRCLE INWARD

S.P.   Standing, right arm in front horizontal position, club in regular grip.
M.   Make a vertical circle with the club on inside of forearm. The elbow bends slightly.

23.   COMBINATION OF INWARD AND OUTWARD VERTICAL CIRCLES

S.P.   Standing, right arm in front horizontal position, club in reverse grip.
M.   Make a vertical circle outside as in No. 21, then make a vertical circle inside as in No. 22.

24.   VERTICAL CIRCLE AT SIDE

S.P.   Standing, right arm in front horizontal position, club in regular grip.
M.   Swing the club down to the right side, make a vertical circle with the club near the right hip. Continue the movement, extending the club to the rear. Reverse the swing and, making another small circle near the hip, return the club to the starting position.

25.   V SEAT ROLL

This is a "fun" exercise, not a real club swinging movement.

S.P.   Long sitting on the floor, club in right hand.

M.   Lift both legs in a V seat, roll the club around to the left side. The head of the club will move in an arc under the legs to the left. Repeat to the opposite direction.

SKILLS PERFORMED WITH TWO CLUBS

Swinging Movements

1.   STEP-HOP WITH ARM SWINGING

S.P.   Standing, clubs at sides, held in regular grip.
M.   Step-hop on right foot as right club is swung high over the head, and left knee is bent to the chest, left club swung to the rear. Arms should be kept straight. The body may be bent forward as in an Indian step-hop.

2.   ARM CIRCLING IN CRAWL

S.P.   Right arm over head, left to side, regular grip.
M.   Circle the right arm forward and simultaneously circle the left arm backwards.
Variations: a. Do the same movement with a leap forward on the right, push with the left and leap again on the right.
    b.   Do the same movement with steps forward.
    c.   Do the same movement with the arms as a waltz turn step is performed.
    d.   Do the same movements backward, arms circling backward as in a back crawl.

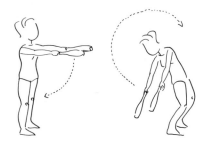

3.   BODY WAVE

S.P.   Standing, both clubs horizontally in front of body, regular grip.

M.   Swing both clubs to the right side, downward, and to the rear as the body performs a body wave. Reverse to the opposite side.

Variation: Do a regular body wave, clubs moving on either side of the body in a backward circle.

Dropping Movements

4.   DROP FROM OVER HEAD

S.P.   Standing with arms stretched over head, regular grip.

M.   Drop the clubs as the arms are brought down to 1st position. The clubs are resting on top of the forearms, the index and middle fingers on the head, thumb on the neck, palms down. Swing the clubs downward and outward and upward back to the original position.

Variation: Take a couple of running steps simultaneously dropping the clubs to 1st position on the forearms, then leap as the clubs are swung and lifted over head.

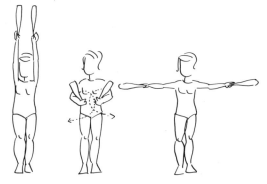

5.   DROP FROM OVER HEAD TO SIDE HORIZONTAL

S.P.   Standing with arms stretched over head, regular grip.

M.   Drop the clubs as in No. 4 to the 1st position, clubs resting on the forearms; swing the clubs downward and outward as both arms are swung to a side horizontal position.

Variation: Do the same movement with a step turn (chaînes) with clubs in on the half turn; end to the sides on completion of the turn.

6.   DROP FROM HORIZONTAL TO OVER HEAD

S.P.   Standing, arms horizontally to the sides, reverse grip.

M.   Bend the elbows and let the clubs fall to 1st position resting on the forearms, then swing the clubs downward, outward, upward, in front of the body.

Kips

7.   FALSE KIP

S.P.   Arms horizontal.

M.   Do a false kip with both clubs (see Grips and Techniques).

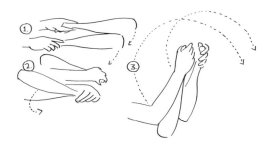

8.   FALSE KIP FROM FRONT HORIZONTAL

S.P.   Arms in forward horizontal position, regular grip, palms downward.

M.   Kip the club outside of the forearm, bend both elbows and circle the elbows inward and upward; swing the clubs out to a horizontal position again, finishing with hands in reverse grip.

9.   REGULAR KIP

S.P.   Arms horizontal to the sides.

M.   Do a regular kip with both hands (see Grips and Techniques).

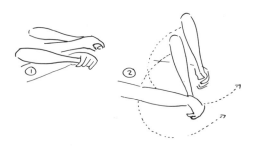

10.   REGULAR KIP IN FRONT

S.P.   Arms horizontal in front, palms facing downward, regular grip.

M.   Kip the clubs outside, bend the elbows and bring the clubs downward and inward to the body, clubs resting on the forearms; circle with the forearms upward and inward, elbows bent, and circle the clubs back to original position.

11. REGULAR KIP OVER HEAD

S.P. Arms stretched over head.
M.   Do a regular kip.

Circling Movements

(Review material for single club.)

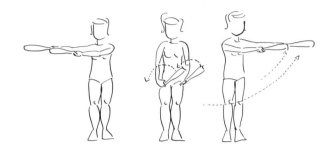

12. FRONT CIRCLE TO OPPOSITE SIDE

S.P. Both arms horizontal, to the right side; arms
      parallel.
M.   Make a circle in front of the body with both
      clubs ending on the opposite side. Reverse
      the movement back to the right side.

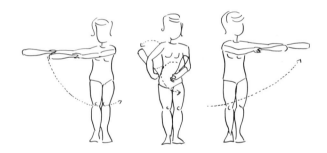

13. SIMULTANEOUS FRONT AND BACK CIRCLES

S.P. Standing, arms horizontal and both to the right
      side.
M.   Left arm makes a circle in front of the body
      and simultaneously the right arm makes
      a circle in the rear, both arms then swing
      to the left side, ending in a side horizontal
      position.

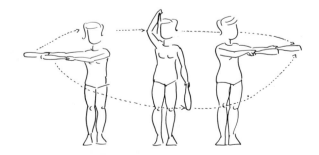

14. SIMULTANEOUS FRONT AND REAR SWING

S.P. Both arms to right side in a side horizontal
      position, arms parallel.

M.   Left arm swings downward and over to the left
      side as simultaneously the right club swings
      behind the head, both ending to the left
      side. Reverse the movement to the opposite
      side.

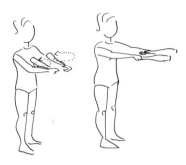

15. HORIZONTAL CIRCLES

S.P. Standing, arms in front horizontal position.
M.   Perform horizontal circles, both clubs moving
      in circles first to the left side and then to
      the right.

16. VERTICAL CIRCLES

S.P. Standing, arms in front horizontal position.
M.   Vertical circles, both outside of the forearms,
      then both inside the forearms. When out-
      side circling, the grip must be a reverse
      grip; inside circling, the grip is a regular
      grip.

17. VERTICAL CIRCLES AT THE SIDES

S.P. Standing with arms in front horizontal position.
M.   Bring clubs down near the hips and make a
      vertical circle, then swing the clubs back
      as far as possible. Reverse the circle and
      return to the original position.
Variation: Both clubs are first circling near the
      right hip, then reverse sides.

18. BALLET POINT WITH VERTICAL
     CIRCLES AT SIDES

S.P. Body in a ballet point, right foot forward, arms
      horizontally in front of body.
M.   Swing the clubs down to the sides near the hips
      and do outside circles, starting backward
      and ending to the rear in a hyperextension
      of the arm. Reverse the circle and return
      to the starting position.

19.   CIRCLING IN FRONT AND BACK OF ARMS

S.P.   Standing, arms horizontal to the sides, regular grip.

M.   Both clubs are circled in front of the forearms inward with a regular grip. Change to a reverse grip and circle the clubs in back of the forearms.

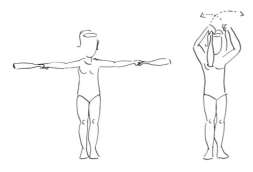

20.   FROM HORIZONTAL POSITION, HEAD CIRCLING

S.P.   Arms in sideward horizontal position.

M.   Right hand makes a circle in front of the head as the left makes a circle in back of the head; both end in the original sideward horizontal position. Alternate sides.

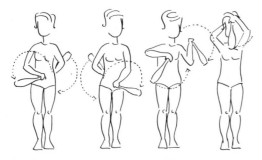

21.   FRONT AND BACK CONTINUOUS CIRCLES

S.P.   Arms horizontally to the sides.

M.   Both clubs move simultaneously, as noted below:
Right hand circles in front of the body, continues in a circle in back of the body, continues in front of the head, continues in back of the head.
Left hand circles in back of the body, continues in a circle in front of the body, continues in a circle in back of the head, continues in a circle in front of the head. These movements are done in a smooth continuous movement, elbows bent and clubs close to the body.

CLUB EXERCISE TO MUSIC

Music: Russell record 31a, Ballet, Les Cygnets.

Starting position: From dropping movement, clubs resting on forearms, hands at waist.

1.   Swing both clubs to the right side, arms in parallel side horizontal position.

2.   Front circle to the left side and back to the right (see Skill 12).

3.   Simultaneous front and back circles to the left, then to the right (see Skill 13).

4.   Waltz to the right side, arms circling in a crawl (see Skill 2c). Then do a quarter turn to the right and do a ballet point with vertical circles at the sides (see Skill 18).

5.   Repeat No. 4 (above) to the left side.

6.   Turn one-quarter to the right to face front; do a head circling from the horizontal position (see Skill 20).

7.   Circle in front of body by swinging arms downward, across low in front of body; continue in circles back to horizontal position.

8.   Front and back continuous circles as in Skill 21; finish with arms at sides.

9.   Kip and swing the arms out to the original side horizontal position.

10.   Repeat from No. 6 to No. 10 (above) and finish in the starting position.

Chapter 7   Ropes

Rope activities include use of the rope for stretching exercises, in swinging movements as a club or dumbbell; in individual rope jumping and partner rope jumping, and in rope climbing. Some material on rope climbing is included because a number of schools do use rope climbing as a means of developing shoulder girdle strength in girls.

Rope activities are primarily for developmental purposes and for group demonstrations. Rope jumping is an excellent means for developing endurance, and it will also strengthen the feet and legs. Because it is such a physically demanding activity, it should be alternated with other activities. When performing rope jumping for any length of time, the class should be divided into groups, to allow for alternate activity and rest.

Rope jumping performed by children takes on various patterns and is like singing games—it varies from one part of the country to another. Individual rope jumping as described here is used primarily by women. Men use rope jumping to develop feet and legs and, although women may have the same purpose, they tend to be more artistic in the type of movements performed, the manner in which the jumping is done, and in the patterns developed.

EQUIPMENT

Some persons consider a No. 8 or 9 sash cord as the best for rope jumping. A manila rope, nylon rope, or hemp rope that is not more than one-half inch in diameter can be used. The length of the rope is measured by having the person stand on the rope with one foot, arms stretched horizontally to the sides. The rope should be long enough for the arms to be completely stretched to the sides at shoulder height. Usually 10 to 12 feet is the correct length of the rope. The length of the rope is important so it can be swung from the wrists with the proper technique. For school use, rope may be bought by the coil or number of feet, cut to the correct length, and taped at the ends to avoid fraying.

TECHNIQUES

1. <u>Rope jumping</u>. The rope should be held with three fingers, with most of the action coming from the wrist and with the arms held horizontally to the sides, elbows slightly bent. The first swing of the rope starts from the shoulders and then the movement is in the wrists. The feet should be extended in the air with toes pointed, and the movement should be light and springing with no noise upon landing. The jump need not be high—just sufficient for the rope to go smoothly under the feet.

2. <u>Rope Swinging</u>. The swinging is done from the shoulders, elbows bending with the movement. The rope may be swung in vertical, lateral, or horizontal planes.

3. <u>Patterns for Rope Jumping</u>. The following are suggested patterns which lend themselves well to large groups doing rope jumping:

   a. Divide the class into two lines, each starting at opposite rear corners of the gymnasium. Do a leap or step-hop diagonally to the opposite corner, lines crossing at the center. This may also be done with partners side by side.

   b. Class in a single circle, jumping toward the center and backing away from the center.

   c. Class in a double circle, side by side and facing each other or back to back.

   d. Class in line formation on the floor. The forward line jumps across the floor, followed by the other lines. This allows each line to have a rest period.

   e. Using the schottische step as a basic pattern, do a regular schottische dance with rope jumping.

MOVEMENTS

Girls will enjoy rope jumping barefooted either in the gymnasium or on a lawn. In most European countries rope jumping is performed out-of-doors as well as in the gymnasium. If the rope jumping is done on a concrete playground, tennis shoes should be worn.

Because of the strenuous nature of rope jumping, alternate the groups or alternate the skills; i.e., some jumping, then some rope swinging, and perhaps some stretching exercises with the rope.

The use of music adds to the enjoyment of rope jumping, and develops more rhythmical body action. Schottische rhythm or slow waltz is best for beginners, although marches or polkas may be used. The jumping pattern should fit the musical phrasing, thus the music should be chosen with care. Even popular music may be used if the rhythm is good. Popular music will interest students, especially if they are creating their own sequences or patterns.

Stretching Exercises with Ropes

To use the rope as an aid in stretching exercises, fold the rope over twice so that it is about two or three feet in length. Grasp the ends of the rope in the hands for most stretching exercises. The rope may also be folded and knotted as in swinging movements.

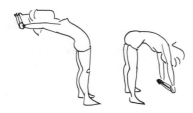

1. OVERHEAD STRETCH

S.P. Standing, arms over head, end of the rope held in each hand.
M.   a. Stretch the arms over the head and arch the body backward as much as possible.
      b. Bend the trunk forward touching the floor with the rope and hands.

2. SIDE BENDING

S.P. Standing, arms stretched over head, end of the rope held in each hand.

M.   Keeping the arms extended and the rope taut, bend to the right side and then to the left.

3. TRUNK TWISTING

S.P. Standing, arms stretched forward in front of the body, holding onto the ends of the rope.
M.   Twist the body from side to side, keeping the rope taut, and keeping the arms horizontal.

4. LEG STRETCHING

S.P. Long sitting, end of rope held in each hand in front of body.
M.   a. Hook the rope around the right foot, bend the knee to the chest, extend the leg upward, bend the knee, return the right leg to long sitting.
      b. Repeat with the left leg.
      c. Repeat with both legs.

5. SIT-UPS

S.P. Back lying, arms stretched over head, end of the rope held in each hand.
M.   a. Keeping the arms stretched and the rope taut, come to a sitting position.
      b. Bend forward bouncing the trunk forward, touching the rope to the floor in front of the feet.

S.P. = Starting Position   M. = Movement

6. V SEAT WITH ROPE

S.P. Long sitting, rope end held in each hand.

M.   Draw the knees to the chest and pass the feet through the rope. Extend both legs to the ceiling in a balanced seat or V seat. Bend the knees and bring the feet through the ropes again to long sitting.

7. UPPER BACK STRETCH

S.P. Face lying, arms stretched over head, rope end held in each hand.

M.   Keeping the arms extended and the rope taut, lift the upper back as high as possible. Hold the position for a second and return to face lying.

8. LOW BACK STRETCH

S.P. Face lying, arms at the sides, rope end in each hand.

M.   Hook the rope over the feet and pull the legs backward, arching the back and lifting the upper back. This is like a "cradle" or back-bend position. Hold the position for a few seconds, return to back lying.

Note. This is a good preliminary stretch for developing a back bend.

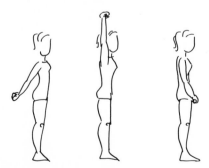

9. SHOULDER DISLOCATION

S.P. Standing, end of rope held in each hand in front of body.

M.   Bring the rope over the head and down the back as far as possible. Return the rope to starting position.

Using the Rope as a Club or Dumbbell

Fold the rope over twice and tie a knot in the top. Hold one end of the rope and swing it as you would a club.

10. ARM CIRCLING

S.P. Standing, holding onto one end of the rope with the right hand.

M.   Keeping the right arm straight, make a circle forward, upward, and backward. When the rope is in front of the body, quickly change the rope to the left hand and repeat to the left side.

Note. Rhythmically, it is better to circle each arm three times and then change.

Variations: a. The swing may be in the opposite direction.
   b. Circle the arm as above, but add a twisting of the body to the side of the rope turning.
   c. Perform a figure 8 with the rope: i.e., circle the rope in the right hand downward and backward and forward; quickly change hands and circle the left forward, upward, and backward.
   d. Do all of the above walking forward or backward.

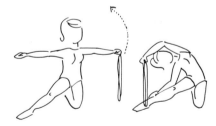

11. CIRCLING AND BOUNCING

S.P. Half kneeling on the left knee, right leg extended to the side, rope in left hand at the side.

M.   Swing the rope over the head and bounce the trunk to the right over the right leg.

Variation: Circle the rope over the head and then bounce over the right leg. The circling may be done three times, bouncing three times, or set it to a rhythmical pattern. Alternate sides.

12.   KNEELING AND CIRCLING

S.P.   Kneeling on both knees, rope in right hand at side.

M.   Swing the rope backward in a circle. As the rope is swung to the rear, bend the knees, sitting on the heels, trunk slightly twisted to the right. As the rope swings over the head and forward, return to an upright kneeling position. Repeat several times and then alternate sides.

Variation: Do the same movement, but instead of sitting on the heels, arch the back (see sketch).

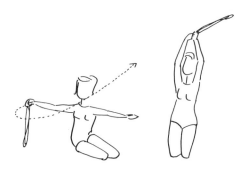

13.   SITTING AND CIRCLING

S.P.   Sitting on the right hip, both legs bent, feet to the left side, rope held by the right hand at right side.

M.   Swing the rope across the front of the body in a circle, twice. On the third circle, as the rope is over the head, rise to both knees catching the rope in both hands, then shift to the left hip as the rope is shifted to the left hand. Alternate sides.

14.   CIRCLING WITH TRUNK BOUNCING

S.P.   Long sitting, rope in right hand at the side.

M.   Circle with right arm backward and forward three times. On the finish of the third circle the rope hits the floor in front of the feet. Quickly change the rope to the opposite hand and repeat to the left side.

Variation: The arm may just swing back and forth rather than make a circle with the rope.

15.   STANDING TRUNK CIRCLING

S.P.   Standing in wide stride, rope in right hand at the side.

M.   Swing the rope to the right side, back, left side, and front as the trunk is bent in the same direction. Alternate directions.

16.   TRUNK CIRCLING IN LYING POSITION

S.P.   Long sitting, rope in right hand.

M.   Bend forward over the legs, making a wide circle with the rope on the floor as the body bends forward to right side, then goes to back lying. Drag the rope on the floor in a circle. As the rope is over the head in the back lying position, quickly change hands and continue the circle to the left, ending in a long sitting with rope in front of the feet.

Rope Swinging

The rope is folded in half; i.e., the two ends of the rope are brought together. The swing may be with one or both hands.

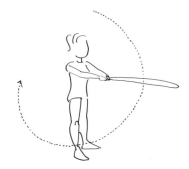

17.   SIDE CIRCLING

S.P.   Standing, holding both ends of the rope in both hands, hands held at right shoulder.

M.   Circle the rope in forward circles.
Variations: a. Circle the rope in backward circles.
   b.   Circle the rope from side to side in a figure 8; i.e., circle the rope backward on right side and when the rope is in front of the body, swing the arms to the left side and circle the rope downward and backward to the left side.
   c.   Body wave to the right side as the rope is swung to the rear and over head. May also be done to left side.
   d.   All circling movements may be done while moving forward or backward, either walking or with dance step.

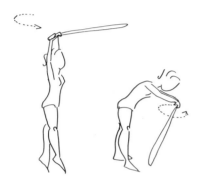

18.   OVERHEAD CIRCLING

S.P.   Standing, holding both ends of the rope in both hands, hands held together and over the head.
M.   Perform horizontal circles with the rope around the top of the head.
Variations: a. Do the same movement walking forward or backward.
   b.   Do the same movement performing a chaînés turn.
   c.   Do a horizontal circle over the head with a forward step, and a low horizontal circle in front of the body, trunk slightly bent forward with backward step. Reach forward with the left arm (see sketch).
   d.   Do the same movement as c, but with a waltz turn.

19.   LOW CIRCLING WITH JUMP

S.P.   Standing, holding both ends of the rope in right hand, to the right side.

M.   Swing the rope low to the left side. As the rope almost hits the left foot, jump over it and continue the circle. Repeat to opposite side.
Variations: a. Do a few running steps and then leap, legs split in air.
   b.   Do a few running steps and then leap, forward leg straight, rear leg bent.

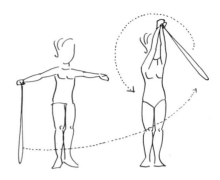

20.   ROPE CIRCLING TO CHANGE ROPE POSITION

S.P.   Standing, rope ends held in right hand, to the right side.
M.   Swing the rope forward across the body toward the left, continue the circling as the right arm is brought over the head. Reach upward over the head with left hand and take the left end of the rope with the left hand. Continue the circle to the front of the body. Separate the rope ends and bring the right hand across to the left side over the head and finish with the rope in back.

21.   HORIZONTAL SWING

S.P.   Standing in wide side stride, weight to right side, rope in right arm to right side.

M.   Swing the rope from the right to the left side keeping the arm horizontal. Bend the knees and shift the weight to left foot as the rope swings to the left. Continue swinging back to the right, rope still in the right hand, or change hands when the rope is to the left side.

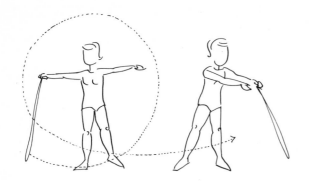

22.   CIRCLE AND SWING TO THE SIDE

S.P.   Standing, in wide side stride, weight to the right, rope in right arm to the side.

M.   Make a circle of the rope in front of the body, starting downward to the left; complete the circle and swing the rope to the left hand. The weight is transferred to the left side as the rope is swung to the left side and transferred to the left hand.

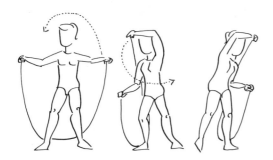

23.   CIRCLING THE BODY

S.P.   Standing in wide stride, weight on left, rope in rear.

M.   Bring left hand to rear over to right side, bring both hands forward to right side, swing right arm across the body and continue the circle around the head and finish in original position.

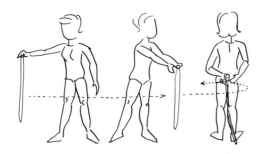

24.   CHAÎNÉS TURNS, ROPE SWINGING HORIZONTALLY

S.P.   Standing, rope in right hand to right side.

M.   Step to the left and simultaneously swing the rope in front of the body. Change the rope to the left hand and step on right foot, swing the rope around the rear to the right hand.

Variation: Do one complete chaînés turn and then swing the rope to the left side with a stretch of the body to the left side. Reverse the turn and the stretch to the right.

Individual Rope Jumping

The jump is a light spring with the feet extended in the air. The arms are horizontal and most of the rope turning is with wrist action. The rope should not touch the floor, but should pass slightly above it. In all forward jumps the rope starts in the rear, and for all backward jumps the rope starts in front.

25.   BASIC JUMP FORWARD

S.P.   Standing, rope in back of the body, arms horizontal.

M.   Jump with both feet as the rope is turned forward.

Variations: a. Jump with the feet apart and then together.

b.   Jump with the feet apart and crossed when together.

26.   BASIC JUMP BACKWARD

S.P.   Standing, rope in front of the body, arms horizontal.

M.   Jump on both feet as the rope is turned backward.

27.   STEP-HOP FORWARD

S.P.   Standing, rope in back of the body, arms horizontal.

M.   Step forward on right foot as the rope is over the head, hop over the rope. Continue the step-hop, alternating sides. This may also be done with the free leg extending forward.

28.   STEP-HOP BACKWARD

S.P.   Standing, rope in front of the body, arms horizontal.

M.   Step backward on right foot as the rope is over the head, hop over the rope as it comes near the floor. Alternate sides. This may be done with the free leg extended backward.

29.   SIDEWAYS LEAP

S.P.   Standing, rope in back of body, arms horizontal.

M.   Moving to the left side. Swing the rope and hop over it on the right foot across in front of the left foot, step to the side with the left, and continue to the left.

When moving to the right side. Swing the rope and hop on the left foot across in front of the right foot, stepping to the side with the right foot.

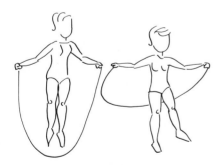

30.   GALLOP TO THE SIDE

S.P.   Standing, rope in back of the body, arms horizontal.

M.   Take a gallop step to the left side as the rope is turned forward; reverse sides.

Variation: The rope may be turned backward and the gallop performed to one side and then changed to the other.

31.   ARMS CROSSED

S.P.   Standing, rope in back of the body, arms horizontal.

M.   a.   Start with a basic jump forward as No. 25, then cross the arms at the elbows and continue jumping with arms crossed, then open arms and do again a basic jump forward; continue the above pattern.

   b.   This may also be done jumping with the rope swing to the rear.

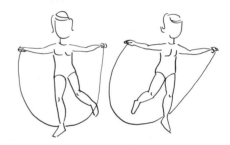

32.   RUNNING STEP

S.P.   Standing, rope in back of the body, arms horizontal.

M.   With a quick turning of the rope do an alternating leap, first on the right and then on the left, in a semi-running movement. This may be done in place, or as low fast leaps across the gymnasium.

Variations: a.   Take three running steps and a leap.
   b.   Take three running steps and an attitude leap.

33.   SPLIT JUMPS

S.P.   Standing, rope in back of the body, arms horizontal.

M.   Do two regular jumps as in No. 25, and on the third jump split the legs forward and backward in the air.

34.   LEAP, PUSH-LEAP

S.P.   Standing, rope in back of the body, arms horizontal.

M.   Leap on the right foot as the rope goes under the foot, push with the left foot in back of the right foot, and hop on the right foot. Continue with the left.

35.   CUT STEP

S.P.   Standing, rope to rear, arms horizontal.

M.   Weight is on right foot. As the rope is over the head, swing the left foot around and in front of the right and hop on it as the rope comes to the floor. Hop again on left foot. Repeat by swinging the right around in front and hopping over the rope with the right, hopping again with the right.

36.   SPEED JUMPING

S.P.   Standing, rope to the rear, arms horizontal.

M.   Jump in the air as the rope turns twice with only one slow jump. Arms must be held horizontally and the rope is swung quickly with most of the movement being in the wrist.

37.   CAN-CAN STEP

S.P.   Standing, rope to the rear, arms horizontal.

M.   Jump on the left, tapping the right foot; jump again on the left and extend the right foot forward. Alternate sides.

Variation: Tap the foot in front, bend the knee, tap the foot in front again and then kick it forward.

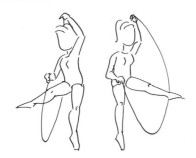

38.   SIDE LEG SWINGING (COWBOY STEP)

S.P.   Standing on left foot, left arm high, right arm low.

M.   Keeping left hand high, swing the rope to the right side, hopping on the left, kick the right leg through the rope; step-hop on the right as the rope is brought around to the left side, kick left leg through the rope, step-hop on left and continue circling the rope. Do in a rhythmical pattern several times.

39.   SCHOTTISCHE STEP

S.P.   Standing, rope to the rear, arms horizontal.

M.   Schottische step forward; i.e., step forward on the right, close the left to the right, and step-hop on the right. The free foot is extended forward or backward on the hop. The rope goes under on the first step and again on the step-hop.

Variations: a. Perform the schottische step to the rear.

b.   Perform the schottische step twice and step-hop four times.

40.   POLKA STEP

S.P.   Standing, rope to the rear, arms horizontal.

M.   Polka step; i.e., hop, step, together step. The rope swings slowly, the step is faster than the hands. Start with the polka step and then add the rope swinging.

41.   HOMBO STEP

S.P.   Standing, rope to the rear, arms horizontal.

M.   Fall diagonally forward on the right foot, touching the left toe to the rear and taking weight momentarily on the left; fall forward again on the right as the left is extended to the rear. Alternate sides. The rope makes two complete swings for each step.

Partner Jumping

42.   PARTNERS FACING

S.P.   Partners stand facing each other. No. 1 has the rope.

M.   No. 1 turns the rope and both persons jump at the same time. It is important to stand very close together.

Variation: Partners facing the same direction, rear person with the rope.

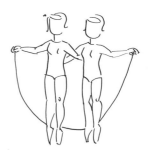

43.   PARTNERS SIDE BY SIDE

S.P.   Standing, inside arm around waist of partner, outside hands holding an end of the rope. Partners standing very close together.

M.   With both persons swinging the rope together, vary the jumping:

a.   Do a two-foot jump forward.

b.   Do a two-foot jump backward.

c.   Do a step-hop forward or backward.

d.   Do a running step or leap forward.

ROPE CLIMBING

Climbing ropes are frequently used as regular equipment in a gymnasium. Although rope climbing is not a competitive activity for women, the ropes can be used to develop shoulder girdle strength and finger strength. Young girls of junior high school age find rope climbing fun; however, it might not appeal to the older girls. The skills performed on the ropes are of value as developmental exercises, and may be used effectively as part of the gymnastic program.

The regulation rope for men's competitive climbing is a three-inch manila rope 20 feet long or more, securely fastened to the ceiling. A tambourine is at the 20-foot level. The rope climb event is not an international one, but is used at many local and national meets. The event for men is a 20-foot climb against time, two trials permitted and the better one to score. Women do not compete in this event, though frequently junior high girls use the score of a rope climb as part of a physical fitness battery of tests. With the advent of other apparatus, the ropes have lost much appeal to girls.

For safety, it is desirable that one girl perform at a time, with one or more spotters and the other students at a safe distance.

Developmental Skills
Using a Single Climbing Rope

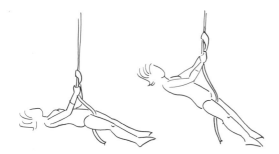

1. PULL-UP

S.P. Supine lying, rope held in both hands at chest.
M. a. Keeping the feet in place and the body rigid, pull up to a standing position using a hand-over-hand pulling movement.
   b. Lower the body to back lying in the same manner.

2. SWING ON THE ROPE

S.P. Standing, grasping the rope with both hands at shoulder height, rope pulled as far as possible to the rear.
M. Run forward with the rope and at the end of the run spring onto the rope, feet resting on the knot at the bottom. Swing forward, backward, forward, and dismount by jumping off at the end of the back swing. To dismount, pull the body upward by bending the elbows, spring back away from the rope.

The same dismount may be done at the end of the forward swing.

3. CHINNING ON THE ROPE

S.P. Standing, grasping the rope high above the head.
M. Keeping a tight grip, hands on the rope, bend the elbows pulling the body upward, head to hands. Lower to standing position.

4. PIKE HANG

S.P. Standing on the floor, grasping the rope with both hands over head.
M. Pulling upward with both hands, lift the legs directly forward on either side of the rope in a good pike position.

5. INVERTED HANG

S.P. Standing, grasping the rope above the head.
M. Holding the rope with both hands, swing the legs up and over the head, placing one foot in front and one in back of the rope and locking the rope between the legs. Hold the inverted position for a few seconds, then return to standing.

Page 60 — Modern Rhythmic Gymnastics

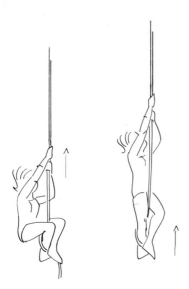

6. CLIMBING WITH FOOT AND LEG LOCK

S.P. Standing, reaching upward with both hands, grasping the rope over the head.

M. Pull the body upward, swinging the right leg around the rope so that the rope passes across the right foot. The left foot steps on the rope across the instep. Reach upward with the hands as the rope is made fast with the foot clamp, bring the feet up as close to the body as possible, and continue the movement.

7. CLIMBING WITH STIRRUP LOCK

S.P. Standing, reaching upward with both hands and grasping the rope over the head.

M. The rope is on the right side and is brought under right foot and over left foot, closing the feet, clamping tightly on the rope. Reach upward with the arms, pulling the body upward, and again use the stirrup position with the feet. Continue the movement. This may be done with the rope on the opposite side.

8. CROSS-LEG CLIMB, OR SHINNY UP (EASIEST FOR GIRLS)

S.P. Standing, reaching upward with both hands and grasping the rope over the head.

M. Pull the body upward with the hands as the legs overlap the rope. The rope passes over the instep of the foot and is clamped to the foot by the back of the ankle of the other foot. Continue the movement.

9. CLIMB WITH HANDS ONLY (VERY DIFFICULT FOR GIRLS)

S.P. Standing, reaching upward with both hands and grasping the rope over the head.

M. The body weight must be shifted from side to side, which is done by kicking the legs forward with the knees slightly bent. Reach upward with the right hand, then the left, in a hand-over-hand movement.

Note. This may be used by girls to descend the rope.

10. DESCENDING WITH ROPE BETWEEN THE ARCHES OF THE FEET

S.P. In a climbing position on the rope, ready to descend.

M. The rope remains between the arches of the feet; legs slightly bent. Lower self with hand-over-hand movement.

11. DESCEND WITH CROSS-LEG POSITION

S.P. In climbing position on the rope, ready to descend.

M. The legs are crossed, right over left, and the rope is gripped between the ankles. Descend by bending the knees and lowering the hands alternately.

12. DESCEND WITH STIRRUP HOLD

S.P. In climbing position on the rope, ready to descend.

M. The rope passes down the right side, under the right foot and over the top of the left foot. Open and close the foot position and lower the hands.

Stunts Using Two Ropes

13. PIKE POSITION OR TUCKED POSITION

S.P. Standing between two ropes, grasping each rope at shoulder height.

M. a. Holding onto the ropes, lift the legs in a tucked position to the chest.
   b. Lift the legs in a pike position.

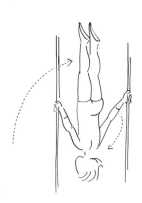

14. INVERTED HANG

S.P. Standing between the ropes, grasp each rope at shoulder height.

M. With a spring from the feet, kick up to an inverted position, hold the position for a few seconds and then return to standing.

Spotting: There should be two spotters, holding at the shoulders.

15. SKIN THE CAT

S.P. Standing between the ropes, grasping each rope at shoulder height.

M. Kick up into an inverted position and bring the feet down over the head rearways, and hang. Let go with the hands and land on the feet.

Spotting: There should be two spotters, one on each side holding at the shoulders.

16. SKIN THE CAT AND REVERSE

S.P. Standing between two ropes, grasping each rope at shoulder height.

M. Kick up with the feet into an inverted position, bring the feet down rearways until the toes touch the floor, push off with the toes, go up back to an inverted position, drop feet down forward.

17.   NEST HANG

S.P.   Standing between two ropes, grasping each rope at shoulder height.

M.   Kick up into an inverted position. Bending the ankles, lock the feet over the rope above the head. Still holding onto the ropes, arch the body as in a cradle position; hold the position, either come out forward or skin the cat rearways to the floor.

Spotting: There should be two spotters one on each side, supporting the shoulders.

ROPE EXERCISE TO MUSIC

Square Dance Using Rope Jumping

Performed in a square (four couples). Couple 1 with back to music, Couple 2 at right of Couple 1, Couple 3 across from Couple 1, Couple 4 at the left of Couple 1. The square should be large for jumping, and may be smaller for other movements. Use any good square dance record, fitting the movements to the musical phrasing.

1. Bow to Your Partner
    Folding the rope four times, holding it over the head with both hands, place the right foot forward and bow to your partner.

2. Bow to Your Corner
    Turn and face your corner, bow in the same way.

3. Promenade the Circle
    Turning to the left, moving clockwise, do a two-step forward, swinging the rope in both hands over the left shoulder (rope ends together). Go completely around the circle, returning to place. End facing the center and moving backward, making the circle large. Couples in a side-by-side position with inside arms around waist of partner, jumping with one rope which is to the rear.

4. Forward and Back
    Couples 1 and 3 in side-by-side position with one rope. Jump three step-hops toward each other, change the rope to the front and do three step-hops backward, changing so that each has her own rope to the rear—stepping apart.

5. Forward and Back
    Couples 2 and 4 do the same as No. 4 movement.

6. Forward and Pass Through
    Couples 1 and 3—each doing a step-hop with individual ropes, change places, turn around and change back to original places.

7. Forward and Pass Through
    Couples 2 and 4 do the same as No. 6.

8. Form a Star to the Right, Then to the Left
    Moving toward the center with the right hand, rope in right hand and middle of rope held in left hand, end to the left. Do a two-step around the circle to opposite sides, change hands to the left in the star, return to place.

9. Grand Right and Left
    Stepping backward with four steps and getting rope ready in the rear, move clockwise passing right shoulders with person on the left first, then passing left shoulders with the next person. Alternate until you return to your own position. Do a schottische as you pass each person.

10. Buzz Step
    Grasping your partner about the waist with the right hand, rope held in right hand and to the left side in the left hand. Right feet and hips together, push with the left foot in a buzz step in a circle; change hands and do buzz step in opposite direction.

11. Step to the side and, grasping the rope over the head, bow to your partner.

Schottische Using Rope Jumping

Use schottische record, and fit the movement to the musical phrasing.

12. Entrance
    Partners in a side-by-side position (Movement 43, page 58) using one rope (one person holds her rope), starting at one corner of the gymnasium, do a step-hop forming a circle. End forming a double circle, facing counterclockwise, and quite a distance apart.

13. Schottische Step Forward
    Do two schottische steps forward, and take four step-hops in place; repeat.

14. Schottische Apart and Together
    Do two schottische steps, moving sideward away from partner.
    Do a turn in place with four step-hops.

Do two schottische steps, moving sideward toward partner.

Do a turn in place with four step-hops.

15. Schottische Forward and Swing

Do two schottische steps forward (partners side by side in double circle moving counterclockwise). With rope in outside hands, do three rope swings in place, change ropes to in front.

Do two schottische steps to the rear.

Do three rope swings in place, change ropes to in front for cowboy step—facing center.

16. Cowboy Step

Do seven cowboy steps making a circle to the left; change hands.

Do seven cowboy steps making a circle to the right; change rope to both hands for swinging.

17. Swing

Facing center, rope held in both hands at right shoulder, four circles to the right, four circles to the left, eight circles alternating right and left.

18. Schottische to Center and Can-can

Do two schottische steps toward the center of the circle.

Do four can-can steps.

Do two schottische steps backward.

Do four can-can steps.

19. Exit

Moving around the circle counterclockwise in double circle, each person does a continuous schottische step.

Chapter 8   Hoops

Hoops were first used by the Gymnastikschule Medau of Coburg, Germany, and from there the use of hoops in gymnastics has spread to many countries. At first, the hoops were used for group demonstrations and were just held in various positions. Used in this way, the hoops had little physical developmental value. Within a short time, however, numerous new and difficult techniques were developed and the hoops became a part of the competitive group gymnastics for women.

Hoop techniques require big movements and they help to develop strength, coordination, and flexibility in the upper extremity. Students find the hoop techniques easier than the Indian club techniques.

EQUIPMENT

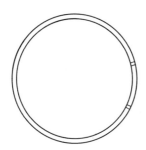

Hoops are made by steaming a piece of hardwood 1 or 1-1/2 inches wide into a circle and closing the ends together. Some hoops are made of aluminum pipe and painted in various bright colors. Size of the hoop varies in different countries. For example, the Russian girls use large hoops while the regulation size in some other countries are approximately:

Width, 1-1/4 inches
Inner diameter, 27 inches
Thickness, 1/3 inch

A medium size hoola hoop may be used if wooden or aluminum hoops are not available.

TECHNIQUES

Hoop exercises are classified into:
Swinging
Jumping
Circling
Tossing

In the swinging, circling, tossing movements the hoops are held in a horizontal plane, a frontal plane across in front of the body, a back plane across in back of the body, or a side plane moving forward and backward alongside the body.

The movement with the hoop should be a smooth, flowing one, with arm, leg, and body movements coordinated with the hoop movements.

In all movements a regular grip is used with the palm facing as follows:

Palm facing forward
Palm facing backward
Palm facing upward
Palm facing downward
Palm facing inward
Palm facing outward

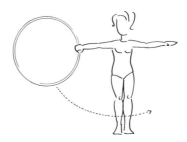

1.   SWINGING MOVEMENTS

Swinging movements are done with a straight arm, and the movement starts from the shoulder. If the hoop is swung in a frontal plane across in front of the body, it is best to use a palm backward grip. Swinging movements may be done with one or both hands.

2.   JUMPING MOVEMENTS

If the hoop is swung forward and the jump is into the hoop, the arms are straight. To leave the hoop, the arms are bent and at the end of the movement the arms are straight again. The movement is just the reverse when swinging the hoop backward.

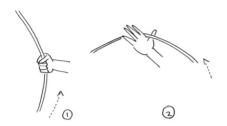

3. CIRCLING MOVEMENTS

The circling movements start from wrist action. Circle movements performed in front of the body or in back of the body may start with either an inward or outward circling of the hoop. When circling in front of the body the grip is with the palm forward. Circle the hoop inward or outward by straightening the fingers and thumb, releasing the grasp of the hoop. The hoop circles between the thumb and index finger and on the palm and back of the hand.

When circling in back of the arm, start with the same grip (palm facing forward), but immediately after the start and the fingers have straightened, turn the hand downward as the hoop will circle around the thumb, palm to the rear, hoop moving behind the arm and body. This is only on the first circle. If circling is continued, then the hoop should circle around the straight fingers.

Changing the hoop from the right to left hand during circling should be done with a continuous movement. This can be achieved only by placing the free hand near the circling hand. If changing in front of the body, put the hands close together in the same position with little fingers toward each other. If changing in back of the body, the index fingers are together for the change. In back circling, a swing should be given so that the hoop will rise vertically above the head.

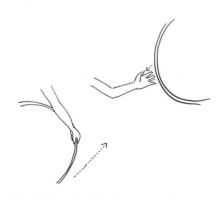

4. TOSSING MOVEMENTS

Tossing can be started either from the

shoulder or wrist. Let the hoop go at the end of the swing, and catch the hoop between the thumb and index finger.

5. HOOP ROLLING

The hoop may also be rolled as a fun exercise. For example, run beside it or jump through while it is rolling. Children like to do this kind of movement.

MOVEMENTS

Swinging Movements

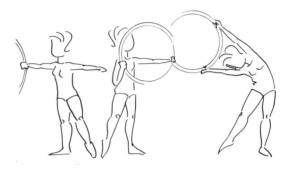

1.   SWING AND LEAN

S.P.   Arms in side horizontal position, hoop in right hand, palm to rear, feet in wide side stride, weight on right foot.

M.   Swing the hoop down in front of body, to the left, grasp it with left hand, palm forward. Transfer weight to the left, lean to the right side. Swing the hoop over the head to the left and back to original position.

2.   SWING FORWARD AND BACKWARD

S.P.   Standing, feet together, hoop in right hand at the side, palm inward.

M.   Holding the hoop with right hand, swing the hoop forward and backward. Let the knees bend with the movement. Reverse sides.

Variations: a. Step forward and backward with the swinging of hoop.

b.   Swing the hoop forward, change hands, swing it backward on the opposite side.

c.   Do chassé steps forward while doing variation b.

S.P. = Starting Position   M. = Movement

3. BALLET POINT

S.P. Standing in front stride, left foot forward, hoop in right hand at side, palm inward.

M. Bend forward over left foot, swinging hoop to the rear; change hands in the rear, swing the hoop forward transferring weight to left foot in front. Reverse the movement to the opposite side.

Variations: a. Do the same movement with a step forward.

b. Do the same movement with a chassé backward on the backward swing, and a chassé forward on the forward swing.

4. BACK ARCH

S.P. Standing, left foot forward, hoop in right hand at side, palm upward.

M. Swing the hoop upward in front of body, both hands swing forward. Keep the left arm extended forward and, with a backward bending of the body, bring the hoop to the rear. Swing the hoop back to original position.

5. BODY WAVE

S.P. Standing feet together, both arms extended forward, hoop in right hand, palm upward.

M. Swing the hoop downward and backward and upward, while simultaneously doing a body wave. Finish with palm facing outward. Twist the hoop outward twice, and finish in original position, palm upward.

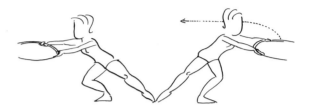

6. HORIZONTAL SWING IN FRONT AND BEHIND BODY

S.P. Standing, hoop held to right side with both hands, palms inward to hoop, hoop horizontal.

M. Swing the hoop horizontally across the body to the left, changing weight. Turn the hoop backward, palms upward, and do a horizontal swing in back of the body; transfer weight, turn the hoop forward to original position.

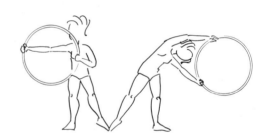

7. HOOP TURN WITH SIDE STRETCH

S.P. Standing, hoop held horizontally to right side, right palm forward, left palm backward.

M. Cross the right arm horizontally over the left in front of the body, half turning the hoop, and to a side stretch to the left while transferring weight to the left foot. Reverse the movement and return to the starting position.

8. HORIZONTAL TURNS

S.P. Standing, holding the hoop in both hands in front of body, arms horizontal, palms inward.

Hold the hoop with a three-finger grasp; i.e., thumb, index, and middle fingers.

M.   Moving the fingers, turn the hoop inward or outward.

Variation: Do the same turning of the hoop while doing a waltz turn.

Jumping Movements

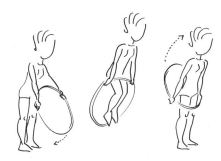

9.   FORWARD JUMP

S.P.   Standing, hoop in front of body, arms horizontal, palms downward.

M.   Swing the hoop downward and jump over it as in rope jumping.

10.   BACKWARD JUMP

S.P.   Standing, hoop held above head, palms upward.
M.   Swing the hoop downward in back of the body and jump over it as in a backward rope jump.

11.   STEP-HOP FORWARD

S.P.   Standing, hoop as in No. 9.
M.   Do a step-hop over the hoop.

12.   STEP-HOP BACKWARD

S.P.   Standing, hoop as in No. 10.
M.   Do a step-hop over the hoop.

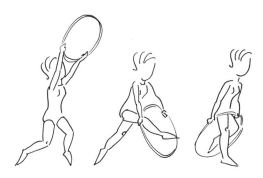

13.   LEAP, BACK FOOT BENT

S.P.   Standing, holding hoop diagonally upward, palms inward.
M.   Run three steps forward and bring the hoop downward and leap over it with right foot, left knee bent to the rear.

14.   WALTZ TURN

S.P.   Hoop horizontal to right side, right palm forward, left palm backward.
M.   Step on left to left, swing hoop down in front and step through it with right foot; turn to the left and step left foot through the hoop to the right (end standing inside hoop), bring hoop upward over the head, palms facing forward, turn hoop downward and return to original position.

Circling Movements

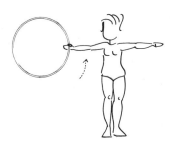

15.   CIRCLING

S.P.   Standing, arms in side horizontal position, hoop in right hand, palm forward.
M.   Circle hoop starting inward.
Variations: a. Circle hoop starting outward.
    b.   Chassé on the left while circling hoop inward.
    c.   Chassé on the right while circling hoop outward.

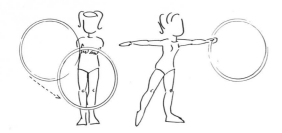

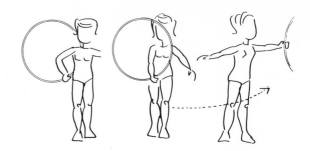

16.   CIRCLE IN FRONT OF THE BODY AND CHANGE

S.P.   Standing, hoop in right hand, palm forward.
M.   Circle the hoop inward, change hoop to left hand, swing it to the left side and stretch to the left side. Reverse the movement to the right.

19.   CIRCLE BACK AND SWING ACROSS FRONT

S.P.   Standing, hoop in right hand, palm forward, arm in side horizontal position.
M.   Circle the hoop inward in back of the body with a very fast change and grasp the hoop, palm backward. Swing the hoop in front of the body and change to left hand.

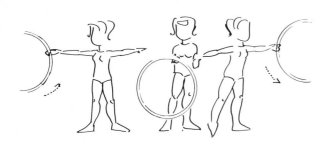

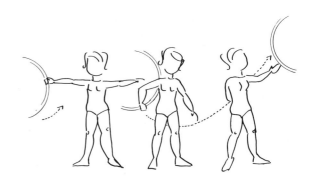

17.   ALTERNATE HAND CIRCLING

S.P.   Standing, hoop in right hand, palm forward.
M.   Circle the hoop with right hand inward, change in front of the body, continue circling outward on the left hand. Reverse direction.

20.   CIRCLE FRONT, BACK, AND CHANGE

S.P.   Standing, hoop to right side, palm forward.
M.   Circle the hoop inward, then change the palm to facing backward, and circle inward in back of the body. Swing the hoop in back of the body to the left, catch with left, and reverse movement.

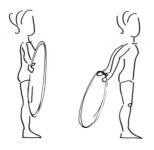

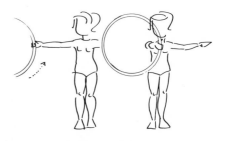

21.   CIRCLE FRONT OF HEAD

S.P.   Standing, hoop in right hand, arm horizontal, palm forward.
M.   Circle the hoop inward, bring the right hand in front of the body, continue the circling. Stop the movement, or change to left hand by regrasping the hoop.

18.   CHANGE HANDS BEHIND BODY

S.P.   Standing, hoop in right hand, palm forward.
M.   Swing the hoop downward and inward in back of the body, change hands in back of the body and swing the hoop to the left side.

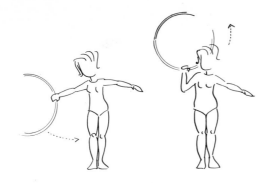

22.   FIGURE 8 BACKWARD

S.P.   Standing, right arm horizontal, hoop in right hand, palm backward.

M.   Circle inward in front of body, change to palm upward and bend elbow and circle hoop inward in back of the body.

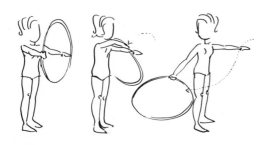

23.   FIGURE 8 SIDEWARD

S.P.   Standing, right arm in front extension, hoop in right hand, palm inward.

M.   Swing the hoop backward outside of the left shoulder, turn the palm upward, circle backward outside of the right shoulder.

24.   HORIZONTAL CIRCLE IN FRONT OF BODY

S.P.   Standing, right arm in side horizontal position, palm downward.

M.   Circle the hoop horizontally in front of the body between the index finger and thumb around the hand. Change to the left hand.

25.   HORIZONTAL CIRCLE IN FRONT OF BODY AND FRONT OF HEAD

S.P.   Right arm to side horizontal, holding hoop, palm downward.

M.   Circle the hoop horizontally in front of the body and gradually raise the arm over the head, continuously circling the hoop in a horizontal plane.

Variation: Do a waltz turn or chaînes turn, doing a horizontal circle in front of the body, body bending slightly forward and circling over the head as the body turns.

Tossing Movements

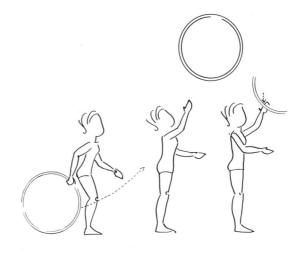

26.   STAND AND TOSS

S.P.   Standing, arms at sides, hoop in right hand, palm inward.

M.   Toss the hoop upward in front of the body with wrist action and catch hoop with the left hand. Alternate sides.

27.   RUN, RUN, TOSS, AND LEAP

S.P.   Standing, arms at sides, hoop in right hand, palm inward.

M.   Run, run, and toss the hoop upward on the leap, right leg in front. Catch the hoop with left hand and hold a scale, swinging the hoop to the rear toward the extended leg.

28.   CHANGEMENT

S.P.   Standing, hoop in right hand, palm inward, arm at side.

M.   Jump into the air changing feet, and simultaneously toss the hoop upward and catch it with the opposite hand.

Variation: Do a split jump while tossing the hoop upward (see sketch).

29.   TOSS OVER HEAD

S.P.   Standing, weight on right foot, right arm in side horizontal position, palm forward.

M.   Toss the hoop over the head and catch it with left hand, while transferring weight to the left.

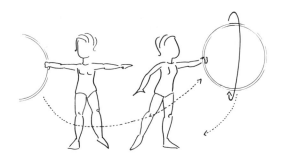

30.   TOSS IN FRONT OF BODY

S.P.   Standing, weight on right foot, right arm in side horizontal position, palm backward.

M.   Toss the hoop downward in front of the body to the left side. Catch hoop with left hand, palm forward; turn palm to rear, and toss the hoop to the right side.

31.   OUTWARD CIRCLE AND TOSS OVER HEAD

S.P.   Standing, right arm in side horizontal position, palm forward.

M.   Circle the hoop outward and toss it above the head and catch hoop with the left hand. Alternate sides.

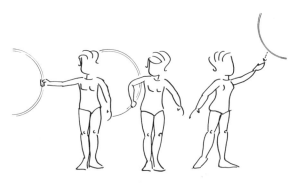

32.   FRONT AND BACK CIRCLES AND TOSS BEHIND BODY TO OPPOSITE SIDE

S.P.   Standing, right arm horizontally to side, palm forward.

M.   Circle inward in front of body, circle inward in back of body and toss the hoop in back of the body. Catch the hoop with left hand.

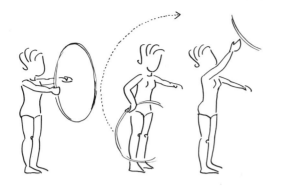

33.   CIRCLE AND TOSS TO FRONT

S.P.   Standing, hoop in right hand, palm inward, arm in front horizontal position.

M.   Circle hoop outside of right arm starting downward. Catch the hoop on the finish of the circle, toss the hoop backward and forward and catch it with the same hand, or change hands.

HOOP EXERCISE TO MUSIC

This may be performed to waltz rhythm, modern speed.

1. a.   (2 measures) Swing and lean (No. 1) on right side.
    b.   (2 measures) Waltz turn (No. 14) to left.
    c.   (4 measures) Repeat No. 1 and 2 to opposite side.

2. a.   (1 measure) Hoop turn to side stretch (No. 7).
    b.   (1 measure) Turn hoop over, hoop on left side, left palm forward, right palm backward.
    c.   (2 measures) Repeat No. 3 and 4.

3. a.   (1 measure) Turn hoop to horizontal and do a half turn to left.
    b.   (2 measures) Run, run, leap to left (No. 13).
    c.   (1 measure) Turn hoop over head and do half-turn left.
    d.   (2 measures) Run, run, toss leap to right side (No. 27), end in scale.

4. a.   (2 measures) Do a body wave, hoop in left hand (No. 5).
    b.   (2 measures) Do a figure 8 sideward (No. 23), finish hoop to left side facing front.

5. a.   (2 measures) Circle in front and change (No. 16) while simultaneously doing a chassé to the right side.
    b.   (2 measures) Repeat No. 11 to left side.

6. a.   (2 measures) Outward circle and toss over head (No. 31).
    b.   (2 measures) Repeat No. 13 to left side.

7. a.   (2 measures) Repeat circle in front and change (No. 16) in place on right side.
    b.   (2 measures) Repeat No. 15 on left side.

8. a.   (2 measures) Turn 1/4 to left, circle outside of left hand and toss to rear (No. 33).
    b.   (2 measures) Catch with right hand, swing right arm with hoop downward and backward, ending in a ballet point (No. 3).

Chapter 9　Wands

Use of the wand in exercise is excellent in building strength and in relaxing the performer so that more natural movements are possible. The wand may be held shoulder distance apart or at the ends, depending upon the movements. Students are usually more interested in performing an exercise with which an object is used, hence ordinary movements take on new interest.

Elementary school children are especially enthusiastic about the use of wands, although they may be used effectively at all school age levels. The exercises using wands should be taught in a large area with ample space between students. The exercises may be performed inside the gymnasium or outside in the school yard.

EQUIPMENT

Wands are usually made of beechwood, although any hardwood doweling may be used. They should be about 36 to 39 inches in length and about 1 or 1-1/4 inches in diameter. The wand should be enameled in various bright colors to make it attractive.

MOVEMENTS

The following exercises are some of the more frequently performed movements using the wands, but created movements are possible.

1. STEPPING OVER THE WAND

S.P.　Standing, gripping the wand at the ends in an over grip.

M.　Step one foot over and then the other, ending with the wand in back of the buttocks. Reverse the movement by stepping one foot and then the other, ending with the wand in front of the body as at the starting position. Start with the hands in a wide position, and gradually bring the hands closer together to make the movement more difficult.

Variation: Step over the wand with one foot and then the other, and carry the wand up to over the head.

2. JUMPING OVER THE WAND

S.P.　Standing, holding the wand at the ends in an over grip.

M.　Jump twice in place and on the third jump, spring over the wand; repeat the two jumps in place, and jump over the wand back to starting position.

3. SQUAT STEPPING OVER THE WAND

S.P.　In squatting position, hands at the ends of the wand.

M.　Remaining in squat position, climb over and back. Gradually bring the hands closer together as the movement is perfected.

4. CRAB WALK

S.P.　"Crab walk" position; i.e., back to floor, weight on hands and feet.

M.　Holding the wand in the hips by contracting the abdominal muscles, try to walk forward and backward.

5. HOOK SIT-UPS WITH WAND

S.P.　Hook sitting, holding wand under the bent knees.

M.　Rock back and go to hook lying; come to hook sitting, holding the wand under the bent knees.

6. ANKLE TOSS OF WAND

S.P.　Hook sitting, wand at the ankles.

M.   Slightly extend the legs and lift the wand into the air with the legs, catch it with both hands.

7.   LEG STRETCHING

S.P. Hook sitting, wand held in both hands and wand under one foot.
M.   Stretch the leg upward, holding onto the wand which remains under extended foot; reverse the feet.

8.   V SEAT WITH WAND

S.P. Hook sitting, wand under both feet, hands at end.
M.   Stretch legs upward into a V seat balancing on the buttocks. Return to hook sitting.

9.   LEG STRETCHING AND V SEAT

S.P. Combine exercises 7 and 8 as follows: hook sitting, wand under one leg, held at the ends.
M.   a. Stretch the right let upward and return.
     b. Stretch the left leg upward and return.
     c. Stretch both legs upward and return.

10.   KNEE LIFT

S.P. Hook sitting, wand under the knee, held at ends.
M.   Lift one leg extending the knee, then the other; and then both legs, holding the wand under the knees throughout the movement.

11.   LONG SITTING TO V SEAT

S.P. Long sitting, wand stretched over head, held at ends.
M.   Bring the wand forward and squat the legs through the wand to a V seat and bring them back trying not to touch the wand.

S.P. = Starting Position   M. = Movement

12.   WAND PULL-UP

S.P. Face lying, wand vertical, hands grasping it at the base, arms straight.
M.   Using a hand-over movement, try to climb up the wand to the top, ending in an arched trunk position. Return in the same hand-over-hand manner.

13.   STANDING TO LYING WITHOUT HANDS

S.P. Standing, wand in back of shoulders, grasped at ends.
M.   Lie down on the abdomen without help of hands. Return to standing without help of hands.

14.   STANDING LEG STRETCH

S.P. Standing, arms extended over head, hands grasping wand at the ends.
M.   Bring the wand down in front of the body, hook one foot on the wand and extend the leg forward balancing in a straight position on one leg; return the foot to the floor. Repeat with opposite foot.

15.   WAND CATCHING

S.P. Standing, arms extended forward, grasping wand in over grip.
M.   Let the wand drop and quickly catch it.
Variations: a. Throw the wand up and catch it.
     b. Throw the wand up with left hand and catch with the right. This will develop reflex action, in preparation for the uneven parallel bars.

16.   WAND TOSSING

S.P. Standing, grasping the wand in front of the body.
M.   Toss the wand up over the head and make a half turn and catch the wand.
Variation: Throw the wand up and make a whole turn and catch it.

17.   WAND TOSSING TO PARTNER

S.P.   Standing facing a partner, wand held in both hands in front of body.

M.   Toss the wand across to partner.

Variations: a. Have each partner throw across, one tossing the wand high, the other low (see sketch).

b.   Practice catching with both hands pronated (facing floor) on the catch.

c.   Practice catching with both hands supinated (facing upward) on the catch.

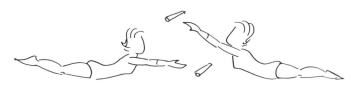

d.   Face lying, lifting the upper back. A rolls the wand on the floor to B, and B tosses her wand to A (see sketch).

18.   ARM STRETCH

S.P.   Standing, grasping the wand in front of body at shoulder height.

M.   Keeping the elbows straight, lift the arms up over the head and back as far as possible. This is excellent stretch for the pectoral muscles, and develops strength for dislocate movements on the uneven parallel bars.

19.   SIDE BENDING

S.P.   Standing, grasping the wand at the ends, arms stretched over head.

M.   Keeping the arms straight, bend the trunk to the right side, then to the left side.

20.   TRUNK FLEXION AND EXTENSION

S.P.   Standing, grasping the wand at the ends, arms straight in front of body.

M.   Bend the trunk and touch the wand to the floor. Extend and hyperextend the trunk bending backward as far as possible, arms straight and reaching upward and backward.

21.   ARM BENDING AND EXTENDING

S.P.   Standing, arms low in front of body, arms extended, grasping wand at the ends.

M.   a.   Bend the arms bringing the wand to the floor.

b.   Extend the arms forward horizontally.

c.   Bend the arms bringing the wand to the chest.

d.   Extend the arms upward.

e.   Bend the arms bringing the wand to the chest.

f.   Extend the arms downward.

22.   WAND LIFT FRONT TO BACK

S.P.   Standing, grasping the wand in front of the body in a wide position.

M.   Lift the arms up over the head and down to the back; return to starting position. Try to keep the elbows straight. This is excellent for learning dislocate shoulder movements on the uneven parallel bars.

23.   TRUNK TWISTING

S.P.   Standing, grasping the wand shoulder distance apart, arms horizontal.

M.   Holding the wand with arms straight, twist the trunk from side to side.

24.   TRUNK TWISTING, WAND IN REAR

S.P.   Standing, wand over shoulders, hands grasping ends.

M.   Twist trunk from side to side.

25.   TRUNK TWIST AND BEND

S.P.   Standing with feet apart, grasping ends of wand.

M.   Twist the body to the right as far as possible; try to touch the left end of the wand to the right toe; reverse the movement.

26.   SITTING, TRUNK BENDING

S.P.   Sitting with legs spread far apart, arms horizontal, hands grasping wand in front of body.

M.   Bend the trunk forward, touching the right toe with the wand, then the left.

Variation: Do the same movement in straddle standing position.

27.   WAND SWINGING

S.P.   Standing, arms sideward horizontal. Wand in right hand, as if the wand were a continuation of the right hand.

M.   Swing the wand across front of the body and catch it with the left hand; reverse the movement.

28. WAND CIRCLING

S.P. Standing, arms sideward horizontal, wand in right hand as if the wand were a continuation of the arm.

M. Swing the wand in a complete circle and then catch it with the left hand; reverse the movement.

29. WAND SWINGING IN REAR

S.P. Standing, arms sideward horizontal, wand in right hand.

M. Swing the wand across the low back of the body and catch it with the left hand; reverse the movement.

Variation: Swing the wand upward across the shoulders and catch it with the opposite hand.

30. TRUNK AND ARM BENDING

S.P. Standing with feet apart, grasping the wand in front of body.

M. a. Lift straight arms over the head and bend the elbows placing the wand at the shoulder blades.

b. Holding the arm position, bend the trunk forward to right angle.

c. Straighten trunk and extend arms upward over head.

d. Return wand to front position.
   This may be varied by stretching the arms forward on the trunk bending.

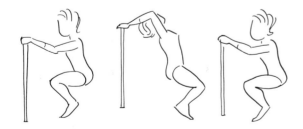

31. SQUAT BACK BEND

S.P. Squat sitting, holding the end of the vertical wand.

M. Turn and twist the body to the left, ending with the back to the wand (like a back bend); twist back to original position. Repeat to the right.

32. SQUAT THRUST

S.P. Squat sitting, right hand on the floor, left hand on top of the vertical wand.

M. Thrust the legs to the rear and return to the squat position; reverse the hand position and repeat.

33. SQUAT WAND CIRCLING

S.P. Squat position, both hands on top of the vertical wand.

M. Holding onto the wand, squat jump in a circle around the wand.

Variation: Holding onto the wand, keeping arms straight and body in a side leaning position, run around the stick. (Similar to a coffee grinder stunt.)

34. VERTICAL RUN-AROUND

S.P. Standing erect, place the wand in a vertical balanced position.

M. Let the wand go and then run around the wand and try to catch it before it falls.

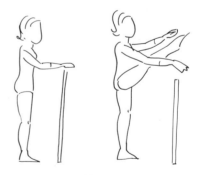

35. KICK OVER WAND

S.P. Standing, wand vertical, held at the end by one hand.

M. Lift one leg over the wand and catch the wand before it falls. Reverse the legs.

Variation: Using a scissor kick, try to jump over the wand with both legs and catch the wand before it falls.

36. WOODCHOPPING

S.P. Standing, holding onto one end of the wand with both hands.

M. Bring the wand up over the head and to one side, swing it downward to the floor as in a chopping movement without touching the floor with the wand.

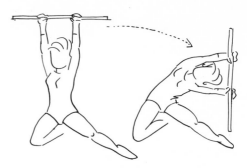

37.   BACK BENDING

S.P.   Standing, holding onto the wand at one end with both hands.

M.   Bend the trunk backward, touching the floor with the wand in back of the body. Return to erect position.

Variations: a. Touch the wand in front of the body, then swing it up over the head and bend backward touching the floor with it in back of the body (see sketch).

   b.   Standing, trunk bending forward, sideward, backward, and to the opposite side, touching the wand in a circle as the trunk is circled.

40.   HALF KNEELING—SIDE BENDING

S.P.   Kneeling on right knee, left leg to the side, wand held over head, arms straight.

M.   Bounce over the left leg to counts 1, 2; stretch arms over head on count 3; change legs on count 4. Reverse sides.

41.   KNEELING TRUNK TWIST

S.P.   Kneeling, knees about 13 inches apart, wand held in back of shoulders.

M.   Twist the trunk and bend forward touching the right end of the wand to the right side in front of right knee. Come to erect position and twist and bend to the left.

38.   TRUNK CIRCLING

S.P.   Standing, holding onto the wand at the ends.

M.   With arms held straight and extended:
   a.   Bend the trunk forward.
   b.   Bend the trunk to the right side.
   c.   Bend the trunk backward.
   d.   Bend the trunk to the left side.

Variation: Continue the bending until there is a complete circling of the trunk with no stopping.

42.   PLOUGHSHEAR

S.P.   Back lying, hands over head, holding onto the ends of the wand.

M.   a.   Bring the feet up over the head into the ploughshear position, feet placed through the wand.
   b.   Sit up, wand under the knees.
   c.   Roll back to ploughshear position.
   d.   Disengage feet and return to original back lying position.

39.   BACK LEAN

S.P.   Kneeling, legs apart at knees, heels together, arms over head holding onto the wand.

M.   Lean backward as far as possible and return.

Part III APPARATUS AND COMPETITIVE GYMNASTICS

Chapter 10   Introduction to Apparatus and Competitive Gymnastics

The apparatus used by women consists of the Swedish box and horse, horizontal bar and uneven parallel bars, balance beam, trampoline, stall bars, and climbing ropes. The apparatus used in competition are the horse, uneven parallel bars, trampoline, and balance beam. The other apparatus mentioned are frequently used in schools and recreation centers as part of a developmental or fitness program. The specific skills for each apparatus are given in the following chapters.

The teaching of skills on apparatus presents a difficult problem. It is undesirable to have a large group standing or sitting while one student performs on a piece of apparatus. Likewise, it is of utmost importance that safety be observed at all times. Spotting should be taught along with each skill, and the "buddy method" or "student assistant" method is the most effective to use with large groups. With careful organization, several pieces of apparatus can be used at one time, thereby giving more activity and making the class more interesting and challenging to the student.

The ingenuity of the teacher is important when adequate apparatus are not available. If a horse is not available, a Swedish box can easily be constructed and most of the basic vaulting can be learned over the box. (See chapter on Vaulting.) Also, if a balance beam is at hand, but no horse, vaulting can be learned over the balance beam. Should a balance beam not be available, a beam 4 by 4 inches and 16 feet long, securely held on two stall bar stools, can give the feeling of height and basic balances can be learned. A home-made beam is not difficult to construct. If uneven parallel bars are not available, many of the hanging and circling movements can be learned on the horizontal bar. Sometimes the men's regular parallel bars, lifted as high and as low as possible, can be used to give a feeling of some of the movements usually performed on the uneven parallel bars.

Stall bars can be used effectively in developing shoulder strength, and in developing flexibility of the trunk and legs, and large groups can be accommodated at one time. (See Chapter on Warm-up and Conditioning Programs for Gymnasts.)

Climbing ropes are frequently available in schools and, if available, should be used to help develop the shoulder girdle as preliminary to the uneven parallel bars. Climbing movements are included in the chapter on Ropes.

ORGANIZATIONS FOR COMPETITIVE GYMNASTICS

There are four organizations sponsoring competitive gymnastics and the rules of competition may be very similar, but with some variations. The Division of Girls' and Women's Sports (D.G.W.S.), of the American Association of Health, Physical Education, and Recreation, is primarily interested in sponsoring gymnastics within the school program. They have issued rules and competitive routines applicable to the school program. The Amateur Athletic Union of United States (A.A.U.) and the United States Gymnastic Federation (U.S.G.F.) issue rules and competitive routines for meets also. To improve the program of gymnastics in America, the three organizations have been working together lately to develop competitive routines and rules for meets. However, these rules are usually based on the rules set forth by the International Federation of Gymnasts (F.I.G.—Fédération Internationale de Gymnastique). The latter group establishes the rules for all world game and Olympic gymnastic competition, and hence is considered the final authority. The information contained in this book is based primarily on the F.I.G. regulations as currently existing.

HOW TO USE THE FOLLOWING CHAPTERS

In the following chapters the basic regulations are given for each event. Teaching suggestions have been listed and the teacher or coach should read these through carefully before using the material. In each event the skills have been divided into beginning, intermediate, and advanced, so that the performer may develop with continuity and safety. It is hoped that the teacher or coach will consider this progression very carefully and plan skills and routines commensurate with the ability of her students. The suggested combinations and routines for each level have been carefully planned and should be of great help to the teacher. Correct spotting is given for each skill in all of the events, as well as suggested steps in learning the skill. This analysis should be of assistance to both the coach and the performer.

Chapter 11   Balance Beam

The Swedish girls used the balance beam first. It was affixed to the wall and pulled out when in use, folded away when not in use. It was narrower than the presently used beam. It was first used in competition in 1934 in Budapest, at the World Championships.

The balance beam is a typical women's apparatus. Besides good balance, one needs courage and precision in movement. The exercise should use the entire length of the beam, and movement should be over and back several times during the composition. The exercise starts with a mount, then the various types of movements described below are alternated, and it ends with a dismount. The variations of the movements are numerous and it is not possible to describe everything here. After the basic movements are learned, the performer should use her ingenuity and creativity. Almost all movements that can be performed on the floor in dance, tumbling, and free exercise can be duplicated on the balance beam. This permits the individual performer to develop progression in balance beam work and encourages creativity as well.

EQUIPMENT

The regulation balance beam used in competition is 5 meters long (16 feet 3 inches), 10 cm. wide (3.937 inches, although generally considered 4 inches), and 120 cm. high (47.24 inches). The height of the balance beam should be adjustable from 80 cm. (31.5 inches) to 120 cm. (47.24 inches), and usually is considered 4 feet high. The beam is 16 cm. thick (6.3 inches). The material for the walking surface of the beam is made of wood which is smooth but not slippery, and the edges of the beam should be beveled. The stands are made of steel or cast iron. Most manufacturers observe the correct internationally accepted dimensions; however, home construction for school use may not be precise in dimensions.

TECHNIQUES

The skills or movements performed on the balance beam may be divided into the following classifications:

Mounts
Walks or movements

Balance or held positions, either low positions or high positions
Turns
Aerial movements such as jumps or leaps
Rolls
Dismounts

Planning an Exercise

The duration of the balance beam exercise according to F.I.G. rules is 1 minute 20 seconds to 1 minute 45 seconds. The optional exercise done in competition must not contain more than three maintained positions or stops. Each additional stop is a penalty of 0.20 points. The exercise should be continuous in movement, and should give the feeling of confidence, control, and grace of movement. Combinations of the different skills mentioned above should be so used that there is continuous, fluid movement in the exercise from the mount to the dismount. The routine should move freely up and down the beam, using the entire length and a variety of levels. The gymnast should use rhythmical variety because a monotonous exercise is less spectacular. Variations in rhythm create a compositionally stronger routine. For most competition, it is better to do an easier movement with control than a difficult one poorly performed. Major faults on the beam include additional stops above those authorized, loss of balance, lack of sureness, and monotony of rhythm.

Hand Positions on the Beam

The hand positions on the beam are relatively simple, and they depend upon the strength and skill of the performer. The hands may be moved from any one of the following positions to another, as necessitated by the movement. The grips are generally as follows:

1. The over grip the length of the beam (e.g., English handstand). The thumbs are on top, with the fingers grasping the sides of the beam.

2. Under grip (i.e., for forward roll or backward roll). The fingers grasping under the beam, at the distal joint, thumbs upward.

3. The over grip across the beam (e.g., side handstand or straddle mount). The thumbs are on the top of the beam with the fingers grasping the sides or, if the hand is large enough, the thumbs may grasp the opposite side of the beam.

When the hands are not used for support on the beam, they are usually in various ballet positions (see chapter on Dance for Gymnasts).

SAFETY

The following general safety precautions pertain to any work on the balance beam. Specific spotting techniques are explained whenever a movement requires them.

1. Place mats on either side of the beam with double thickness of mats at the ends, especially if a difficult dismount is to be made.

2. Mounts and dismounts should not be made anywhere near the legs or supports of the beam, thus avoiding turned ankles or sprains from landing on uneven surfaces.

3. The beat board should be removed as soon as the mount is made.

4. To learn beginning walks and movements up and down the beam, a spotter should walk alongside the beam, arms extended. The spotter should not take the performer's hand, but the performer may grasp the spotter. If the spotter should take the performer's hand, the latter is liable to be pulled off balance.

5. In learning any move, a spotter should stand on each side of the beam; later, only one spotter may be used with the spotter at the most advantageous point according to the exercise.

6. In competition, the performer should never touch the spotter, although the spotter should be ready, particularly on a difficult dismount. If spotting is needed, it should be done even in competition if the safety of the performer is jeopardized.

7. In the mounts using arm support, elbows should be held straight and directly in line with the shoulders.

TEACHING SUGGESTIONS

1. To acquaint students with the beam, lower it to about two feet, and let the students step on it, walk, turn, or explore movements on it so that fear will be overcome.

2. All the movements on the beam should be practiced on the floor first.

3. Difficult movements should be learned on the low beam first.

4. A pad or rolled towel on the beam may be used for learning shoulder and back rolls, handstand forward rolls, and for other stunts.

5. All mounts can be practiced with two or three students on the beam at one time.

6. All the mounts and dismounts can be practiced either on the Swedish box or horse.

7. Very short combinations of a mount, a movement or two and dismount, may be practiced using 1/2 of the beam so that two gymnasts may perform at the same time. Have one mount at the right end, the other at the middle, both moving to the left end of the beam, or in the same direction.

8. The arm positions may vary with different movements along the beam, but shoulders should be down, elbows should be rounded and held high, and thumbs close to middle fingers regardless of the arm position.

9. The toes must be pointed and the gymnast must be aware of aesthetic line of the body. It is usually easier for the spectator to see faults on the beam because of the silhouette effect of the movement in space.

10. In all movements along the beam, the head should be kept in line with the spine, focus should be on the beam, but head up. The back should be straight, shoulders pulled together. Buttocks should be tight, hips tucked under. Toes pointed and knees straight, except in plié or bent leg positions.

11. All turns should be performed on the half-toe or ball of the foot. In turns the body should be erect and stiff, hips over feet. To think of lifting and turning at the same time helps the performer to turn.

12. To teach the feeling of continuity required for fluid routines, combine skills into short combinations as soon as possible. Also, the use of background music will help the gymnast to overcome the tendency toward lengthy held positions or jerky movements.

13. In composing routines, keep in mind contrast of levels, tempo, force, slow and flowing to sharp movements, and directional changes. Also keep in mind the special flexibility or style of the gymnast.

14. Each time a gymnast falls from the beam analyze the reason, i.e., poor body alignment, poor focus, poor control, or lack of concentration.

MOVEMENTS

Mounts

All mounts can be practiced with two or three students on the beam at one time. Most of the mounts can be practiced on the Swedish box.

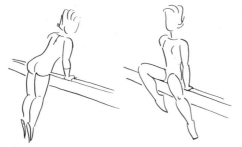

1.   CROSS SEAT MOUNT

M.   Stand facing the beam, both hands on the beam in an over grip. Jump upward and simultaneously push with the straight arms lifting to one hip to sit on the beam. The other leg is extended to the rear.

Spotting: The spotter stands on the opposite side of the beam and assists by grasping at the wrist and shoulder.

Steps in learning: Practice push-up movements to strengthen shoulders and arms.

Movements to follow: The legs may be swung to a V seat, to a crotch seat.

2.   BACK PULLOVER MOUNT

Good for warm-up and may be used by several students at one time. Best for small children.

M.   Stand facing beam, bend knees and grasp the beam with an under grip. Bring legs up and over the beam into a backward hip circle movement. Swing the straight legs downward and end in a straight arm support facing the same way as at start of movement.

Spotting: Spotter should stand on opposite side of beam and may help lift the hips and assist the control on shoulders as the person pulls through.

Steps in learning: Practice the hip pullover on a horizontal bar or uneven bars.

Movements to follow: From a front support, swing one straight leg over the beam to a crotch seat.

M. = Movement

3.   CROTCH SEAT MOUNT

M.   Stand facing the beam. Run and jump to a straight arm support and simultaneously lift one straight leg over the beam and sit on the beam, one leg on either side and both legs straight, hands supporting in the rear.

Spotting: The beat board should be at right angle. Spot on the opposite side of the beam by grasping the shoulder opposite to the leg to be swung over the beam.

Movements to follow: Swing legs to V seat or swing legs backward to a crouch and to standing.

4.   ONE-KNEE MOUNT

M.   The beat board is at right angle to the beam. Jump to straight arm support and simultaneously bend one knee on the beam, hand on either side of the bent knee. The opposite leg is extended to the rear, head is up and back arched.

Spotting: Stand on the opposite side of beam and spot at the shoulders.

Movements to follow: Swing around on bent knee to a knee scale facing lengthwise, swing extended leg forward and stand.

5.   WOLF MOUNT

M.   Use the beat board at right angle. This movement is similar to the squat mount with the exception that one leg is held to the side parallel to the bar. Jump with a straight arm support to squat on one foot, the other leg extended to the side.

Spotting: Stand on the opposite side of the beam and spot at the shoulders.

Steps in learning: At first the extended toe may touch the beam. Later, as the movement is perfected, the leg should be held horizontally in the air over the beam. Practice the movement on the floor, then on a Swedish box or horse.

Movements to follow: Swing the body to lengthwise on the beam in a lunge position—to stand.

Variation: One leg squat facing diagonally.

6. STRADDLE MOUNT

M. Use beat board at right angle. Jump with straight arm support, feet to a wide straddle position on the beam, hands between the feet, arms straight. Head should be up and looking forward.

Spotting: Stand at the opposite side of beam and support the shoulders.

Steps in learning: Reverse the movement by having the performer stand on the beam and assume the correct straddle mount position to get the feeling of the forward body position. Also practice the position on a Swedish box or horse.

Movements to follow: Twist the trunk to a lunge or split.

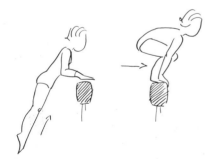

7. SQUAT MOUNT

M. Jump and push off with straight arm support, arms spread, feet landing between hands on the beam, body in a deep squat position.

Spotting: Use the beat board at right angle. Spotter stands on opposite side of beam and supports the shoulders of performer.

Steps in learning: Practice a deep squat position on

the floor, then on a Swedish box or horse (see Vaulting).

Movements to follow: From the squat position, the performer may immediately twist to lengthwise of the beam and stand.

Variations: a. The squat may be done facing diagonally.

b. The squat may be done at the end of the beam.

8. FORWARD ROLL MOUNT

M. Beat board at the end of beam. Standing at one end of the beam, run and jump placing the hands on either side of the beam. Lift the hips and tuck the head and execute a forward roll.

Spotting: A spotter should be on either side of the beam, holding the arm and assisting to keep the hips on the beam.

Steps in learning: Practice a forward roll lengthwise of the Swedish box, or by putting mats across the beam.

Movements to follow: From the forward roll, assume a crotch seat and swing legs back in crouch to standing.

9. HEADSTAND MOUNT

M. The beat board at the end of the beam. Standing at one end of the beam, run and jump, placing hands on either side of the beam. Lift the hips and place the head on the beam, simultaneously lifting the legs to headstand.

Spotting: A spotter should be on either side of the beam, assisting at the hips.

Steps in learning: Practice a headstand to a controlled forward roll on the floor, then on the Swedish box.

Movements to follow: A forward roll.

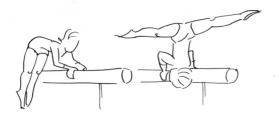

10.   SHOULDER BALANCE MOUNT

M.   Beat board at a slight 45-degree angle to the beam. Run and jump lifting the hips in the air and kick one leg upward to an inverted split, balancing on the shoulder. Hands grasp in an over grip lengthwise of the beam. If approaching from the left, the left hand would be placed on the opposite side, fingers at the side of the beam, thumb on top. The right hand would be on the rear side. At the climax of the movement the split is nearly parallel with the length of the beam.

Spotting: Stand on the opposite side and assist by controlling the shoulders and holding the inverted balance.

Steps in learning: Practice a shoulder balance on the beam by placing the shoulder on beam and kicking up into the inverted position. Practice on Swedish box and horse.

Movements to follow: With a slight twist, place one knee on the beam and do a knee scale lengthwise.

12.   FLANK-LEG SWING TO CROTCH SEAT

M.   Beat board at right angle. From a straight arm support swing both legs to the right. At the height of the beam spread the legs, the left going over the top of beam as the right hand is released. As the left leg gets to the crotch seat, the right hand returns to the beam. (This is similar to a flank vault.)

Variation: Swing both legs over and end in a back support.

Spotting: Stand to the side, grasping left shoulder and elbow.

Steps in learning: Practice a flank vault over the beam, the horse, or the Swedish box.

Movements to follow: Swing to a V seat, or twist body lengthwise and swing legs back to crouch stand position.

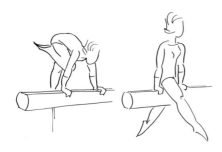

11.   SINGLE-LEG SHOOT THROUGH TO CROTCH SEAT

M.   Beat board at right angle. Run and jump to a front support position as one knee is bent to chest and shoot through to a crouch seat facing forward.

Spotting: Spot to one side grasping the arm.

Steps in learning: Practice lifting the hips high and tucking the leg close to the chest. Practice this movement on a horizontal bar or uneven bars.

Movements to follow: Twist the body facing lengthwise of the beam and swing the legs backward to crouch stand.

Variation: Perform the same single-leg shoot through with the legs held straight as in a stoop vault.

13.   REAR SCISSORS TO CROTCH SEAT

M.   Beat board at right angle. Run and jump with hands on either side, thumbs on top of the beam. Give a slight twist so that the right side is to the beam. Kick left leg backward and bend the trunk forward. As the left leg clears the beam in the rear, let go of the beam with left hand and finish the turn sitting in a crotch seat, facing the opposite direction.

Spotting: Stand on the opposite side of the beam, facing the performer. Grasp the trunk as the body twist is made.

Steps in learning: Practice a front vault to get the leg lift. Practice a flank vault with a body twist.

Movements to follow: Any movements from a crotch seat may follow.

14.   FENCE VAULT OR SCISSOR MOUNT

M.   The beat board is placed almost parallel to the beam. Approach from an oblique angle and do a movement similar to a hitch-kick; i.e., with the left side to the beam, run and lift both straight legs over the beam, left then right as in a vault; end in a side seat position on the right hip.

Spotting: Stand on the opposite side and to rear of performer.

Movements to follow: Swing legs to a V seat and back to crouch standing.

16.   STEP ON MOUNT

M.   Beat board placed almost parallel to the beam. Approach from an oblique angle with the left side to the beam. Run and a one-foot take off from the right foot, simultaneously lifting the left leg and arms and land on the left foot on the beam, either in a squat or an upright position.

Spotting: Stand on the opposite side of the beam and be ready with extended hand to grasp if the balance is not maintained.

Movements to follow: Any movement may follow this mount.

Variation: The mount may also be performed from the end of the beam.

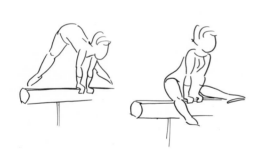

15.   AERIAL STRADDLE MOUNT

M.   Beat board at right angle. The approach is the same as for a straddle mount; however, all of the weight is taken by the hands which should be closer than shoulder distance apart. The legs are held in a wide spread above the beam.

Spotting: Stand on the opposite side of beam, facing the performer, grasping the shoulders.

Steps in learning: Practice the held position on the floor. Practice the held position by hanging from a stall bar or horizontal bar. Practice a straddle vault. Practice the straddle held position on the uneven bars.

Movements to follow: Quickly turn to a crotch seat or go up to a handstand.

Variation: Perform the same movement at the end of the beam continue to half straddle seat turn.

17.   HANDSTAND MOUNT

M.   Beat board at right angle. Run and with straight arm position, hands grasping across the top beam, go to a handstand position. After holding the position for an instant, move out of the position as noted below. The legs may be together or straddled.

Spotting: Stand on the opposite side and catch the shoulders.

Steps in learning: Perfect a handstand on the floor, then gradually on the lowered beam.

Movements to follow: a. From handstand position, continue in a chest roll to front support.

b.   Straddle the legs to a straddle stand on the beam, or free straddle seat.

c.   Squat down to a squat position on the beam.

18.   WALKOVER MOUNT

M.   Beat board at the end of the beam. Run and jump placing hands in over grip on the top of the beam. Lift the hips and split the legs to a walkover (Note: a momentary handstand may be performed, then go into the walkover).

Spotting: Stand to one side and support under the low back with both hands.

Movements to follow: Any movement may follow this mount.

20.   THIEF MOUNT

M.   Beat board at right angle. Jump passing one straight leg over the beam followed immediately by the bent other leg and end in a rear support on the beam. (Note: The hands are placed on the beam after both legs have cleared the beam and are straight.)

Spotting: Spot on the near side of the beam on the side of the first leg, catching the performer at the hips to control landing on the beam.

Steps in learning: Learn the thief vault first, then practice first on the Swedish box or horse, or by putting mats across the beam.

Movements to follow: a. Quarter turn to V seat.
   b.   Swing legs backward to a crouch and to standing.

Low Balances

These are balances that are performed in a low position on the beam; e.g., lying, kneeling, sitting. The performer is low and close to the beam. Most of these movements are fairly easy to perform and each may be followed by a variety of movements according to the ability of the individual performer. All the movements should be practiced on the floor first.

19.   CARTWHEEL MOUNT
(DESCRIPTION FOR LEFT SIDE)

M.   Beat board at the end of the beam. Run and jump, placing left hand on beam, then right as legs are kicked upward (similar to a cartwheel vault). Finish on the right foot.

Spotting: Stand on opposite side of the beam and spot at waist as in performing a cartwheel on the floor.

Movements to follow: Any high balance movement.

Variation: Tinsica mount. The tinsica is a combination of a cartwheel and forward walkover. See the tinsica in the High Balances.

21.   BALANCE SEAT
(CALLED ALSO A V SEAT OR PIKE SEAT)

M.   Sitting on the beam, hands behind the body, lift both legs from a bent position to full extension in the air, balancing on the buttocks with the body in a good pike position. Later, lift the legs from a straight position without bending at the knees first. As the position is mastered, lift the arms to a side horizontal position and balance on the buttocks.

Spotting: Stand to one side of the beam assisting the performer in finding the point of balance.

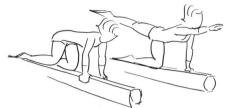

22.   KNEELING SCALE

M.   Facing lengthwise from a kneeling position, one knee behind the other, place the hands in front of the beam, thumbs on top; lift one leg to the rear and as high as possible, arching the body. Later, be able to lift the same arm or opposite arm stretching it forward.

Spotting: Stand to one side assisting the performer in finding the point of balance over the knee.

23.   BALLET POINT

M.   From a standing position, bend the supporting leg and extend the forward leg with the ankle and toe pointed. Bend the trunk forward over the extended leg. The arms may be held to the rear, one curved in front and the other over head, or both to the sides.

Spotting: Stand to one side; little spotting is necessary.

24.   ONE-LEG SQUAT

M.   From a standing position, bend one knee and slide the other foot forward on the beam. Arms are horizontal for balance. Later, be able to go to a one-leg squat position with the leg in front held in the air and parallel to the beam.

Spotting: Let the performer hold the hand of the spotter when learning.

25.   LUNGES

a.   Forward lunge

M.   Facing the length of the beam, bend the forward knee and rear leg along the beam. Get a full extension of the knee and ankle in the rear. Arm position may vary.

b.   Sideward lunge

M.   Facing forward, step with one foot to the side. Bend the supporting knee and stretch the other leg to the side. Arms are usually in second position or horizontal to the beam. The body may lean in any direction.

Spotting: These are simple movements, and the spotter should stand to the side with raised hand in case the performer loses balance.

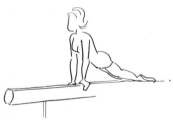

26.   PUSH-UP

M.   From a face lying position on the beam, go into a push-up position, legs extended, ankles extended. Weight is on the straight arms and extended toes.

Spotting: Stand to one side of the performer and assist with balance.

27.   FRONT LYING

M.   Lying prone on the beam, grasp under the beam, lift one leg upward and rest it on the foot of the bent leg, chin resting on the beam.

Spotting: Stand to the side of performer, controlling the shoulders and trunk.

Variation: Front lying without support. From the above position lift arms sidewards.

28.   REAR LYING

M.   From a supine position on the beam, grasp
the beam over the head and on the under
side. Raise the legs vertically. (May also
be done with a scissor movement of the
legs.)

Spotting: Stand to one side and help to control the
body on the beam. Assist the performer
in pinching the elbows together to get
control.

29.   PRETZEL BEND (YOGA PLOUGHSHEAR)

M.   Usually done in combination with a backward
shoulder or backward roll. From supine
position as in rear lying, pull the legs
upward and over the head until they touch
the beam over the head, keeping the knees
straight. Elbows should be pinched together
and the body must bend in a direct line
with the beam.

Spotting: Stand to one side and help by controlling
the hips.

30.   SPLITS

a.   Forward split

M.   Facing the length of the beam, turn the forward leg outward so that the heel will
slide forward in a controlled movement
down to a split on the beam.

b.   Backward split

M.   Facing the length of the beam, place the weight
on the forward leg as in a lunge, then slide
the backward leg to the rear into a split.

c.   Sideward split (Japanese split)

M.   Legs in wide straddle as in a straddle mount,
go down into a split with the legs in a
wide spread position sideward.

Spotting: All of the splits should be controlled on
the floor before attempting them on the
beam. The spotter should stand to one side
and offer her hand to help balance the
performer.

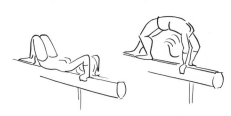

31.   REAR ARCH

M.   From a supine position on the beam, grasp
beam over the head and close to the ears,
hands on top of the beam, slide the feet
in close to the buttocks, one foot in front
of the other, and lift the body in an arch
or bridge.

Spotting: Stand to one side, place hand under low
back and assist in controlling the arched
position.

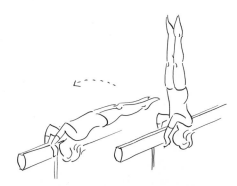

32.   SHOULDER BALANCE

M.   From a supine position pull up into a shoulder
balance. Grasp the bar over the head and
under the beam, turn the head to one side
and lift the legs up so that the balance is
on one shoulder. (Movement is similar to a
shoulder roll.)

Variations: a. The balance can also be at the back of
the neck. The hands grasp over the head
as in a back roll, but the body remains in
the inverted shoulder stand position.

b.   Shoulder stand as in a, with legs split.

c.   Shoulder balance as above, then slowly let
the body down, keeping the body in an arch
with feet together, or one knee bent and
one leg extended.

Spotting: Stand to one side near the head and shoulders. Assist the performer in maintaining
balance.

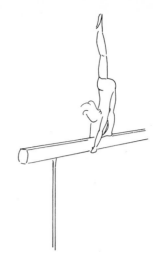

33. SITTING STAG

M.   Facing forward, left leg bent, foot to left buttocks. Sit on the left buttocks, right leg extended to the side (parallel to the beam) or bent back in an attitude, right arm extended to the rear, left hand on the beam, head turned to the right.

Spotting: Stand to the rear of the performer, assisting performer at the hips to maintain balance.

High Balances

These balances are performed in a standing or high position on the beam. All movements should be performed on the floor before performing them on the beam.

35. NEEDLE SCALE

M.   Start from front scale position and lean the body forward, grasping under the beam on either side and near the supporting leg which is kept straight. You may also hold the supporting ankle, or top of the beam with one hand. Bend forward, bringing the head to the knee of the supporting leg while the other leg is brought vertically upward.

Spotting: Little spotting is necessary. Stand to one side and be ready to assist if balance is not maintained.

34. SCALE (ARABESQUE)

M.   Standing on one leg, lift the other leg to the rear as high as possible, both knees straight, toes pointed on the extended leg. The back is arched with the head high. The arm position may vary; i.e., the same arm extended as leg, arms in opposition, or in a second position to the sides. The extended leg may also be held by one hand.

Spotting: Stand to one side and let the performer hold the spotter's hand until balance is maintained.

36. CROISÉ

M.   Standing on one foot, lift the other knee high and slightly across the supporting leg. Arm on the supporting leg side is high, the other arm to the side; or the arm position may vary. Also, the supporting foot may be on tiptoe (see chapter on Dance for Gymnasts).

Spotting: Little spotting necessary. Stand to one side of the beam and offer a hand if needed.

37.   ONE-LEG BALANCE

M.   Usually performed facing forward. Lift one leg from bent position in front to a full extension to the side. You may also kick the straight leg to the side extension and catch the leg with one hand. Hold onto the heel of the extended leg, keeping the supporting leg straight. The opposite arm is high and to the side.

Spotting: Practice the movement holding onto the spotter's hand. When balance is good, let go of spotter's hand.

38.   BODY WAVE

M.   Same movement as performed in free exercise. Standing, one foot in front of the other, hands at the sides or in front of the body, bend the body to a low crouch, the arms swing downward. Arch the body pushing the hips forward as the palms turn upward, continue arching and lifting arms to over head. This may be followed by runs, or the movement may be done while taking several steps.

Spotting: Stand to one side and offer an extended hand.

39.   SIDE BALANCE

M.   Stand facing sideways; raise one leg to the side and lean the body to the opposite side until the body is almost parallel with the beam. Lift the opposite arm so that there is a line from the extended leg through the body and out to the arm.

Spotting: Stand in back of performer to catch her if she is unable to hold the balanced position.

40.   BATTEMENTS (KICKS)

M.   a.   Step forward taking high kicks on each step.
      b.   Step backward taking high kicks backward on each step.
      c.   A sideward kick may be included as a movement from one position to another. Body position and arm positions may vary.

Spotting: Little spotting is necessary. Stand alongside the beam and walk with the performer, offering an extended arm.

41.   ATTITUDE

M.   Standing on one leg, raise one knee as high as possible and carry it backward as far as possible. The raised leg is bent at right angle and the knee is held high. The same arm as raised leg is raised and curved over the head. The opposite arm is raised horizontally, or the arm position may vary.

Spotting: Stand to one side and support on the arm which is raised horizontally.

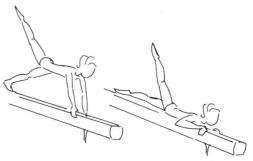

42.   SWEDISH FALL

M.   From standing position, kick one leg backward

and fall forward grasping the beam on either side. Thumbs on top. Keep the extended leg in the air during the fall (see Floor Exercise). This may follow a scale position.

Spotting: Stand to one side of the beam, and assist in controlling the body as it falls to the beam.

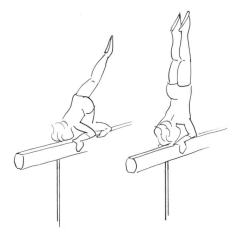

43. HEADSTAND

M. From a crouch or lunge position, bend forward placing the hands on the beam, thumbs on top, fingers on the sides. Taking the weight on the hands and forehead, kick up into a headstand.

Variations: a. From the headstand position, tuck the head and go to a forward roll.

b. From the headstand, split the legs into an inverted split, or spread the legs sideward to an inverted straddle.

Spotting: To learn, have spotters on either side of the beam; lower the beam to learn, or have one spotter standing on something so that she can hold the waist. Later use one spotter helping at the waist.

44. ENGLISH HAND BALANCE

M. To be done facing the length of beam. From standing position, bend forward placing

the hands on the beam, thumbs on top, fingers on the sides. Kick up into a hand balance position.

Variations: a. The position of the legs may vary as in a headstand.

b. From the English handstand, tuck the head and go into a forward roll; i.e., from the handstand, slowly lower by bending the elbows, tuck the head and roll on the upper back, and simultaneously change the hands to an under grip.

c. From the handstand, shift the body weight forward over the hands and straight arms as the legs are swung down backwards to crotch seat position. The body should be straight and the weight should be caught on the inside of the thighs (see sketch).

Spotting: Use two spotters, one standing to one side of the beam supporting the elbow and shoulder of the performer. The other spotter should stand on something so that she can control the handstand by catching the waist or thighs. In variation c each spotter holds with one hand the shoulder of the performer and with the other helps to catch the thigh.

45. HANDSTAND—SCISSOR KICK

M. From a one-leg squat position facing lengthwise, right foot on the beam, left leg extended. Kick with the left, then the right in a scissor movement as the weight is taken on the hands. Return to the one-leg squat position on the opposite foot. This movement may also be started from a standing position.

Spotting: Same as for English hand balance.

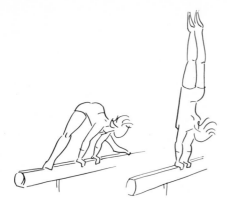

46. SIDE HANDSTAND

M.   From a straddle position, hands grasping the beam with thumbs to rear, fingers grasping opposite side of the beam, lift up to a handstand position bringing the legs together. Also, you may start as a cartwheel but bring legs together (it is easier than the regular side handstand).

Return M.

a.   From the handstand position sideways, slowly bend elbows and, keeping the body arched, lower the body to a front support position.

b.   From handstand position, slowly lower the legs down to a straddle position. The hands must be nearer than shoulder width apart.

c.   From handstand position, slowly lower to a straddle seat. Keep the hips high, move shoulders forward and slowly pike over the beam. When clear of the beam, slowly lower the hips to a sitting position.

d.   Handstand to a squat through to a balanced side seat.

e.   Handstand to a stoop through to a balanced side seat.

Spotting: Stand to one side and control the elbow and shoulder of the performer. If the performer is lowered to straddle seat, or squat, etc., the spotter controls the movement at the hips.

47.   CARTWHEEL

M.   Same as a cartwheel on the floor, except that

it must be very straight. If to the right side: right foot, right hand, left hand, left foot, all touching in sequence on the beam.

Variations: a. Series of cartwheels.
b.   One arm cartwheel.
c.   Dive cartwheel.

Spotting: Stand in back of performer on a raised platform or a Swedish box, control the movement at the waist as in performing a cartwheel on the floor.

48.   CARTWHEEL TURN TO ENGLISH HANDSTAND (ROUND-OFF)

M.   Same as a round-off. Start as in a cartwheel with hands on top of the beam, then turn 90 degrees to an English handstand and come to feet (or continue with any other movement).

Spotting: Spot with overhead spotting or from a raised platform.

49.   FRONT WALKOVER

M.   From a standing position, lean forward placing hands on either side of the top of the beam. Kick one leg over and then the other, splitting the legs in the air. (Performer should see the beam when she puts her leading foot onto it.)

Variations: a. Front walkover, switching legs in the air.
b.   Front walkover, one arm.
c.   Series of front walkovers.

Spotting: Standing to one side on a platform or Swedish box, support under the low back with both hands.

50. BACK WALKOVER

M. From a standing position, lean backward in an arch until the hands touch the beam. Kick one leg over, then the other, splitting the legs in the air.

Variations: a. Back walkover switching legs in air.
  b. Back walkover, using one hand.
  c. A series of back walkovers.
  d. Back walkover to handstand to straddle seat.
  e. Back walkover to split (see sketch).

Spotting: Same as No. 49 Front Walkover.

Variations: a. Series of tinsicas.
  b. Dive tinsica.

Spotting: Stand to the right side of performer on a raised platform or Swedish box and assist the twisting movement at the waist.

52. VALDEZ

M. Sitting on the beam, right leg extended, left knee bent with left foot close to buttocks. Right hand on beam close to buttocks, left arm extended horizontally forward. With a vigorous push of the left foot and a simultaneous whipping of the left arm from shoulder in an upward backward movement, push upward and over to a back handstand.

Spotting: Stand to the right side of the beam and assist at the waist.

53. FLIP-FLOP

M. Standing position, feet together or closed forward stride. Swing the arms downward bending the knees as though sitting on a chair. As the body falls off balance backward, vigorously swing the arms upward over head and then throw the head backward. Push off the beam by straightening the legs. Hands grasp the beam in an over grip as in an English handstand. Land on one or two feet.

Spotting: An overhead belt is preferred when learning this stunt. If hand spotting is used, stand on a raised platform and assist at the waist.

Walks or Movements Along the Beam

The walks or movements along the beam are frequently followed by turns, held positions, etc. The hand positions may vary (see Ballet positions). For compulsory exercises, exact positions are described.

51. TINSICA

M. Stand facing the length of the beam. Step forward on the right, placing both hands on the beam on the right side, as for a right cartwheel. As the hands are placed on the beam, kick the left leg upward, followed by the right into a momentary split position. Place the left foot on the beam, followed by right, and come out as in a forward walkover. Note: A tinsica is a combination of a cartwheel and forward walkover. It may also be done to the opposite side.

54.   WALK FORWARD

M.   Step forward with a definite pointing of the
       toes on each step. Arms may be in various
       positions, or may move from ballet first
       through second to fourth or fifth position.
Variations: a. Walk forward on tiptoes.
       b.   Run forward with small, quick running
             steps.
Spotting: Walk along to one side of the beam, offer-
       ing hand to performer.

55.   WALK BACKWARD

M.   Extend the foot backward on each step, trying
       to move with confidence and keep the body
       erect. Arm positions may vary. Walk may
       also be performed on tiptoes.
Spotting: Same as in No. 54.

56.   SLIDE (SIDEWARD WALK)

M.   Stand facing forward, moving sideward on the
       beam; step with left to the side, close
       right to left, step left sideward again.
       May be done with the feet sliding along the
       beam, or with a slight jump on the close
       so that the feet are lifted off the beam.

Spotting: Spotting should be done in front and in back,
       in case the feet miss the beam.

57.   TOE TOUCH AND STEP

M.   a.   Forward, with weight on left, touch right
             toe forward then transfer the weight to it;
             repeat with left.
       b.   Backward, with weight on left; touch right
             toe backward, then transfer the weight to
             it; repeat with left.

58.   CHASSÉ OR GLISSADE

M.   Facing length of beam, slide-close-slide. The
       foot remains in front; i.e., slide left foot
       forward, close right to left, slide left
       forward again. In a glissade the slide-
       close-slide is frequently used to prepare
       for a step or a leap on the opposite foot.
Spotting: Move alongside the beam, offering a hand
       to the performer.

59.   STEP-HOP

M.   Same as a regular step-hop. The knee may
       be lifted high and the arm positions may
       vary.
Variations: a. Lifted leg is straight in front.
       b.   Lifted leg is straight in back.
Spotting: Move with performer alongside the beam,
       offering a hand for balance.

60. PLIÉ-WALK

M. Bend the supporting leg as the opposite leg is swung from the rear with the knee straight so that the foot swings below the side of the beam, ending in a forward point. Plié-walk backward is just the reverse.

Spotting: Move with the performer alongside the beam, offering a hand for balance.

61. PAS DE BOURRÉE

M. Performed with the feet held in ballet fifth position and up on the toes. The movement should be a gliding one with short steps either forward or backward, with body held rigid. Movement is usually done facing forward and with the shoulder facing the length of beam.

62. RONDE DE JAMBE WALK

a. Ronde de jambe walk forward
M. Walk forward lifting the leg from the rear to the side and forward. Hold the leg straight in the air, make a continuous controlled movement; place the foot forward in a point position, then step forward on it and alternate.

b. Ronde de jambe walk backward
M. Lift the forward leg forward, to the side, and to the rear, and step back on it.

Spotting: Spotter should stand out of the way of the moving leg, but be ready to assist if balance is lost.

63. SKIP

M. May be taken with a highly lifted knee; arm positions may vary.

Spotting: Move with the performer alongside the beam, offering a hand for balance.

64. WALTZ (TWO-STEP)

M. Similar to glissade. Step forward on one foot close to the opposite foot, and step out again; i.e., step forward on right, close left to right, step forward on right. Alternate the step.

Here the movement is low on the beam, while in the glissade there may be a little hop in the movement.

Variation: Waltz turn, make a half turn on each waltz step.

Spotting: Stand to one side of beam, moving with performer and offering extended hand for balance.

65. SCHOTTISCHE STEP

M. May be done forward or backward, and with varying arm positions. The schottische step is three steps forward and a step-hop. The free leg may be extended or bent on the hop.

Spotting: Stand to one side of the beam, moving with the performer and offering the extended hand for balance.

66. MAZURKA STEP

M. This step is a slide-cut-hop. Slide forward on the right foot, bring the left to the right with a cut step, taking the weight on the left with a little hop as the right foot is kicked forward and then bent into the left ankle. Arm positions may vary.

Spotting: Stand to one side of the beam, moving with the performer and offering extended hand for balance.

67. POLKA

M. Facing length of beam, right foot in front. Hop on left foot, step forward on right, step left to rear of right, step right. The sequence is a hop, step together, step, with the upbeat on the hop. Repeat the hop on right, step forward left, step right to rear of left.

Spotting: Stand to one side of the beam, moving with the performer and offering extended hand for balance.

Turns on the Beam

All turns should be performed in a fast but smooth movement. This can be done only if the turn is on the ball of the foot. In all turns the body should be erect and stiff with the shoulders pulled together. Any turn performed on the floor may be performed on the beam, and many variations of the turn are listed below. All turns may be made more difficult by performing them with a leap so that the feet leave the beam.

68. TIP-TOE TURN

M. Stand with one foot in front of the other, close together; rise up on the toes and pivot around on the toes to face the opposite direction. To make a half turn, start with the weight on right foot; swing the left across the right and do a half turn, weight on both feet.

Spotting: A spotter should stand on either side of the beam with arms outstretched, ready to assist the performer should she lose balance.

69. CROUCH TURN

M. Stand with one foot in front of the other, squat down .in a deep crouch (back straight) lifting the heels and pivot around on the balls of the feet in a very low position.

Make a half turn to face the opposite direction.

a. To make a complete turn, start in a crouch position on left foot, swing the right foot across the left and do a half turn, put down the right foot after the left, and complete the turn with the weight on both feet. It should be a fast, continuous movement.

Spotting: Same as turn No. 68.

70. PIROUETTE TURNS

Pirouette inward (see picture)

M. Standing on the left, right foot in the rear. Swing the right foot with bent knee across in front of the supporting foot, and with arms over head (fifth position) turn on the supporting toe. Reverse the action to turn to the right. The turn may be a half turn, a whole turn, or more, depending upon the force given through the swinging leg.

b. Pirouette outward
Start in the same foot position, turn on the left foot to the rear (right) lifting the right leg in front of the body.

c. Pirouette inward or outward with leg extended forward or sideward.

Spotting: Same as turn No. 68.

71. LUNGE TURN TO LUNGE

M. From a forward lunge position, rise on the toes and, twisting the body, turn half way to a lunge facing the opposite direction. Do not change position of the feet.

Variations: a. From a lunge position with right foot forward, push off with the left leg and make a complete turn to the right; the arms may swing around the body to assist the turn.

b. From a deep side lunge position, arms horizontal, swing the back foot forward to a lunge facing the opposite direction (see sketch).

c. From a deep side lunge position, arms horizontal, swing the back foot forward and make a complete turn, ending in the original position.

Spotting: Same as turn No. 68.

72. CHAÎNÉS TURNS

M. Facing sideways, step to the left with left foot, cross the right foot over the left and do a half turn facing the opposite side of the beam. Continue the movement, to the same direction.

Spotting: Same as turn No. 68.

73. JETÉ TURNS

M. Similar to the chaînés turns, but with a small spring. Step on the right to right side, facing sideways. Cross the left foot over the right and spring onto it with a slight leap as a turn is made on the ball of the left foot; step out with the right and continue the turns.

Variation: Give a small leap onto the right, and a small leap onto the left, making a complete turn.

Spotting: Same as turn No. 68.

74. BATTEMENT TOURNEY

M. Facing length of the beam, weight on left foot in front, right leg in the rear; swing right leg forward in a high kick. Holding the right leg in the air, pivot around on the

left foot, ending in a scale facing the opposite direction. This is usually preceded by a glissade as preparation for the movement.

Spotting: Same as turn No. 68.

75. REVERSE BATTEMENT TOURNEY

M. Facing the length of the beam, weight on left foot in front, right foot in the rear, swing right leg forward, then backward in a high battement. As the right leg swings backward, pivot on the ball of the left foot turning to the right.

Spotting: Same as for turn No. 68.

76. STRADDLE SEAT TURN

M. Crotch seat position, hands crossed in front (right over left). The weight is taken on the hands, so when the turn is completed you end with the regular over grip the length of the beam; legs are lifted, the right crossing the beam in front and end facing the opposite direction.

Variation: Do a full turn ending with hands crossed as at the start.

Spotting: Same as turn No. 68.

77. KNEE SCALE TURN

M. Knee scale on the right knee, left leg extended to the rear. Pivot on the knee 180 degrees to face the opposite direction. Help the turn with a trunk twist.

Variation: Do a full turn.

Spotting: Same as turn No. 68.

78.   MODERATE ARABESQUE TURN

M.   Standing on right foot, left leg lifted about 45 degrees, body slightly arched. Do a half or full turn keeping the body position. (With the knee bent, it is an attitude turn, see sketch.)

Spotting: Same as turn No. 68.

Aerial Movements

Aerial movements are those in which the performer jumps or leaps or hops off the beam. The feet must completely leave the beam and the higher the leap, the better. Advanced gymnasts may add a half turn to leaps or jumps.

79.   STEP-HOP

M.   A step-hop is performed with the hop high off the beam.

Spotting: Same as turn No. 68.

80.   SKIPS

M.   A skip with a high lifting movement of the bent knee while the supporting foot leaves the beam.

Spotting: Same as turn No. 68.

81.   AERIAL LEG SWING

M.   Swing the leg backward and forward, with a hop on the opposite foot—hop as high as

possible leaving the beam. To alternate, add a step as follows: Weight is on left foot; swing right leg forward and backward as you hop twice on the left foot, step on the right and alternate the action.

Spotting: Same as turn No. 68.

82.   LEAP

M.   Spring into the air from one foot and land on other foot. The leap may be high or low; there may be a series of leaps, or may be done with steps between.

Spotting: Stand to one side of the beam, moving with the performer and offering the extended hand for balance.

83.   RUNS AND LEAPS

M.   Running steps which gradually get into a leap leaving the beam. Or several quick running steps and a leap.

Spotting: Same as turn No. 68.

84.   LEAP-PUSH-LEAP

M.   This movement is a coupé with a hop. Leap to the left foot, touching the right behind in a pushing movement as the leap on the left is repeated and the right leg is extended to the rear.

Variation: With changement, repeat the movement above bringing the left leg in front of the right.

Spotting: Stand to one side of the beam, moving with the performer and extending hand for balance.

85. STATIONARY LEAPS

M. (These are easiest to do facing lengthwise.)
    a. Split. Jump in the air and with legs in a forward-backward split.
    b. Stag leap. Jump in the air, forward leg bent, the foot touching the knee of the straight rear leg.
    c. Attitude. Jump in the air, holding the forward leg straight and back leg bent in an attitude poise.

Spotting: Same as turn No. 68.

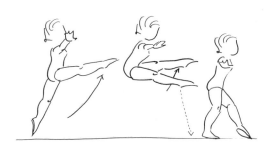

86. CISEAUX (HITCH KICK, SCISSOR KICK)

M. a. Forward ciseaux. Kick right leg in the air; as the right leg begins downward movement kick the left leg in the air and land on the right foot, with the left leg held in the air in front of the body.
    b. Backward ciseaux. Lift the right leg in the air in the rear, quickly change left, end with weight on right, left in the air in back of the body.

Spotting: Same as turn No. 68.

87. TOURS JETÉ TURN

M.   Similar to a battement tourney, but there is a change of feet during the turn. Standing on left foot, kick the right foot forward,

quickly turn to the left as the weight is taken on right foot, and the left leg swings backward in a scissor movement. Finish with weight on the right foot, the left leg backward to a scale.

Spotting: Same as turn No. 68.

88. CABRIOLE

M.   Standing facing length of the beam, right foot in front, arms in third or fourth position. Lift the right leg to a medium forward croisé. Right leg is then thrust into the air, keeping the knee straight, toes pointed. From a demi-plié on the left, the left leg is thrust into the air to beat the calf of the right leg. The beat forces the right leg higher in the air, landing on the left leg in a demi-plié.

Variation: Do the movement with bent legs.
Spotting: Same as turn No. 68.

89. PAS DE CHAT

M.   (This is used on the beam in a forward movement rather than the regular Pas de chat —see Dance for Gymnasts.) Standing facing the length of the beam, right foot in front, arms in second position. Step with the right foot forward, kick bent left leg in the air and as the left leg descends, kick the bent right leg in the air, land on the left foot. There is a moment of suspension in the air.

Spotting: Same as turn No. 68.

90.   SISSONE

M.   Standing on the beam, feet close in fifth position. Plié and spring into the air, springing forward on left foot as right is
extended to the rear; replace the right
foot to the left in closed position; repeat.

Variations: a. Sissone to the rear. The movement
is the same except that the forward leg is
extended in the air.

       b. Sissone with changement. The movement
is the same except that the rear foot is
brought through to a forward closed position, alternating sides.

93.   CROUCH JUMP

M.   Start from a standing or crouch position. Jump
into the air, lifting the feet off the beam
and bending the knees as close to the chest
as possible; return to original position.
The arms may swing foward, upward, or
backward with a slight forward tilt of the
body.

Spotting: A spotter should stand on either side of
the beam with outstretched hand to help
the performer balance.

91.   JETÉ BALLOTTÉ

M.   From a standing position, right foot forward,
spring into the air, right foot opens forward as the left leg opens from a
développé to the rear, land on the right
foot. The movement may also be done to
the rear.

Spotting: Same as turn No. 68.

92.   JETÉ BALLONÉ

M.   Standing with feet together (fifth position),
right foot forward, right shoulder forward. Right foot is lifted to the ankle of
left foot, right knee turned outward. Plié
on the left leg and at the same time thrust
right foot forward and hop on left toward
the right. End in a plié on left foot, the
right foot at the ankle again.

Spotting: Same as turn No. 68.

94.   CHANGEMENT

M.   Standing in fifth position, left foot in front,
spring into the air from both feet and
change position so that the right foot ends
in a front fifth. Point the toes in the air.

Variations: a. The changing of the feet may be done
with a scissor movement.

       b. The body should bend forward as the
arms swing backward and then forward
as the legs change.

Spotting: Same as turn No. 68.

95.   ENTRECHAT

M.   Jump into the air from fifth position and beat
the feet together (see Dance for Gym-
nasts).

Spotting: Same as turn No. 68.

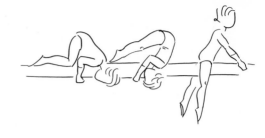

96.   AERIAL CARTWHEEL

M.   Same as aerial cartwheel on the floor excepting that it must be very straight (see Tumbling).

Spotting: Spot with overhead belt or standing on a raised platform grasping gymnast's waist.

Steps in learning: a. Practice on a line on the floor.
   b.   Practice on a floor beam.
   c.   Practice on a lowered regular beam.

98.   FORWARD SHOULDER ROLL

M.   Standing in a kneeling position or deep lunge, place the shoulder to one side of the beam, hands gripping the under side of the beam (or one hand on top, one underneath). Pull the hips up to a pike position, slowly roll forward and finish with the legs vertical, or go immediately into another movement.

Spotting: Spotters should stand on either side of the beam, control the hips as the roll is completed. Assist the performer to change hands to the under grip as the legs finish in the vertical position to give control.

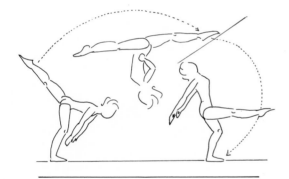

97.   AERIAL WALKOVER

M.   Same as an aerial walkover on the floor excepting that it must be very straight (see Tumbling).

Spotting: Spot with overhead belt, or standing on a raised platform grasp gymnast's waist.

Steps in learning: a. Practice on line on floor.
   b.   Practice on a floor beam.
   c.   Practice on a lowered regular beam.

Rolls

Three kinds of grips can be used for each roll, depending upon choice of the performer: (1) over grip the length of the beam, (2) the under grip, (3) mixed grip—one hand over, the other under. The aim should be to roll smoothly without stopping or breaking the rhythm.

99.   BACK SHOULDER ROLL

M.   (Usually done after a pretzel bend is mastered.) Supine on the beam, hand over head and gripping under the beam, head to one side, elbows close together. Draw the legs up over the body and as they are lowered over the head, place one knee on the beam and complete the roll.

When the legs are over the body, shift the hands to on top of the beam. (Usually, when one knee is placed on the beam, the other is placed to the right side, the left knee should hit the beam first; but some performers find it easier by using the right knee for landing.

When learning, use a folded towel or pad under the shoulder.

Spotting: Spotters should stand on either side of the beam. Assist by lifting hips and shoulder through and placing the knee on the beam.

100. FORWARD ROLL

M.   Standing in a kneeling position or deep lunge, lift the hips in pike position, hands on top of the beam, head tucked close to the body so that the roll is on the upper back. Quickly change the hands to the under grip as the weight reaches the shoulders, elbows pulled close together. Come out of this into a one-leg squat or a V seat.

Beginners should start with the under grip.

Variations: a. Headstand forward roll.
    b.   Handstand forward roll.

Spotting: Same as for forward shoulder roll.

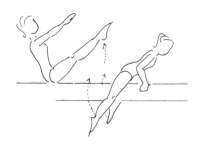

101. WHIP OR SWING FORWARD ROLL

M.   From a V seat position, straddle legs and place hands in over grip on beam, immediately forcefully whip legs backward and upward as the body weight is transferred forward over the arms. The body should be in a layout position above the horizontal (this is the final aim). At the height of the swing forcefully flex the hips (lifting them upward), bend the arms and tuck the head. Change hands to under grip as you roll and the hips are lowered to the beam.

Spotting: Spotters should stand on either side of beam. Support the shoulder with one hand and with the other hand help the leg swing down and up.

Steps in learning: a. Practice free swing of legs downward and back upward. This can be also done on the horse.
    b.   Practice leg swing to push-up position (see No. 26 Low Balances).
    c.   Practice leg swings to layout position, then bend hips and knees and come to squat stand on the beam.

102. FORWARD ROLL WITHOUT HANDS

M.   Start from a lunge, arms in second position. Bend hips and lean forward, slowly lower back of neck to the beam. Roll and keep arms in second position throughout the roll.

Spotting: Grasp at the hips in order to help her to lower to the beam and roll.

103. BACKWARD ROLL

M.   From a back lying position on the beam, reach over the head and grasp the beam with the fingers under the beam. In a tucked roll, bend the knees as the legs reach the overhead or the inverted position, push with the hands which have shifted to top of beam. End on a bent knee or go into knee scale. Advanced gymnasts should place their hands at once on top of the beam since the movement would then be more continuous.

Variation: Backward pike roll. Keep legs straight throughout the roll. This may end in a front lying position or low lunge.

Spotting: Spotting same as No. 99.

104. BACKWARD ROLL TO HANDSTAND

M.   From a back lying position on the beam, roll as for a pike roll; when the legs are almost vertical, push up with the hands and kick up into a handstand. The hands must be on top with thumbs on top, fingers to the sides. (This is a fast movement and there is no time for hand changing.) Keep the legs straight and finish by placing one foot on the beam and come to a standing position (see Tumbling).

Variations: a. From handstand swing legs to crotch seat.

b. Backward roll to headstand.

Spotting: Stand on a raised platform or a Swedish box. Grasp the legs as they are extended upward and help to lift the person to a handstand position.

Dismounts

The dismount provides the final touch to the routine. It is the last thing seen by the judges. Therefore, a correct landing must be practiced. Practice landing by jumping off the beam in a straight body position to landing many times. Land on the balls of the feet first, then push down the heels with the knees slightly bent. The arms may be spread forward or sideward or diagonally to assist in maintaining balance. Immediately straighten knees extending the body upward; simultaneously the arms are placed at the sides, coming to attention. Any excessive movement is an error for which points are subtracted.

105. SIDE SEAT DISMOUNT

M.   From a side seat position lean forward, placing the hand on the beam; swing the outside

leg backward and push upward, lifting the body away from the beam.

Spotting: Assist by supporting the elbow and shoulder of the hand on the beam.

106. JUMPING OFF THE BEAM

M.   In all jumps the body weight should be forward, knees should bend and then straighten as the position of attention is assumed after landing. Start with an upward jump, face sideways for each of the following:

a.   Jump off the beam, ending in a good standing position.

b.   Jump off the beam with a half turn in the air, end with hands touching the beam, facing the beam.

c.   Jump off with a straddle position in the air, end with back to beam (see sketch).

d.   Jump off with a straddle quarter turn in the air, end with the side to beam, one hand on beam.

e.   Jump off in pike position, end with back to the beam.

Spotting: For learning, use two spotters; one behind the beam, the other in front.

107. FRONT VAULT

M.   From a front leaning rest position (push-up) kick one leg upward, then the other and swing the legs over to the side of the beam.

Spotting: Stand on the near side, opposite to the leg swing, and control the performer by grasping elbow and shoulder.

108. ENGLISH HAND BALANCE DISMOUNT

M.   From a standing position, place hands parallel on the beam, facing the length of the beam. Rise to a handstand and do a front vault off. Use double mats for landing area.

Variation: Quarter turn, cartwheel out.

Spotting: Stand on the opposite side, controlling the supporting arm.

109. ROUND-OFF

M.   Stand at the end of the beam, kick left leg upward placing both hands close together in over grip across the beam, as in a side handstand. As the right leg swings upward followed by the left, hold a momentary handstand and come off the beam doing a quarter turn as the legs snap down to the mat. Push with hands after feet have passed the inverted position. End facing the end of the beam.

Variations: a. Round-off at the side of the beam.
            b. Run and round-off.

Spotting: Spotting: The spotter stands behind the performer and grasps the second arm below and above the elbow (in the above example the right arm).

110. CARTWHEEL

M.   (This will be performed at the end of the beam, and the space should be paced off so that the second hand is very near the end.) Lean sideward placing one hand on the beam near the forward foot; elbows must be straight; kick legs up as in a cartwheel but bring them together above the head so you land on both feet.

Variations: a. Cartwheel off side of beam.
            b. One arm cartwheel.
            c. Dive cartwheel.
            d. Quarter, half, or full twist after hands leave the beam.

Spotting: The spotter stands behind the performer and grasps the elbow of the second hand to be placed at the end of the beam.

111. HANDSTAND ARCH OVER

M.   From a handstand position, continue the arch bringing the feet over the mat. Push with hands after feet pass the vertical position.

Spotting: Stand to one side grasping the shoulder and elbow of the performer. Use two spotters at the beginning. The spotters should move with the performer to prevent undercutting.

112. HANDSTAND QUARTER TURN

M.   From a standing position left foot in front or to the left side, place hands in over grip across the beam as if performing a left cartwheel, but bring legs together above the head. After handstand position is achieved, shift the entire weight to the left hand, and raise the right arm sideways, simultaneously the body is forcefully arched and turned a quarter turn to the left as the legs swing down to the mat. The left hand remains on the beam as the gymnast lands with the left side to the beam.

Variations: a. Handstand half turn.
    b.   Handstand quarter or half turn at the end of the beam.

Spotting: In this case the spotter should stand at the side of the beam to the left of the gymnast. As the performer places her left hand on the beam grasp her left arm. As the gymnast is descending give supporting help to her right arm if needed. The second spotter should stand at the right side of the gymnast and help to push her legs off the side of the beam if necessary.

113.   WINDY (ONE-ARM ROUND-OFF SIDE OF THE BEAM)

M.   Standing at the center and facing the length

of the beam, perform a one-arm round-off.

Spotting: Same as in Handstand Quarter Turn No. 112.

Steps in learning: 1. Practice first the handstand quarter turn on the floor then on the beam. 2. Practice windy at the end of the beam.

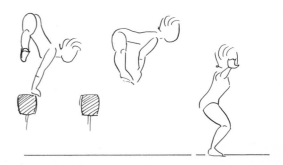

114.   HANDSTANDS

a.   Handstand squat through
    M. From hand balance position, bring legs through in a squat position to the mat. (A strong push from the shoulders and hands is necessary.)
b.   Handstand straddle through (see sketch).
    M. Same movement as above, but the legs are spread in a straddle through.
c.   Handstand stoop through
    M. Same movement as above, but the legs are held straight in a pike position and come through the hands.

Spotting: Use an overhead belt if possible, or spotters on either side grasping the arms of the performer.

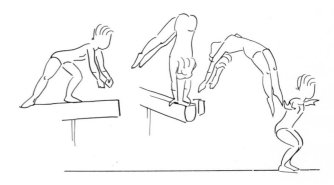

115.   HANDSPRING (OR HEADSPRING)

M.   From near the middle of the beam, lean forward placing the hands on the beam and execute a front handspring in a diagonal direction, landing with the side to the beam.

Variations: a. At the end of the beam (see sketch).
    b.   One arm handspring.

Spotting: Same as No. 111 Handstand Arch Over.

116. WALKOVER

M.   From the end of the beam, do a forward walk-over as in tumbling, but bring the legs together in the inverted position in the air for landing.

Variations: a. Walkover off side of beam.

b.   One arm walkover.

Spotting: Same as for Handstand Arch Over dismount No. 111.

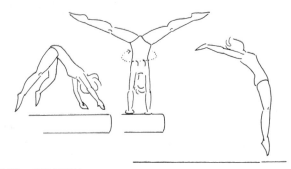

117. TINSICA

M.   From the end of the beam, do a tinsica as in tumbling, but bring the legs together in the air for landing.

Variations: a. Tinsica dismount with quarter, half, or full turn.

b.   Dive tinsica.

Spotting: Same as for Cartwheel Dismount No. 110:

118. VALDEZ (OR BACK WALKOVER)

M.   Sitting on the beam, right leg extended left knee bent with left foot close to buttocks. Right hand on beam close to buttocks, left arm extended horizontally forward. With a vigorous push of the left foot and a simultaneous whipping of the left arm from the shoulder in an upward-backward movement, push upward and over to a momentary handstand, then swing off the beam.

Variations: a. Valdez at the end of the beam.

b.   One arm valdez (see sketch).

Spotting: Stand to the right side of the beam and assist at the waist.

119. AERIAL CARTWHEEL

M.   From the end of the beam, do an aerial cart-wheel as in tumbling, but bring the legs together in the inverted position in the air for landing.

Variations: a. Aerial cartwheel at side of beam.

b.   Aerial round-off at the end or side of the beam.

c.   Aerial cartwheel with quarter, half, or full turn.

Spotting: Use an overhead belt to learn. Later, spotter should stand between the performer and end of beam.

120. AERIAL WALKOVER

M.   From the end of the beam, do an aerial walkover as in tumbling, but bring the legs together in the inverted position in the air for landing.

Spotting: Use an overhead belt to learn. Later, spotter should stand between the performer and end of the beam. A second spotter can be used in front of the performer to check the landing.

121. BACK SOMERSAULT

M.   Standing sideways on the beam, do a back somersault to the floor. It can be performed in a tucked, pike, or lay-out position. Allow double mats for landing.

Variations: a. Back somersault at the end of the beam.
   b.   Run, round-off (land on one foot or two feet, one in front of the other) somersault.
   c.   Back somersault with half or full turn.

Spotting: Use an overhead belt to learn. Then spot at the waist to help the gymnast not to touch the beam.

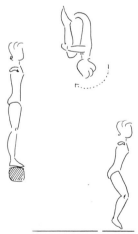

122. FRONT SOMERSAULT

M.   Standing sideways on the beam, do a front somersault to the floor. It can be performed in a tucked or piked position. Allow double mats for landing.

Variations: a. Front somersault at the end of the beam.

   b.   Run forward, take off and front somersault.

Spotting: Same as Back Somersault No. 121.

123. FLIP-FLOP

M.   Standing at the center and facing the length of the beam, perform a flip-flop as in tumbling but hands must be brought together to overgrip the length of the beam.

Variations: a. Flip-flop at end of the beam.
   b.   One arm flip-flop.
   c.   Run, round-off flip-flop.

Spotting: Use an overhead belt to learn. Then spot at the waist.

BEGINNING SKILLS AND COMBINATIONS

Selecting Skills

Usually the beginning gymnast will select from the following skills for the beginning balance beam exercise.

Mounts

   Front support mount
   Cross seat mount
   Crotch seat mount
   One knee mount
   Squat mount
   Straddle mount
   Wolf mount
   Single leg
   shoot through

Balances

   V or balance seat
   Knee scale
   Ballet point
   Lunge
   One-leg squat
   Shoulder balance
   Scale
   Croisé
   Attitude
   Splits

Movements along the beam

   Walks: forward and backward
   Slide
   Running
   Chassé
   Glissade
   Step-hop
   Skip
   Waltz
   Leap
   Leap-push-leap
   Schottische
   Mazurka

Turns

   Tip-toe turn
   Squat turn
   Lunge turn to lunge
   Battement tourney
   Chaînés

Aerial movements

   Changement
   Leaps
   Skips
   Gallop
   Several hops changing legs

Rolls

   Forward shoulder roll

Backward shoulder roll
Forward roll
Backward roll

Dismounts

   Side seat dismount
   Front vault
   Jumping off beam, half turn,
      straddle or pike
   Round-off
   Cartwheel
   Headspring
   Handstand arch over

Beginning Combinations

1. Front support mount; crotch seat; swing legs backward to squat; forward walk; tip-toe turn; step-hop; scale; half turn jump off.

2. Crotch seat mount; V seat; one leg squat to stand; glissade; reverse battement tourney; lunge; forward roll; swing legs backward to squat and turn; backward walk; straddle jump off.

3. Wolf vault mount; turn one leg squat and stand; running steps and leap; tip-toe turn; waltz steps; one leg squat; back shoulder roll to knee scale; front vault dismount.

1.

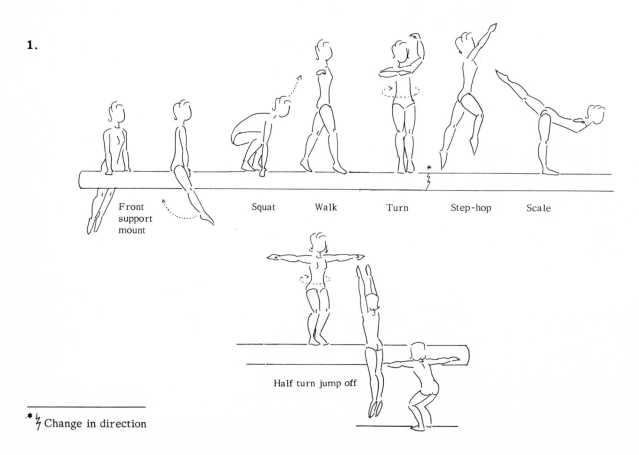

Front support mount · Squat · Walk · Turn · Step-hop · Scale

Half turn jump off

* ⸎ Change in direction

2.

Crotch seat mount · V seat · Squat · Glissade · Reverse battement tourney

Lunge · Forward roll · Squat and turn · Straddle jump off

3.

Wolf vault mount · Squat · Run and leap · Turn · Waltz

Squat · Back shoulder roll · Knee scale · Front vault dismount

*⚡ Change in direction

4.

Straddle mount   Lunge   Forward roll   V seat   Squat

Stand   Chassé   Turn   Scale   Run and leap   Round-off dismount

4. Straddle mount; twist to lunge; forward roll; V seat; swing legs backward to squat and stand; chassé; tip-toe turn; scale; run and leap; round-off dismount.

INTERMEDIATE SKILLS AND COMBINATIONS

Selecting Skills

Usually an intermediate gymnast, in addition to beginning movements, will select from the following skills.

Mounts

> Fence vault mount
> One leg squat on end or middle of beam
> Forward roll mount
> Aerial straddle mount
> Headstand
> Rear scissors to crotch seat
> Flank, leg swing to crotch seat
> Shoulder balance mount

Balances

> Needle scale
> Headstand
> English handstand
> Handstand scissor kick
> Cartwheel
> Walkover, front and back

*⁴⁄₇ Change in direction

Movements Along the Beam

These movements are the same as the beginning moves, but are performed with sureness and with elegance.

Turns

> Tours jeté
> Straddle seat turn
> Knee scale turn
> Moderate arabesque turn
> Lunge spin or turn
> Pirouette turn

Aerial movements

> Squat jump
> Straddle jump
> Leaps
> Ciseaux (scissor kick)

Rolls

> Headstand forward roll
> Handstand forward roll
> Backward roll to headstand
> Whip or swing forward roll

Dismounts

> Handspring
> Handspring quarter turn
> Handstand--squat, straddle, or shoot through
> Walkover
> Tinsica

Intermediate Combinations

The mounts and dismounts may be given just to get on and off the beam.

1. Forward roll mount; swing legs backward to squat and stand; waltz steps; tip-toe turn; handstand quarter turn dismount.

2. One leg squat mount; running steps forward; handspring dismount.

3. Straddle aerial mount, straddle seat turn, backward roll to headstand, knee scale, front vault dismount.

1.

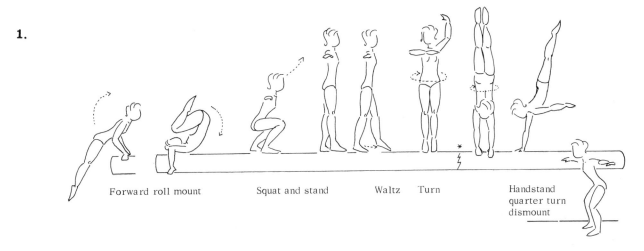

Forward roll mount   Squat and stand   Waltz   Turn   Handstand quarter turn dismount

2.

One leg squat mount   Run   Handspring dismount

3.

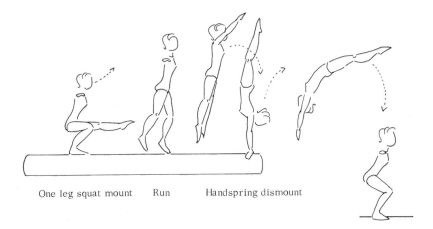

Straddle aerial mount and turn   Backward roll Headstand   Knee scale   Front vault dismount

*⌁ Change in direction

4.

Rear scissors   Squat   English handstand

Forward roll   Whip forward roll   Side seat dismount

4. Rear scissors to crotch seat, swing legs back to one leg squat, English handstand-forward roll, whip forward roll, side seat dismount.

ADVANCED SKILLS AND COMBINATIONS

Selecting Skills

Usually an advanced gymnast, in addition to intermediate movements, will select from the following skills.

Mounts

> Handstand mount
> Step on mount
> Walkover mount
> Cartwheel mount
> Thief vault mount

Balances

> Cartwheel to English handstand
> Side handstand, stoop through
> Cartwheel in series or one arm
> Walkover--front or back in series,
>   or one arm
> Handspring
> Valdez
> Backward roll to handstand
> Tinsica
> Dive tinsica
> Dive cartwheel
> Aerial cartwheel
> Flip-flop

Movements Along the Beam

Movements along the beam are similar to intermediate skills but are performed with sureness and elegance.

Turns

Advanced gymnasts include some of the same turns as the intermediate, but increase the degrees or revolutions of some turns. They include jump turns in their routines, for example:

> Tours jeté turn
> Leap with half turn
> Stag leap with half turn
> Pas de chat (cat leap) with half turn

Aerial movements

> The turns listed above
> A series of large leaps
> Aerial cartwheel
> Aerial walkover

Rolls

> Backward roll to handstand
> Dive forward roll
> Forward roll without hands

Dismounts

> Aerial cartwheel
> Aerial walkover
> Back somersault
> Front somersault
> Round-off somersaults
> Flip-flop
> Round-off, flip-flop

Advanced Combinations

The mounts and dismounts may be given just to get on and off the beam.

1. Run obliquely, step on mount, to one leg squat position; immediately half turn and kick to English handstand-forward roll; whip forward roll; side seat dismount.

2. Straddle aerial mount, then press to handstand; squat between hands; quarter turn to stand, ciseaux, pas de chat, hop with legs extended to the rear, jump off dismount.

1.

Squat   English handstand   Forward roll

Whip forward roll   Side seat dismount

2.

Straddle aerial mount   Handstand   Squat and quarter turn   Ciseaux

Pas de chat   Hop   Jump off dismount

3.

Walkover mount   Cartwheel   Quarter turn and cabriole backward

Cabriole forward   Steps   Arabesque turns   Croisé   Jump off

*⌁ Change in direction

4.

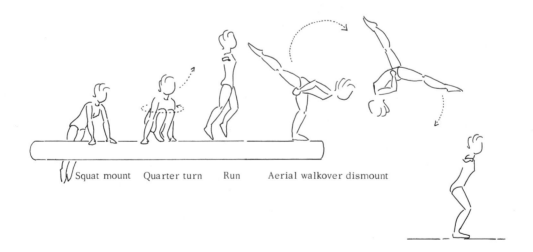

Squat mount   Quarter turn   Run   Aerial walkover dismount

3. Walkover mount at end of beam; immediately continue with a cartwheel; quarter turn, cabriole backward, cabriole forward; step, step, moderate arabesque turn (1-1/2 turns) finish in croisé, jump off.

4. Squat mount, quarter turn; run, aerial walkover (or aerial cartwheel), dismount.

BEGINNING EXERCISES

1. One knee mount on right knee.

2. One quarter turn to left to knee scale, left leg in rear.

3. Swing left forward in front of right and stand.

4. Plié walk, right, left, right.

5. Standing scale, left leg to rear.

6. Swing left foot to beam in front of right and do a tip-toe turn to the right.

7. Step-hop left, step-hop right, step-hop left, step-hop right.

8. Forward lunge, left foot forward.

9. In a lunge, turn to face the opposite direction.

10. From the lunge do a forward roll. Go to a balance or V seat, swing legs to rear to standing.

11. Running steps forward, squat, squat turn.

12. Changement.

13. Chassé left, chassé right.

14. Dismount—round-off at the end of the beam.

| One knee mount | Knee scale | Stand | Plié walk | Scale | Turn |
| 1. | 2. | 3. | 4. | 5. | 6. |

| Step-hop | Lunge | Turn | Forward roll | V seat | Stand | Run and squat turn |
| 7. | 8. | 9. | | 10. | | 11. |

| Changement | Chassés left and right | Round-off dismount |
| 12. | 13. | 14. |

*⚡ Change in direction

INTERMEDIATE EXERCISES

1. Forward roll mount.

2. Whip forward roll.

3. Swing legs back to a squat position.

4. Skip left, skip right, skip left.

5. Step on right and do a moderate arabesque turn to right.

6. Run left, run right, run left, and split leap (right foot forward).

7. Land on right foot, battement left forward and step into deep lunge.

8. Deep lunge turn (360 degrees) to split.

9. Backward roll to one-leg squat on left foot, right leg extended.

10. Step on right foot to crouch turn to left.

11. Leap left, push right, leap left. Repeat to opposite side.

12. Swing left leg forward to left cartwheel.

13. One fourth turn to scale (right leg to rear).

14. Reverse battement tourney.

15. Waltz step forward.

16. Pirouette turn to left (360 degrees).

17. Tinsica dismount.

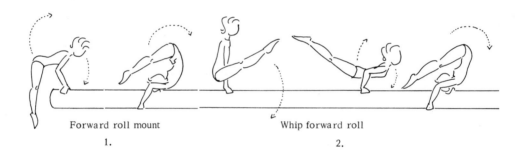

Forward roll mount   Whip forward roll
        1.   2.

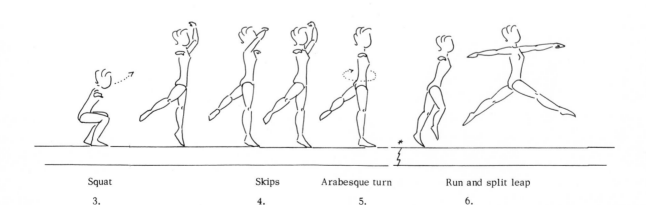

    Squat   Skips   Arabesque turn   Run and split leap
     3.   4.   5.   6.

*⚡ Change in direction

Battement   Lunge turn to split   Backward roll to squat   Crouch turn

7.   8.   9.   10.

Leaps   Cartwheel   Quarter turn to scale

11.   12.   13.

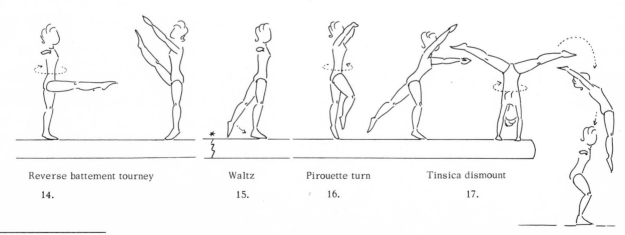

Reverse battement tourney   Waltz   Pirouette turn   Tinsica dismount

14.   15.   16.   17.

*⁄ Change in direction

ADVANCED EXERCISES

1. Step on mount at the end of the beam, end in moderate arabesque.

2. Run left, run right, run left, split leap (right foot in front).

3. Battement left, back bend with leg lift.

4. Back walkover, back walkover to handstand, swing legs down to crotch seat position.

5. Back roll to needle scale.

6. Waltz forward with half turns.

7. Moderate arabesque turn (360 degrees), end in a front croisé.

8. Step, battement tourney.

9. Front walkover, cartwheel with one hand, quarter turn to scale.

10. Close the rear foot, jump to a backward arch leap with one foot straight, other bent.

11. Pirouette turn, body wave.

12. Run, round-off, back lay-out somersault dismount at end of beam.

Step on mount   Run and split leap   Battement and back bend
1.   2.   3.

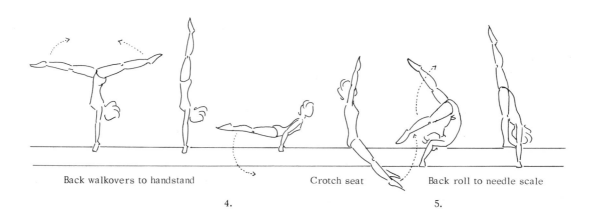

Back walkovers to handstand   Crotch seat   Back roll to needle scale
4.   5.

Waltz with half turns   Arabesque turn to croisé   Battement tourney   Front walkover   Beginning of cartwheel

6.   7.   8.   9.

Cartwheel with one hand   Quarter turn to scale   Backward arch leap   Pirouette turn

                                                     10.   11.

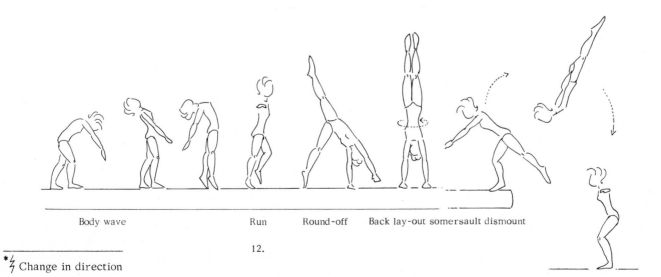

Body wave   Run   Round-off   Back lay-out somersault dismount

12.

*⚡ Change in direction

Chapter 12   Floor Exercise

Floor exercise is probably the most spectacular and artistic of all the events for women. It combines flexibility, agility, and strength in a continuous pattern of movement; and is planned in a design that is pleasing to observe. Floor exercise combines the movements from ballet, from tumbling, and includes other movements which do not belong in either category. It affords creativity and artistry on the part of the performer, and allows for individuality. Floor exercise is similar to dance in that it must have design, it is held within boundaries of space, and it allows freedom for individual experimentation.

The area for floor exercise in competition is 39-1/3 square feet (12 x 12 meters). The performer should use all of the area, and should plan a choreographic design that allows for the best use of each corner and of all the space. The compulsory floor exercise composition is usually very specific and detailed. For national and international competition, specific details are given for each movement of the floor exercise composition. For school work, the teacher may make up the "compulsory" floor exercise composition.

Optional compositions in floor exercise do not follow any specific pattern; the gymnast is allowed freedom to create her own sequence of movements. Naturally, the composition should include tumbling, ballet, some floor exercise skills, some standing skills, and some aerial skills. These must be continuous and flow readily from one to the next in a fluid artistic pattern. Held positions and strength movements are not acceptable. The composition must be performed in a time limit of one to one and one-half minutes, and it must be performed to one instrument only, according to the international rules.

The composition should contain easy and difficult acrobatic and tumbling movements connected smoothly with dance. It should cover the entire area. Every line of the exercise should contain an element of difficulty and all of the floor area should be covered. The sequence must be original, and make the grace, suppleness, and dynamism of the gymnast stand out. The routine should be according to the temperament of the gymnast. The exercise should be progressive with an increase of difficulty as the routine reaches the end.

All kinds of music may be used. If classical music is used, it must be appropriate to the movement. If small parts of a musical composition are used rather than the whole theme, the selection must be in good taste and rhythmically correct. Small pieces of folk music may be used, but again the music must be correctly combined. Modern jazz music may be used; however, it should be carefully selected and should suit the composition and the temperament and movement of the gymnast. Variety in rhythm is important to express the execution of the gymnast and for spectacular interest.

The music may begin before the gymnast starts her exercise, but the music must end directly with the final pose of the gymnast, otherwise deductions will be made. The musical accompaniment should finish in a logical fashion with the end of the exercise. Only one instrument is authorized for the accompaniment of the floor exercise. Whenever possible, the music should be composed to fit the floor exercise.

TEACHING SUGGESTIONS

1. A fast warm-up to jazz music is a good way to begin class because this type of music puts the students into a happy mood and relieves their tensions.

2. Sequences or combinations should be started as soon as a few skills are learned so that grace and flow of movement are emphasized from the beginning.

3. In school situations where mass floor exercise must be done, the sequences should be planned to move in specific direction so that large groups may perform a short sequence at the same time.

4. Stress should be given to develop aesthetic arm and body positions to give artistic line to movements, and the gymnast must learn how best to present skills for the spectator or judge to view.

5. The teacher should help the student to be able to see and feel the movement. The student must be made aware of the correct positioning and incorrect positioning.

6. Major accepted form should be discussed in class, such as balance, pointed toes, straight knees, full extension, and good body alignment.

7. Discuss judging and point deductions with students.

8. Let students judge each other's performance. This will make them more aware of their own and others' form breaks.

9. As students progress they should practice within correct floor area limits so that movements will be contained within the required floor space, and consideration will be given to angles, diagonals, curves, and straight lines in the floor pattern.

10. Movements should be practiced with music at all times.

11. Let the students create their own dance and tumbling combinations. This will help them to discover the limitless possibilities of movement.

12. Difficult tumbling sequences should be perfected on mats before performing on the floor.

13. It is better to have students perform the skills well, within the level of their mastery, than to do poorly those which are above their present accomplishment.

14. Students should be given opportunity to develop optional routines so that creativity and individual personality may be developed.

15. Practice of floor exercise routines, either compulsory or optional, should be done several times in their entirety, then the poorly performed skills or combinations should be practiced separately.

MOVEMENTS

Floor exercise includes tumbling (see also Tumbling chapter), dance (see chapter on Dance for Gymnasts), and some special floor exercise skills. The special floor exercise skills may be divided into floor skills, standing skills, skills performed in the inverted position, and aerial skills. All poses should be held for only an instant and should go immediatly into the next movement. The following are some of the more common floor exercise skills:

Floor Skills

1. LOG ROLL TO TUCK SIT

S.P. Back lying, arms extended over head.
M. Roll to the left side, then to front lying, and to right side (making a 360-degree turn); rise to a tuck sit position, hands supporting in the rear. A scissor movement of the legs may be done in the tuck sit position.

2. KNEE SCALE

S.P. Kneeling on the right knee, left leg extended upward and backward as high as possible, right arm extended forward.
M. The position above is held for an instant and moves immediately into another movement.
Example: From a knee scale, take the weight on both hands; with a high back scissor kick, come to standing.

3. BODY SWEEP

S.P. Kneeling on the right knee, right arm on the floor.
M. Stretch the left foot backward and rotate the leg outward. Stretch the left arm over head, and get a continuous line from the left hand to the left toe.

4. BALANCE OR V SEAT

S.P. Long sitting. (The movement may also be initiated out of a roll, etc.)
M. Lift the legs and balance on the seat in a V or pike position. Arms may be to sides or to the rear; or the hands may grasp the ankles.

S.P. = Starting Position   M. = Movement

5.   SITTING LEG LIFT

S.P.   Long sitting.

M.   Keeping the straight right leg on the floor, lift the left leg upward as high as possible. Tilt the body slightly backward and lift both arms upward over head as in a fifth position, but with the elbows closer together.

Suggested sequence: Hold the above position for an instant, and do a back shoulder roll to a knee scale.

6.   ONE-LEG SQUAT

S.P.   Standing.

M.   Slide one leg forward and bend the supporting knee, sitting on the heel.

7.   FLANK TURN

S.P.   Push-up.

M.   Push with the feet and swing both legs to the right side bending the hips. Lift the right arm as the legs swing under it. Finish in a long sitting position.

8.   SIT TURN

S.P.   Hooking sitting.

M.   Swing around on the buttocks, keeping the hook sitting position. Make a complete turn, end facing original position.

9.   HIP CIRCLING AROUND

S.P.   Front lying.

M.   Swing both legs to the right as the weight is taken on the left hip. Swing legs forward and to the left as weight is transferred to the right hip; end in a front lying position.

10.   HOOK SITTING TO STRADDLE LEAN

S.P.   Sitting, right leg extended in the air, left knee bent, foot at buttocks.

M.   Swing the right leg upward, taking weight on the left hand and left foot, do a half turn to the left, ending in a straddle lean.

Variation: Starting from a straddle seat, do the same movement.

11.   SUPINE ARCH

S.P.   Back lying.

M.   Placing hands directly under the shoulders, push the body upward, taking the weight on the hands and the toes; body arched, head backward.

12.   BRIDGE

S.P.   Back lying.

M.   Bend knees placing feet on the floor and simultaneously place the hands on the floor near

the shoulders. Push the chest upward as the arms straighten and the body forms a bridge.

13. KNEELING TURN TO SPIRAL UP

S.P. Kneeling on right knee—may be in scale or other movement.

M. Bring the left knee across in front of the right knee, place the weight on it as you turn to the right; step again to the right on the right knee, step on the left foot, then on right foot as the turn is continued to the right in a spiral movement.

14. HALF KNEELING, SIDE BEND

S.P. Kneeling on left knee, right leg extended to the side.

M. Bend the trunk to the right side over the right knee, right arm parallel to leg and left arm reaching upward.

Suggested sequence: Kneeling scale No. 2, to half kneeling No. 14, to spiral up No. 13.

15. HALF KNEELING, BACK BEND

S.P. Kneeling on left knee, right toe placed to the side.

M. Bend trunk to the left, weight on left knee and right toe. Left arm is low in front of body, right arm curved over head.

16. HALF KNEELING WITH BACK ARCH

S.P. Kneeling on left knee, right toe in front.

M. Extend the left leg backward so that it is in a semi-split. Weight taken on the lower left leg and the right toe. Both arms over head; body arched backward.

Suggested sequence: Do this movement, then slide right leg outward and forward into a split, bringing body forward over the right leg.

17. HALF KNEELING WITH LEG LIFT

S.P. Kneeling on left knee, right leg to side.

M. Lift the right leg upward to the side, tilting the body to the left. Arms in horizontal position to the side.

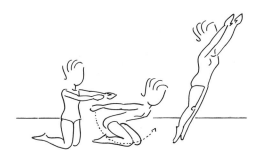

18. KNEELING, JUMP TO STAND

S.P. Kneeling, arms in front.

M. Sit downward toward heels, swing the arms downward and, with upward swing of the arms, simultaneously push from the knees and insteps and come to a standing position.

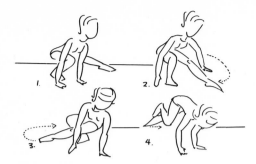

19.   PINWHEEL

S.P.   Squat position, hands on floor in front of the body, weight on right foot, left extended to the side.

M.   Bring the left leg in a circle movement forward in front of the body, lifting one arm and then the other as the leg passes under them. Continue the left leg around and take the weight on the hands as the left leg passes under the right foot.

Suggested sequence: From standing, do a one-leg squat and into a pinwheel, continue to a straddle headstand or handstand.

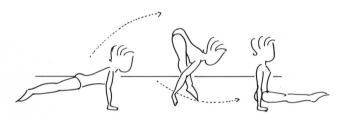

20.   SHOOT THROUGH

S.P.   Front support (push-up position), weight on hands, legs extended to the rear.

M.   Push with the feet and lifting the hips as high as possible, shoot the straight legs through the hands to a long sitting.

Variations: a. Do a mule kick or handstand, and swing the legs down through the hands in a shoot through.
    b.   Squat through.
    c.   Straddle through.

21.   SPLIT

S.P.   Standing in front stride, right leg extended forward.

M.   Slide forward until both legs are extended. The

arms may be extended to the side, or front and back. Trunk may be arched backward, or bent over the forward leg.

22.   JAPANESE SPLIT

S.P.   Side straddle stand.

M.   Spread legs sideward until they form a split on the floor.

23.   STRADDLE LEAN

S.P.   Long sitting, legs widely spread.

M.   With arms horizontal, or holding onto the ankles, bend the trunk forward, bringing the chin to the floor.

24.   SPLIT TURN

S.P.   Split on the floor, left foot forward.

M.   Swing the right leg straight forward in an inverted split and simultaneously lie on the back. Swing the legs apart in a wide spread, then swing left leg to an inverted split (left foot near the head); meanwhile turn halfway around or completely around to the left. Continue tucking the right leg to the side under the left leg and come to kneeling position, and continue with another movement.

25. VALDEZ

S.P. Long sitting, right leg extended, left knee bent with left foot close to buttocks. Right hand on floor near buttocks, left arm horizontally forward.

M. With a vigorous push of the left foot and left hand, and a simultaneous swinging of the right arm from the shoulder in an upward and backward movement, push upward and over into a back handstand.

Standing Skills

The following movements are in the standing position, or start from a standing position. See also chapter on Dance for Gymnasts.

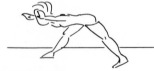

26. STRADDLE STAND

S.P. Standing, feet apart.

M. Bend trunk forward 90 degrees with a flat back. Arms stretched horizontally.

Suggested movements to follow: Tuck the head and do a straddle roll.

27. BODY WAVE

S.P. Standing, feet together or one in front of the other; arms at sides.

M. Lift the arms slightly forward and bend the knees and hips, swing the arms backward and upward as the body executes a waving motion in an arched position by pushing the hips forward.

Variation: Do the same only with one arm to one side.

28. SCALE (ARABESQUE)

S.P. Standing.

M. From a standing position, raise one arm forward as the body is bent forward, and the opposite leg as arm is lifted to the rear.

Variations: See Arabesque, in chapter on Dance for Gymnasts.

29. SWEDISH FALL (FORWARD DROP)

S.P. Standing.

M. Fall forward landing on the hands which are placed in line with the shoulders. The arms are straight and then bend as the head is brought to the floor. Lift one leg as the fall is executed.

Suggested movements to follow this: a. The leg that is extended in the air may be twisted to the back as the body twists in the same way, and come to a long sitting position.

b. The leg extended in the air may bend and then push up to a half kneeling position as in 14, 15, 16, or 17.

30. BACK BEND WITH LEG LIFT

S.P. Standing.

M. Keeping weight on the left leg, lift the right leg upward as high as possible, and simultaneously bend the trunk backward, arms over head.

Suggested movement to follow: Back walkover.

31.   NEEDLE SCALE

S.P. Stand in a scale as in No. 28.

M.   Bend forward until the hands touch the floor,
      or one hand may be on the floor and the
      other on the ankle of the supporting foot.
      The extended leg is raised toward the
      ceiling.

Suggested movement to follow: Do a forward roll to
      a V seat.

32.   ONE-LEG BALANCE

S.P. Standing, arms at sides.

M.   Keeping the weight on the left leg, lift the
      right leg sideward and upward holding
      the heel with right hand.

33.   ALLUSION

S.P. Standing on left foot, arms horizontal, right
      leg in forward point.

M.   Step onto right foot, kick left leg forward in a
      high battement, simultaneously swing arms
      overhead. With a forceful downward swing
      of the left foot, twist the body to the left.
      The head comes down near the right knee
      as the left leg is kicked high to the rear
      in a needle scale. Do a half turn on the
      right foot as the left leg continues in the
      air. Twist the body to the left and end
      facing the left foot which comes to a for-
      ward battement position; continue to a
      split with the left leg forward, or to a
      front walkover.

Spotting: Stand to the left side; with the right hand
      hold the left wrist of the gymnast, and
      with your left hand hold the back of the
      neck to help the gymnast with the turn.

Skills Performed in the Inverted Position

Use all tumbling skills such as tinsica, handsprings, etc. See also chapter on Tumbling.

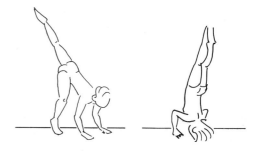

34.   HEADSTAND

S.P. May be started from various positions.

M.   Place hands on the floor, shoulder distance
      apart. Lift the legs straight supporting
      the weight on the hands, tilt the body for-
      ward placing the head on the floor in a
      tripod position between the hands, weight
      on the hair-line. Extend both legs upward
      into a headstand.

Variations: a. From a front lying position, pull up
      into a pike position and then up into a
      headstand.

      b. From a straddle stand, or straddle lean,
      pull up into a headstand.

      c. Pull up from a front lying to a headstand
      with the legs spread to the sides, or split.

Suggested movements to follow: The headstand should not be held for more than three seconds.

a. Do a forward roll to a V seat.
b. From the headstand, push up with the arms into a handstand, and arch out as in a walkover or limber.

37. YOGI HANDSTAND

S.P. Handstand.

M. This may be taken from a regular handstand, or with a push-off from both feet and immediately performing the yogi balance. The hips are forward with the legs backward so that the body is in somewhat of a pike position. The head is tucked, looking at the toes.

35. HANDSTAND

S.P. Standing.

M. Bend forward placing the hands shoulder distance apart on the floor, and kicking one leg upward, immediately followed by the other. Find a point of balance without too much of an arch in the low back; hold for three seconds, then go into another movement.

38. CARTWHEEL

S.P. Standing.

M. (Cartwheel to the left side.) Kick the left leg upward and place it forward on the mat, bending forward as the weight is taken on the left hand, then on the right. Arms are straight and shoulder distance apart. Legs are split in the air. Land on the right, then on the left foot as the body ends facing the original position. There should be an even 4-count rhythm; i.e., left hand count 1, right hand count 2, right foot count 3, left foot count 4. The cartwheel should be practiced on both sides.

Variations: a. Cartwheel from a run.
b. One hand cartwheel.
c. Dive cartwheel—run and dive into the cartwheel.

Spotting: Stand on the opposite side to the kick-up, hands crossed, left hand crosses over the right and grasps right waist of the performer, assisting the performer through the movement by lifting at the waist.

36. HANDSTAND TURN

S.P. Handstand with left foot in front.

M. Place right hand across the body in the same line as left foot, fingers toward left foot. Immediately half turn to the left, placing the left hand down upon completing the half turn.

Spotting: Stand in front near the left shoulder. Catch at waist to assist the turn.

39. CARTWHEEL TO SPLIT (TEACH FIRST ON MAT)

S.P.   Standing, side to the mat.
M.   (Cartwheel to left side.) Kick the left leg upward and place it forward on the mat, bending forward as the weight is taken on the left hand, then on the right. Arms are straight and shoulder distance apart. Legs are split in the air. Now lift the left arm, shifting all the weight to the right hand, and cut the right foot to a split position; hips must be close to the right hand.

40. FRONT WALKOVER

S.P.   Standing.
M.   Placing both hands on the floor shoulder distance apart and parallel, kick one leg upward over the head, followed by the other. The legs are split in the air. Continue the movement until the leading leg touches the floor and then the other foot lands in a front stride position. To stand up again, push forward with the hips and arch out of the movement, the head coming up last and the arms come over the head. It is important that the whole foot be placed on the floor in landing.

Variations: a. Front walkover, switch legs in air.
       b.   Front walkover, one arm.
       c.   Front walkover ending in split.
Spotting: Stand to one side, one hand under the low back and the other assisting to lift the shoulders.

41. BACK WALKOVER

S.P.   Standing.
M.   Bend the trunk backward, arms over head, until the hands touch the floor. Kick one leg up and over the body, followed by the other. Legs are split in the inverted position. Land with one leg, then the other.
Variations: a. Back walkover, switch legs in air.
       b.   Back walkover using one hand.
       c.   Back walkover to handstand, stoop or straddle through.
       d.   Back walkover to split.
Spotting: Stand to one side, one hand under back and the other hand under the leading leg. Give assistance by helping to lift the leg up and over.

Aerial Skills

In these movements the gymnast leaves the floor, as in a leap. All tumbling skills are used, such as forward somersaults, etc. See the chapter on Tumbling.

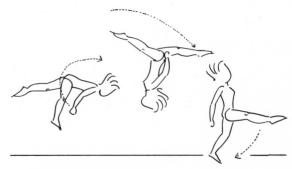

42. AERIAL WALKOVER (SEE NO. 29 TUMBLING)

S.P.   Standing at one end, facing a long mat.
M.   With a run and a take-off from one foot, bend forward swinging the arms downward and backward as the head is pulled strongly backward. Kick the leading leg strongly

to the rear. Continue the movement of a walkover, but keep the body extremely arched, elbows pulled close to the body. Don't drop the upper body lower than the position of a good front scale.

Spotting: Use an overhead belt or hand belt.

43. BUTTERFLY

This is similar to a tours jeté done in a horizontal position.

S.P. Standing in wide stride with weight on right foot, body bent slightly forward, arms to the side.

M. Bend low to the right, bending the right knee. As the recoil is made, swing the arms up and over and twist violently to the left and very low. Straighten the left leg and push hard with it as the right leg is kicked out and up. Follow through with the body flinging it in a low twist to the left as the left foot follows the right. Land on the right foot, the head near the right ankle, continue the slanting whirl by whipping around to the left to the original position.

44. LEAPS

Below are described a few of the various leaps which may be used in floor exercise.

S.P. Standing or moving from another stunt to get necessary motion.

a. Stag leap
M. Leap upward and while in the air, the back leg is extended and the forward knee is

bent with the foot touching the knee of the extended leg. For example, if the right leg is extended sideward and backward, the left knee is bent. The left arm is over the head, the right arm parallel and back to the right.

b. Cat leap
M. Jump into the air, knees to the side and bent so that the feet are together under the body. Arms in third or fifth position.

c. Tuck leap
M. Jump into the air, bringing both knees upward to the head, head bent forward, arms backward in hyperextension.

d. Backward arch
M. Body arched, both knees to rear. Jump into the air, both knees bent, feet in the rear, both slightly arched, left arm stretched upward, right arm backward.

e.   Side extension

M.   Leap to the right side on the right leg, left leg to side extension, body facing forward, right arm stretched diagonally over head, left arm to the side extension.

f.   Aerial Split

M.   Run and leap into the air, legs in a split with right leg forward and left leg back, arms horizontal right to the rear, left arm forward, body slightly arched with focus forward and upward.

BEGINNING SKILLS AND COMBINATIONS

Selecting Skills

Usually the beginning gymnast will select from the following skills for her floor exercise combinations.

Ballet and dance

    Arabesque
    Battements (kicks)
    Rond de jambe
    Attitude
    Ballet point
    Croisé
    Chassé
    Glissade
    Chaînés turns
    Battement tourney
    Balancé
    Lunge
    Waltz step
    Waltz turn
    Body wave
    Hop and variations
    Kneeling turn to spiral up
    Half kneeling side bend

    Half kneeling with back arch
    Sissonne
    Swan jump
    180-degree turn on one foot
    Low spiral body stretch
    Running
    Skip
    Jump
    Turns on both feet

Tumbling

    Forward rolls
    Backward rolls
    Cartwheel
    Round-off

Other movements

    Knee scale
    Hip circle around
    Split
    Straddle lean
    Body sweep
    Balance or V seat
    One leg squat
    Swedish fall
    Scale
    Headstand
    Bridge
    Sit turn
    Handstand
    Headstand forward roll

Note: For combinations with original music see Floor Exercise for Women, directed by Blanche Drury and Andrea Bodo Schmid, original music by Adelia Spangenberg. Hoctor Records, Inc., Waldwick, N.J., HLP 4011.

Beginning Combinations

1.   Perform in eight measures of 3/4 time. Balancé to left, both arms to left, balancé to right, both arms to right, three walking steps forward 1, r, 1, battement tourney, scale (arms crossed in front), Swedish fall, hip circle to left, touch toes (in long sitting), backward roll to squat, jump up with 1/2 turn, arms circling from first through fifth and to sides.

2.   Perform in eight measures of 3/4 time. Balancé right, balancé left, waltz step forward right, waltz step forward left, waltz turn to right arms low second, right shoulder dip, arms opening to second; kick left in forward battement, cartwheel left, turn 90 degrees in moderate arabesque arms in third (right arm high).

1.

Balancé Walk Battement tourney Scale Swedish fall

Hip circle to left Toe touch Backward roll Jump turn

2.

Balancé Waltz Shoulder dip Battement

Cartwheel Arabesque turn

3.

Plié   Battement   Cartwheel

Lunge and arm circle   Headstand   Forward roll   Stand   Plié

4.

Chaînés   Cartwheel   Turn   Scale

Swedish fall   Headstand   Forward roll   Attitude

3. Perform in eight measures of 2/4 time. Start on toes, left foot in front, left arm forward, right to rear. Plié twisting body slightly, changing arms. Repeat plié. Battement left, cartwheel, turn 90 degrees to deep lunge, arms circling downward, backward, and forward, headstand with left foot on right knee, forward roll, stand to right foot forward, end in deep plié right arm forward, left to rear.

4. Perform in eight measures of 4/4 time. Chaînés turn right; chaînés turn right; step right, batte-

ment left, left cartwheel; 90-degree turn stepping to scale, arms in second; Swedish fall; pull up to headstand; forward roll to stand on right in attitude, arms third, right high.

INTERMEDIATE SKILLS AND COMBINATIONS

Selecting Skills

An intermediate gymnast may select from the following skills for her floor exercise combinations.

Ballet and dance

Half kneeling with left lift
Tours jeté
Pas de ciseaux forward
Pas de ciseaux backward
Cabriole
Waltz run turn
Rond de jambe turn with body twist
Entrechat
Pas de chat
Jeté ballotté
Changement de pieds
Pirouette (360-degree turn on one foot)
Stag leap
Tuck leap
Split leap
Sauté with back arch
    (jump, arching body, trying to touch
    head with feet)

Tumbling

Back extension
Headspring
Neckspring
Handspring
Tinsica
Walkover handspring
Flip-flop
Round-off flip-flop

Other movements

Handstand forward roll
Front walkover
Back walkover
Valdez
Cartwheel to split
Shoot through
Split turn
Allusion
Needle scale
One-leg balance

Intermediate Combinations

1. Perform in six measures of 4/4 time. Step back on left foot, arms in fifth, right leg lifted forward; step forward on right as left leg is lifted to rear and both arms are to the rear; three running steps and a hop (Japanese hurdle); handspring; headspring; forward roll to stand with sauté. Three steps forward and jump upward, bending left leg, and end in a deep bend half kneeling on left, right foot in forward point, left arm forward, right to rear.

1.

Run   Handspring   Headspring

Forward roll   Sauté   Run   Jump   Deep bend

2.

Cartwheel   Split

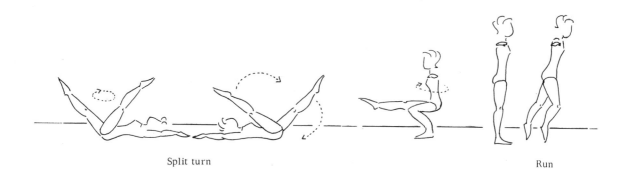

Split turn   Run

Tuck leap   Squat turn   Back walkover   Croisé

2. Perform in six measures of 4/4 time. Cartwheel-split, split turn 360 degrees, standing up; two running steps, close; tuck leap; squat turn 360 degrees, back walkover, and hold in croisé.

3. Perform in six measures of 4/4 time. Three running steps and hop (Japanese hurdle), tinsica step forward to lunge, arms in second; forward roll without hands ending in long sitting; valdez to standing pose.

4. Perform in six measures of 4/4 time. Attitude turn, three running steps and hop (Japanese hurdle), round-off, flip-flop landing on one foot and turn 180 degrees and hold in front stride with body arched, arms to rear; battement, and one arm front walkover to split.

3.

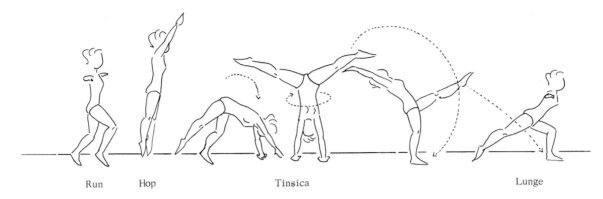

Run   Hop   Tinsica   Lunge

Forward roll   Valdez   Stand

4.

Attitude turn   Run   Round-off   Flip-flop   Turn

Stride   Battement   One arm walkover   Split

ADVANCED SKILLS AND COMBINATIONS

Selecting Skills

Advanced skills are similar to intermediate skills but they are performed with a higher amplitude and performed more gracefully. Aerial cartwheels, aerial walkovers, all somersaults, a series of flip-flops, and a series of aerial butterflies are all advanced skills.

Advanced Combinations

To develop advanced combinations substitute some of the skills listed above into an intermediate combination, i.e., instead of doing a walkover handspring, do an aerial walkover.

BEGINNING EXERCISES (THE CLOCK AS A GUIDE)

As stated, floor exercise composition must be performed in a time limit of one to one and one-half minutes, and performed in a space of 39.33 square feet. With young performers, direction presents a problem and the following suggestions are offered as a means of assisting the student to become oriented in space.

By superimposing the face of a clock in the floor exercise space, the student can orient herself to directions. Thus, 12 o'clock is always directly forward, and 6 o'clock is directly backward; 3 o'clock is directly to the right and 9 o'clock is directly to the left, with the other numbers giving an oblique focus.

Following is a simple floor exercise composition, showing the use of the clock for focus and orientation in space:

1. Start at 7 o'clock facing 1 o'clock. Do a body wave, finish with a kick of the left foot.

2. Step left, right, and kick left foot in a left cartwheel, to 1 o'clock.

3. At the end of the cartwheel, glissade directly backward toward 5 o'clock and do a battement tourney, ending in a scale facing toward 8 o'clock.

4. Moving directly across the space from 5 o'clock to 8 o'clock, do a Swedish fall to a front lie.

5. Pull up into a headstand, roll out of the headstand to a one-leg squat. Turn in the one-leg squat and spiral to standing, end facing 11 o'clock.

6. Moving directly forward to 11 o'clock, run forward, left, right, left, and do a stag leap with right foot forward, land on the right foot, step with the left into an arabesque turn to the left, end facing 4 o'clock.

7. Moving from 11 o'clock backward to 4 o'clock, do two chaînés turns, a cartwheel, and round-off. End in a lunge facing 11 o'clock.

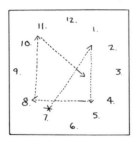

Body wave   Walk   Cartwheel

1.   2.

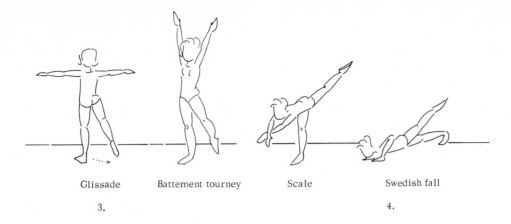

Glissade   Battement tourney   Scale   Swedish fall

3.   4.

Headstand   Squat   Run   Leap   Arabesque turn

5.   6.

Chaînés   Cartwheel   Round-off   Lunge

7.

INTERMEDIATE EXERCISES (NUMBERS AS A GUIDE)

Another plan for the orientation of the student within the floor exercise space is to divide the space into eight parts, as noted below. For those who have had ballet or dance orientation, this might be the easier plan to follow. The simple floor exercise composition shows the use of this plan. (For those familiar with stage terms, such terms may be substituted for the numbers. However, this is a little more cumbersome, and the numbers are generally preferred.)

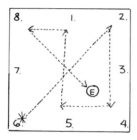

1. Start at 6, moving to 2. Do an arabesque turn to the left.

2. Do a few running steps and handspring, headspring, forward roll to stand.

3. Moving from 2 to 4, do two chaînés turns and a cartwheel left (end cartwheel facing 6).

4. Moving from 4 to 6, glissade and tours jeté (end tours jeté facing 4, left leg in scale).

5. Moving from 5 to 1, do a straddle roll forward from the scale, keep the left leg in the air and twist to a straddle stand facing 1. From the straddle position pull up into a headstand, legs moving together over head. Drop down to the left knee, right leg to the side. Step on the right knee across the left, then the left knee in a spiral turn to the left up to standing. End facing 1. Do a standing back handspring, end facing 1.

6. Moving from 1 to 8, run toward 8 and do a split leap, ending in a ballet point facing 4 (turn).

7. Moving from 8 to 4, do a walkover handspring, cartwheel and tinsica. From the tinsica do a high battement (kick) facing 4, and end in a lunge.

Arabesque turn   Run   Handspring   Headspring   Roll
1.   2.

Stand   Chaînés   Cartwheel   Glissade   Tours jeté
3.   4.

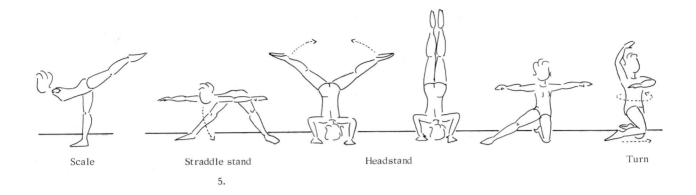

Scale   Straddle stand   Headstand   Turn

5.

Back handspring   Run   Split leap   Point   Walkover handspring

6.

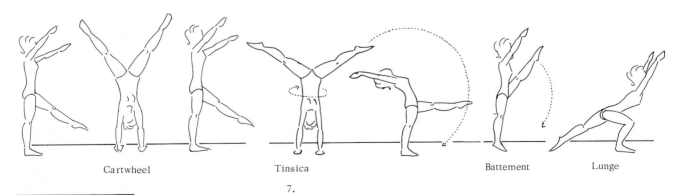

Cartwheel   Tinsica   Battement   Lunge

7.

*⚡ Change in direction

ADVANCED EXERCISES (THE CLOCK AS A GUIDE)

1. Start by standing at 7 o'clock facing 1 o'clock— in good posture. Do a moderate arabesque turn on right, left foot to rear.

2. Do a few running steps forward to handspring, then a forward roll, stag leap, glissade left and tours jeté, ending in scale on right foot, left leg extended to rear, facing 5 o'clock.

3. Step kick right leg to battement forward, allusion (ends in split).

4. Swing legs from split to seat and do a seat turn ending facing 1 o'clock.

5. Do a backward roll, back extension, half turn to face 5 o'clock.

6. Do three chaînés turns and facing 10 o'clock.

7. Do a few running steps, round-off, two flip-flops, half turn to dive front walkover, pirouette turn ending 7 o'clock.

8. Run, run, leap (back leg bent, front leg extended on leap).

9. Kick rear leg to battement tourney, end facing 10 o'clock.

10. Back walkover, back arch and shoot through with one leg ending in split, split turn to stand, and two steps circling around.

11. Continue to run, aerial walkover, rond de jambé turn with a twist, end facing 12 o'clock.

12. Do a few running steps and round-off, flip-flop, back tucked somersault; jump straight up in the air and land in a lunge position. Hold the lunge position for a second, then finish at attention.

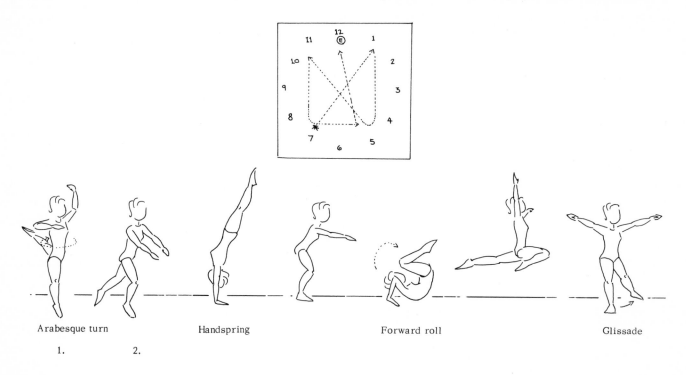

Arabesque turn   Handspring   Forward roll   Glissade

1.   2.

Tours jeté   Scale   Battement   Allusion   Split   Seat turn

*⚡ Change in direction   3.   4.

Backward roll   Back extension   Chaînés   Run   Round-off   Flip-flops   Half turn

5.   6.   7.

Front walkover   Pirouette turn   Run   Leap   Battement tourney   Back walkover

8.   9.   10.

Split   Split turn   Aerial walkover

11.

Rond de jambe turn   Run   Round-off   Flip-flop   Back tucked somersault   Lunge

12.

Chapter 13   Uneven Parallel Bars

Previous to 1938 women used the even parallel bars, at slightly lower height than those used for men. In 1938 the uneven parallel bars were introduced in Czechoslovakia at the Sokol Games, and were used at the World Championships at Prague in 1938. They were officially accepted in 1952 at the Olympic Games, and have been used as part of the competition for women ever since.

The uneven parallel bars have been readily accepted because they offer to the woman performer an opportunity for using more flowing and swinging movements than strength movements. They combine some of the movements of the parallel bars with some of the thrilling movements commonly used on the high horizontal bars for men. They offer a great challenge to the performer, and yet graduated movements on them can be executed by the novice as well as by the advanced performer.

EQUIPMENT

The height of the upper or high bar is 2.30 meters (7' 6-1/2''); the height of the low bar is 1.50 meters (4' 11'').

In competition the height of the bars cannot be adjusted, but the width of the bars may be adjusted by the performer by moving the low bar only in or out to a minimum width of 48 cm (1' 6-7/8'') and a maximum of 68 cm (2' 2-3/4'').

TECHNIQUES

Positions

Rather than listing the many terms here, the terms will be explained as the movement is described. The most important positions of the gymnast on the apparatus are listed.

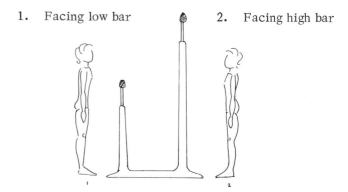

1. Facing low bar   2. Facing high bar

3. Front support   4. Rear support

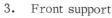

5. Front lying position   6. Rear lying position

Grips

7. Regular (over grip). With thumbs turned toward each other and grasping the bar on opposite sides from the fingers (hand pronated).

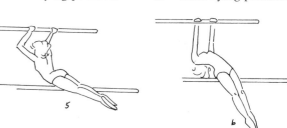

8. Reverse (under grip). The opposite of regular grip. Thumbs point in opposite directions (hands supinated).

9. Combined (mixed grip). One hand is in regular grip, the other in reverse grip.

10. Eagle grip (dislocate grip).

11. Wide grip. With hands wide apart the grip may be any of the above grips.

Planning an Exercise

In competition it is important that suspension and swinging movements with releases and regrasps dominate the routine. Support exercises should be used only as temporary or passing positions. A routine on uneven parallel bars should consist of a mount, stunts, or movements involving both the low and high bar, swinging, kipping, and circling movements, releases and regrasps, and a dismount.

There should be a continuous flow of movement in the routine. Two short stops are permitted for momentary positions of balance and/or as a brief period of preparation prior to a difficult movement. Stops in excess of these are penalized 0.2 point each time. There is no time limit for the performance on uneven parallel bars in competition. Most routines have approximately 12-18 movements. In competition there is a compulsory and an optional exercise. Of utmost importance in the compulsory exercise are form, fluency, and correctness of execution. In the optional exercise the performer is free to combine and perform any moves in any sequence. Again, form is very important but originality and difficulty of execution are also considered. Major faults are stops, poor continuity, extra swings, and breaks in execution.

SAFETY

Only general safety precautions will be considered here. Specific safety and spotting positions will be given with each movement.

It is important to check the equipment before each practice, to see that all supports are securely in place. Mats should be placed underneath the bars and around the bars, with double thickness for dismounts. If a beat board is used for mounting, it should be removed immediately. Two spotters should assist in learning new movements. The spotters should stand in the most advantageous spot according to the movement. Detailed position of spotters will be given with each movement. It may be desirable to have a person sit on or hold the base of

the bars during any "flying" movements, to avoid a rocking of the base of the bars. Most commercial bars have some form of stabilization through a bracket which is fixed at the top of the high bar post, and at the other end to the base of the apparatus. The apparatus may also be fastened to the floor to give maximum stability.

TEACHING SUGGESTIONS

1. Activity on the bars requires strength. Exercises should be given for developing strength in the upper arm, shoulder girdle, and abdominal region.

2. The beginning student should be given opportunity to explore movements on the bars as a means of overcoming fear. This is particularly true of the high bar, where the feeling of height may be a problem. For the beginner the held positions, simple combinations of movements, are important for developing confidence.

3. In class situations it is usually desirable to have a sequence of a mount, one or two movements and a dismount. This allows more students to be on the bar during the class period.

4. One-bar movements can be learned at the horizontal bar, adjusted to the correct height.

5. It is better to practice two or three moves together than to practice a single movement, with the exception of difficult movements. The reason for short sequences of movements is to get the performer into the movement and out of it, and this way teach the feeling of continuity required for fluid routines.

6. Throughout the routine, legs should be straight and together, except in moves requiring straddling of the legs, tucking, or squatting.

7. Throughout the routine the toes should be pointed.

8. The object in routine work is to make everything look easy and not to struggle through the moves.

9. Dismounts must have manual support (i.e., no somersault dismounts from standing on the bar), though a hecht is all right because there is body contact.

10. The mount and dismount should be in harmony with the rest of the routine.

11. Do not let the gymnast perform beyond her ability. The importance and progression of difficulty in the exercise is apparent, but too much emphasis is sometimes placed here. Proper technique and good execution, rather than profuse difficulty is preferred. Over-emphasis on difficulty opens the gymnast to possibilities of too many breaks in continuity and increases the possibility of poor performance.

12. Though there is no time limit on the uneven bar routine, six difficulties and approximately twelve moves are desired.

13. Sitting and standing positions must be very brief and used only as preparations. No hesitations are allowed, but two preparations for difficult moves including the dismount are permitted. Other stops are penalized by 0.2 each time.

14. Repetition of the same movement will be penalized, such as a predominance of straddle glide kips or the same circling movements.

15. A Reuther board may be used for mounts, but should be removed immediately for safety reasons.

16. Elements from a compulsory exercise may be used in the optional, providing the sequence is different. However, there is a 0.3 penalty for using the same mount or dismount.

17. Almost all movements herein listed may be performed facing in the opposite direction from that described. Simply reverse the facing positions at the beginning and end of each movement.

MOVEMENTS
Mounts

1. STRAIGHT ARM SUPPORT MOUNT

M. Standing facing the low bar (may also be performed facing the high bar), arms shoulder distance apart, hands grasping the bar with regular grip (fingers on top, thumbs underneath). Jump into the air and simultaneously push down on the arms straightening the elbows. End with the weight resting on the upper thighs, arms straight, back straight and slightly arched, head up and toes pointed.

Dismount: Bend at the hips letting the legs drop slightly, then lift the hips and push with the arms, spring backward away from the low bar.

Spotting: One spotter should stand to either side of the center of the low bar and grasp the arm of the performer, grasping the wrist and above the elbow. A second spotter may assist by standing behind the performer and helping to lift her by grasping at the waist.

M. = Movement

Steps in learning: Lower the bar to about shoulder height of the performer. The mount may also be practiced on a horizontal bar.

Correction of errors: The performer must learn to time the jump and the pressing down of the arms so that the movements occur simultaneously. The performer must strengthen the arms and shoulders, and remember that the elbow is in its strongest position when completely locked in extension. The point of balance on the thighs must be adjusted to the height of the performer. Arching the body and keeping the chest high will assist in balancing the body at the low bar.

Suggested Movements to follow: a. Reach to the high bar with left hand and swing the left leg across the low bar to a crotch seat or stride support position.

b. Reach the high bar with right hand and twist on the hips to a riding seat or cross seat on the right hip.

2. BACK-HIP PULL-OVER MOUNT

M. Note: This may also be performed on the high bar. Stand facing the low bar with hands grasping the low bar in an over grip. Pull in toward the bar with the arms and kick one leg from the hip upward and over the top of the bar, immediately following with the other leg. Continue the circling of the bar until the body finishes in a straight arm support position on the low bar.

Dismount: Dismount the same as for Straight Arm Support Mount No. 1.

Spotting: Stand to one side in front of the low bar to help the performer lift the hips toward the bar. A second spotter may also help to lift the hips toward the bar. After the legs are lifted and up and around the bar, quickly shift the help to the arms, in order to stabilize the performer's elbows.

Correction of errors: The performer must learn to kick the leg straight up from the hips. Also, the hips must be kept as close to the bars as possible, so that the movement is in a pike position with the bars at the hip angle. Watch the movement until the hips are curved over the bar, then lift the head to straight arm support. The arms must be kept bent to help to bring hips close to the bar.

Suggested movements to follow this mount: The performer ends in a front support position on the low bar, so she may move to any position suggested for Straight Arm Support Mount, such as placing one leg over the bar and doing a mill circle forward.

3.   SHOOT OVER LOW BAR (FROM LONG HANG ON HIGH BAR)

M.   Start behind the high bar facing the low bar. After a few approaching steps, jump and grasp the high bar, hands over the top of the bar, thumbs around the bar. The movement can also start from a standing position. Immediately the legs are swung forward under the low bar, then backward. At the end of the back swing the hips are bent sharply and the legs lifted over the low bar, finishing with the legs together, toes pointed, and thighs resting on the low bar. The shoot over can be performed in a squat, straddle, or pike position.

Dismount: Transfer hands to low bar and push away from the low bar by lifting the hips. End with back to the low bar.

Spotting: Stand behind the performer and assist by lifting the waist.

Steps in learning: a. From a hanging position practice the beat swing only.

b.   The performer should first try to lift the legs up and over the low bar in a tucked position.

c.   From the hanging position on the high bar, spread the legs apart as they are lifted up and over the low bar.

d.   From the hanging position on the high bar, pike the legs as they are lifted up and over the low bar.

Correction of errors: The performer should be sure to grasp with the thumbs around the high bar so that the hands will not slip on the swing. Practice hanging and coming to a tuck position, then a pike position from a hang. Any apparatus may be used to perfect the pike position, as this depends upon abdominal strength to a great extent.

Suggested movements to follow: a. Back hip pull-

over to high bar, ending in a balanced swan on the high bar (see Balance or Held Positions).

b.   Double-leg bounce to hip pull over to high bar (see Connecting and Miscellaneous Movements).

4.   SINGLE-LEG SWING UP MOUNT

M.   Start facing the low bar. Jump and tuck one leg through the arms over the low bar. Swing down and under the bar, and then pull with the arms and by whipping the free leg straight from the hip, rise to on top of the low bar. End in a crotch seat or stride support position, facing the high bar.

Variations: a. Keep the leg straight as it shoots through the arms.

b.   Run and jump swinging one leg up over the low bar and continue as above.

c.   Start between the bars (or facing in the opposite direction from the above). If performed starting between the bars, the high bar may be grasped as the performer rises to the top of the low bar. This may be done in one continuous movement.

Dismount: Grasp the high bar with both hands, swing the rear leg over the top of the low bar so that both feet are facing the high bar, swing off the high bar.

a.   Drop backward toward the rear leg, tuck both legs and skin-the-cat off.

Spotting: Stand to one side, give extra help by assisting the whip of the straight leg. Also help by lifting the hips up and over the low bar.

Steps in learning: Practice a skin-the-cat movement on the ropes or horizontal bar. Practice on the horizontal bar to get a quick tuck of one leg, bringing it up and through the arms.

Correction of errors: The performer must learn to whip the straight leg backward from the hips and, at the same time, press downward on the arms as the elbows are straightened and the hips are lifted to on top of the bar. When attempting to squat through, keep the arms straight and bring the legs up to the chest and lean forward from the shoulders.

Suggested movements to follow this mount: In stride support position, mill circle forward. In stride support position, mill circle backward (see Circling Movements).

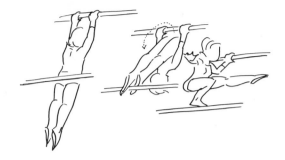

5. SKIN-THE-CAT TO BASKET MOUNT

M. Stand between the bars, back to the low bar. Jump and grasp the high bar, pike at the hips and bring the legs between the arms and continue in a basket or skin-the-cat. End in a one-leg squat on low bar.

Variations: Perform the basket as above, but let the thighs (rather than one foot) rest on the low bar, shoulders in dislocate position; right hand is released, lift the left foot backwards and turn to a cross seat position, resting the weight on left thigh, left hand holding the high bar.

Dismount: Flank or rear vault off the low bar.

Spotting: Assist in placing the foot on the low bar in the basket; also assist by holding at the hips in the twisting movement.

Correction of errors: Keep the hips high on the turn. This can be aided by pulling up on the hand on high bar.

Movements to follow: a. From the squat position out of the basket, go to a standing scale or pull-away.

b. Perform a single- or double-leg bounce over the high bar.

c. Perform a single-leg stem rise to the high bar.

d. For variation, when the thighs are resting on the low bar, do a V seat.

6. CROSS SEAT MOUNT

M. Start standing between the bars facing the length with the right shoulder toward the low bar and the left shoulder toward the high bar. From this position, jump up and grasp the high bar with the left hand in an over position, and grasp the low bar with the right hand. Immediately straighten the right arm and swing the legs up over the low bar,

legs held close together, ending in a cross seat position.

This movement may also be done facing the opposite direction.

Dismount: From cross seat position, perform a rear vault with quarter turn to dismount. Continue to swing the legs up and out as the hips are lifted off the low bar. Let go of high bar with left hand when turning. Quickly change the right hand position to a thumb outward position from the thumb inward position of the mount.

Spotting: Stand facing the low bar to the left of the performer, and grasp the right arm holding it straight as the performer swings up and over the low bar. A second spotter may stand beside the performer and help to lift the legs up and over the low bar.

Steps in learning: Practice swinging the legs back and forth from a hanging position until the performer can easily pike the hips. The left hand on the high bar should be about shoulder distance in front of the position of the right hand on the low bar. The left elbow may remain in a bent position and rest part of the forearm on the high bar as additional support when learning. (Note: Keep the elbow off the bar.) The right arm should be directly under the shoulder with the elbow straight to give maximum support.

Correction of errors: The ankles should be extended and the pike should be from the hips. Also, the supporting right arm should be held straight.

Suggested movements to follow this mount: a. From the cross seat position, lift the legs to a V seat and rise to a standing position for a scale.

b. Any of the movements following mount No. 3 (shoot over low bar).

7. CROTCH TWIST MOUNT

M. Standing between the bars (left arm to high bar), jump and grasp the high bar with both hands in a mixed grip, the left hand in front. Swing the legs up and over the low bar, legs spread and ending with the weight on the right thigh, left leg in the air. Continue to roll to the right, lifting the left foot over the low bar ending in crotch position and with the left hand on the high bar.

Dismount: Rear vault with quarter turn dismount.

Spotting: Stand between the bars as soon as the hips are lifted up and over the bars. Assist in the twisting and turning of the body.

Steps in learning: The performer should have a good crotch seat and be able to keep the legs in a good pike position. The body and legs must be kept firm as the rolling and twisting position is performed.

Correction of errors: The leg must be kept straight and the toes pointed. Practice in quick changing of hand position if the mixed grip position is necessary. The rolling action is on top of the thigh.

Suggested movements to follow this mount: If the performer ends in a crotch position facing forward, a mill circle forward may be performed.

   a. Knee swing up from a crotch position and grasp the high bar and stem rise or back hip pull over to the high bar.

8. DOUBLE LEG STEMRISE MOUNT

M.   Stand in back of the high bar, facing the low bar. Jump and grasp the high bar and tuck the feet to the low bar. Push with both feet and rise to a straight arm support on the high bar, facing the low bar.

Dismount: a. Grasping the low bar in reverse grip, slide down the bars and skin-the-cat off the low bar.

   b. Hang down from the high bar and jump off.

Spotting: Stand between the bars to one side. Assist by a boost at the hips.

Correction of errors: Keep the arms at shoulder distance apart. Keep the body slightly arched in the front support position and rest on the thighs.

Suggested movements to follow: Any movements from the high bar; e.g., cast off flying hip circle.

9. VAULT MOUNTS (TO CATCH HIGH BAR)

M.   Use a beat board for each mount, start facing the low bar.

   a. Flank vault. The right flank is described, although this may be performed on both sides. Run forward and place the hands on the low bar. As the legs are lifted from the hips in a straight position up and to the right over the low bar, quickly grasp the high bar with the right hand. End facing the high bar in an inner seat position.

   b. Squat vault. Jump with legs in bent position over the low bar, catching the high bar.

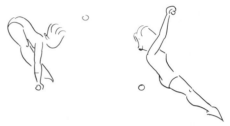

   c. Stoop vault. Run and jump to a stoop vault over the low bar and immediately catch the high bar (see sketch).

   d. Straddle vault. Jump with the legs in straddle position over the low bar, catching the high bar.

Variations: a. All the above mounts may end in a rear seat on the low bar without catching the high bar.

   b. Do a half turn to long hang from any of the above.

   c. Straddle swing back over low bar to glide kip after any of the above. (Note: This must be done immediately from a forceful beat swing.)

Dismount: Swing off from the high bar.

Spotting: Stand between the bars and grasp the gymnast at the waist to help her to grasp the high bar and also to assist with the half turn if it follows. A second spotter may stand in front of the low bar to help the gymnast to clear the bar by lifting the hips if necessary.

Steps in learning: a. Practice all the above vaults first over a horse.

   b. Practice the vault over a horizontal bar after successfully mastering the movements over the horse.

Correction of errors: The most important thing is to be able to time the movement to catch the high bar.

Suggested movements to follow these mounts: a. Back hip pull over to high bar.

   b. Mixed grip half turn to flying hip circle.

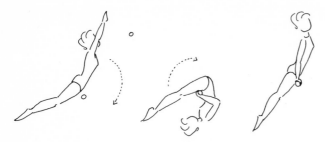

10.   FRONT HIP CIRCLE MOUNT

M.   Using a Reuther board, either face the low bar or face the high bar. Run and take-off, arching the body into an almost horizontal swan. The upper thighs should contact the low bar while the body is arched in a swan position, arms extended upward. Immediately after the thigh contact, bend the hips whipping the upper body and arms downward under the low bar. Maintaining a good pike position, rotate around the bars. As the body passes under the low bar, grasp the bar in a regular grip and pull the upper body to a position directly over the hands as the legs swing to the rear. End in a front support position.

Variations: a. Tuck front hip circle mount. Tuck when rotating around the bar.
    b. Free front hip circle mount, to catch the high bar. (Note: This must start from facing the high bar.)

Spotting: The spotter stands in front of the low bar. First place one hand momentarily on the calves as the body is in the swan arched position. This will control any forward thrust. As soon as the legs are bent, place a hand under the back, pressing it upward. Immediately switch to grasping the elbow, assisting the gymnast to a front support position.

Correction of errors: The body should be arched until touching the bar, then a forceful piking action is necessary for circling the bar.

Suggested movements to follow this mount: Any movements from front support, e.g., back hip circle.

11.   FULL TWIST TO FRONT HIP CIRCLE (WITHOUT HANDS)

M.   Using a Reuther board, face the low bar. Run and jump upward making a full twist in front of the low bar to a front support on the low bar and immediately into a forward hip circle without hands. The twist must start from the hips; when about halfway in the twist turn the head and shoulders to follow the hips. The body must be slightly tipped forward. This movement is similar to the full twist to front drop on trampoline.

Spotting: Use an overhead twisting belt if possible or spotters on either side in front of the low bar (see Front Hip Circle Mount No. 10).

Suggested movements to follow this mount: Any movements from front support on the low bar may be performed.

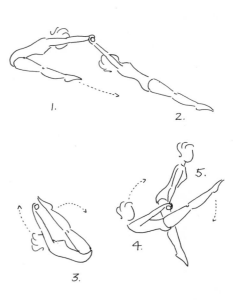

12.   GLIDE KIP MOUNT

M.   This may be done from a position facing outward or inward. Stand facing the high bar, hands on the low bar in over grip. Jump into the air lifting the hips up and backward, head in normal position, and glide forward with the feet a few inches off the mat. Upon reaching the full extension position, pike the body sharply and bring the ankles up toward the bar. Continue the gliding action from the ankle up through the leg until the bar is at hip level, head is forward; then kick outward and downward with the legs, pulling strongly with the arms and finish in front support.

Variations: a. Single-leg shoot through glide kip. This is easier than the double-leg kip. Until the toes touch the bar, the movement is the same as above; then on the glide kip, shoot one leg through between the arms and over the top of the bar. The spotter should assist as in the Single-leg Swing Up Mount. (No. 4)

  b. Glide with legs in straddle position.
  c. Glide kip—catch high bar. Same as the regular kip. The hand release is when the hips contact the low bar.
  d. Glide kip—catch high bar with eagle grip.
  e. Glide kip—half turn catch high bar.

Dismount: Use any previous dismounts from a front support position.

Spotting: a. On the hip lift to the rear, the spotter should stand beside the performer and push at the hip to get a good pike position (left hand).

  b. In the gliding position, press under the hips to give the feeling of a full extension (right hand).

  c. At the pike, support the low back with one hand and try to push the hips to the bar with the other.

  d. On the kick outward and downward, assist the leg movement.

Steps in learning: This can easily be practiced on a horizontal bar. Practice just lifting the hips upward and backward and gliding forward. Practice the lifting of the hips in a swinging pike position. Learn first the stem-rise and kip between bars.

Correction of errors: The timing of the pike from the full extension must be practiced so that it is caught at the exact instant. The pike position must be with the hips close to the low bar. Do not grasp the bar tightly, but let the hand slide with the movement.

Suggested movements to follow this mount: The performer ends in a front support on the low bar, and any move into any position from this may be performed, e.g., forward hip circle.

13.   GLIDING KIP IN HIGH BAR

M.   Standing behind the high bar, run and jump with an over grasp on the high bar. Swing legs in a pike over the low bar and extend the body in an arched position over the low bar. Swing back and when the hips are pulled back in a pike position, swing the legs outward and downward pulling strongly with the arms and finish in front support position on the high bar.

Spotting: Stand to one side in back of the high bar, and give the hips a boost to lift them over the high bar. A second spotter should stand between the bars to one side, to help lift the body up and over the low bar.

Steps in learning: This is an advanced mount and should not be attempted until a gliding kip mount on the low bar is perfected.

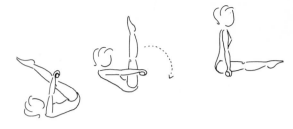

14.   GLIDING KIP—DOUBLE LEG SHOOT THROUGH

M.   Perform a gliding kip (see previous description) facing the low bar. On the kip part shoot both legs through the arms and over the top of the low bar and at the same time pull very hard with the arms, ending in a rear support position on the low bar.

Variations: a. Straddle seat position. Perform the movement as above, but end in a straddle seat position on the low bar.

  b. The same movement may be performed in the opposite facing position and catching the high bar on the completion.

  c. Glide kip, double leg shoot through, straddle cut, catch low bar or high bar.

  d. Glide kip, double leg shoot through, dislocate, release, regrasp low bar, glide kip.

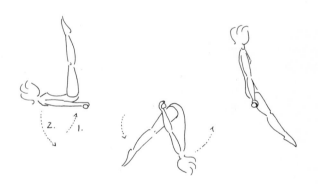

15.   REAR KIP MOUNT

M.   The movement is the same as for the gliding kip-double leg shoot through mount until the legs are completely through the hands in the pike position—then allow the movement to reverse and, keeping the buttocks close to the bar, push with the shoulders, head backward, and end in a rear support position on the low bar.

Variation: Rear kip in straddle seat position.

Spotting: Same as for gliding kip, but with assistance at the shoulders and hips.

Suggested movements to follow these mounts: Catch the high bar and continue with any desired movement.

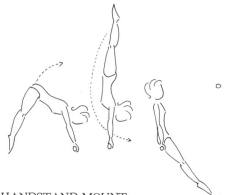

16.   HANDSTAND MOUNT

M.   Using a Reuther board, facing low bar. Run and jump to a handstand on the low bar. After holding the position for an instant, move out of the position as noted below.

Spotting: Stand between the bars and help at the shoulders.

Suggested movements to follow this mount: a. Hip circle to front support on low bar.

b.   Squat or stoop through between hands to a rear support (see Shoot Through—Connecting and Miscellaneous Movements)(see sketch).

c.   Straddle on low bar to a straddle sole circle backward.

d.   From the handstand, let thighs lean against high bar, release grip, raise upper body to grasp high bar in a regular grip, finish in a rear support on high bar.

Balance or Held Positions

Balance positions are held only momentarily, and should allow for a natural movement to another position or to a swinging movement. For the beginner, these positions may be held for a longer period of time so that she gets the feeling of the bars and develops security and a feeling of successful performance.

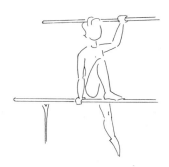

17.   SEAT BALANCE (ONE-LEG CROUCH SEAT)

M.   Sitting on low bar, left leg extended, right foot on the bar, knee bent close to the body. Right hand is in regular grip on the low bar in back of and close to the buttocks. Left hand is in hook grasp on the high bar.

Spotting: Stand on the outside of the low bar, grasping the right elbow.

Steps in learning: The performer must learn to sit with ease on the buttocks. The left leg should be completely extended and the ankle extended.

Suggested movements to follow this position:

a.   From this position the performer may swing the left leg to the rear and come to a standing position, a standing scale.

b.   Both legs may be extended in a V seat.

c.   Any hanging or swinging movements may follow it.

18.   V SEAT

M.   This is the same as the seat balance excepting that the person extends both legs in the air while sitting on the low bar. With perfection, the right arm may be released and held to the side.

Spotting: Same as No. 17 above.

Suggested movements to follow this position: Same as No. 17 above.

19.   ONE-LEG SQUAT

M.   The right foot is on the low bar, with the body in a squat position. The left leg is extended and should be held above the bar. The right hand is on the low bar in front of the right foot, and the left hand is in a regular grasp on the high bar.

Spotting: Hold at the right elbow.

Steps in learning: The performer should be able to perform a one-leg squat position on the floor. The balance should be over the right foot.

Suggested movements to follow this position: The performer may step into a scale by swinging the extended leg (left) to the rear and holding on with the left hand only to a standing scale; or the performer may swing around on the ball of the foot and face the high bar for a swinging movement.

20. SQUAT STAND

M. From a front support position on the low bar, swing the legs forward and then forcefully backward to a free front support position (see Cast→Swinging Movements). At the height of the rear swing bring the knees to the chest and place the toes on the bar between the hands.

Spotting: Spotter stands in front of the bar to one side of the performer and supports the wrist and arm of the gymnast. A second spotter stands between the bars and assists in lifting the hips upward to help the gymnast to squat on the bar.

M. Standing with right foot on the bar (ball of foot), left leg extended in a scale to the rear, facing the high bar with both hands on the high bar in a hook or over-grasp position. Extend both arms, and both legs, pulling away from the high bar as the body holds the scale position.

Spotting: Like the scale, this is a secure position and little spotting is necessary.

Steps in learning: The performer should learn to extend the arms quickly, and to keep the weight on the ball of the right foot.

Suggested movements to follow back pull-away:
a. Swing the extended leg over the high bar to a mill circle on the high bar.
b. Swing the extended left leg over the high bar, right hand in reverse grip, cross left hand over right in regular grip, then swing the other straight leg over the high bar, ending in a swan or front support on the high bar.

21. SCALE

M. Standing with the right foot on the low bar, left arm holding onto high bar, extend the left leg to the rear and the right arm forward. Try to lift the arm and extended leg to get an arch throughout the body.

Spotting: This is a simple move and the performer has complete control of the position by her hand on the high bar.

Steps in learning: Full extension of the arm and leg should be accomplished. This is a very simple way to acquaint the performer with the feeling of height, and to stress line and form. This movement may be followed by any movement from a standing position done on the high bar.

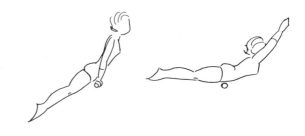

23. SWAN BALANCE

M. This may be performed facing inward or outward, and on either the low or the high bar. From a front support position find the point of balance on the thighs at the groin. Keep the body arched, legs extended and toes pointed and lift the arms sideward or upward off the bar. Each person will find a point of balance on the hips or upper thighs.

Spotting: If performing a swan on the low bar, facing outward, spotter should stand in front of the performer and let her transfer her arms from the bar to placing her hands on the spotter's shoulders, then gradually letting go of the bar.
b. Spotter may stand to one side and assist in balancing at the waist.
c. On the high bar, spot by holding the legs.

Steps in learning: a. Practice the swan position on the floor.
b. Practice the position on any object that is off the floor; e.g., a box or horse or horizontal bar.

Suggested movement to follow this position: Hip circle forward.

22. BACK PULL-AWAY

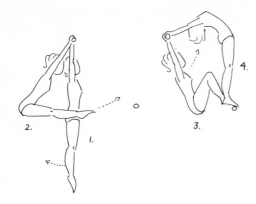

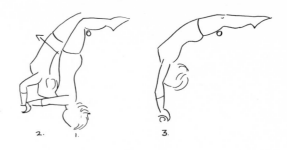

24.   ARCH THROUGH

M.   From a long hang on high bar, facing low bar, at the end of the rearward swing, pike and quickly place the feet on the low bar. As soon as the feet are on the low bar, bend the knees and push the head and shoulders forward arching the body through the bars, end in a rear standing, changing hands to over grip.

Spotting: Stand between the bars, assisting by pressing upward against the back to get the arch.

Suggested movements to follow this position: This movement is a good one to use after an "eagle catch" in order to place the gymnast in a position for any other move from standing on the low bar; e.g., straddle jump over high bar.

26.   ARCH BACK FROM KNEE HANG

M.   From double-knee hang on the high bars, facing the low bars, reach backward and grasp the low bars with both hands in a regular grip. Straighten the elbows as the body is arched with the high bar continuing to be under the knees.

Spotting: One spotter should stand outside of the low bar and grasp the performer at the right elbow and wrist. Another spotter may stand between the bars and help lift the body upwards at the shoulders.

Steps in learning: a. Get the feeling of a double-knee hang from the high bar.

b.   Practice the arched position by doing a handstand against the wall, or against stall bars.

25.   REAR ARCH

M.   Squat on the low bar with left foot, back to the high bar, grasping high bar with both hands. Lift the right knee upward with toe pointed as the arms and left leg are straightened.

Spotting: Little spotting is needed for this movement.

Steps in learning: Be able to perform a good backbend on the floor.

Suggested movements to follow this position: a. Tuck under the high bar, kick bent leg backward and push to a front support on the high bar (single leg stem rise).

b.   From standing on low bar, straddle jump backward over high bar to hang on high bar.

27.   ARCH BACK TO BACKWARD HIP CIRCLE

M.   Assume an arch back position. From the complete arch back position place one foot on high bar and, with a slight push, come to a momentary handstand; then swing the legs downward and under the low bar in a backward hip circle, ending in front support facing the high bar.

Spotting: Stand to one side supporting the wrist and arm.

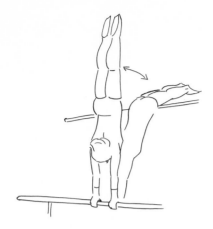

Spotting: Stand in front of the low bar to one side of the performer. Support the wrist and shoulder during the handstand and straddle hold.

Suggested movements to follow this position: a. From the straddle position on the low bar swing the legs under the low bar to a pike position, hanging on the low bar, and perform a kip to front support on the low bar.

    b. From the straddle position on the low bar do a straddle seat circle backwards.

28.   SIDE HANDSTAND

M.   From a front support position on the high bar, raise the arms horizontally and reach forward grasping the low bar with a regular grip. Push the body off the high bar to a handstand position, hold the handstand momentarily and return to original position or follow with one of the suggested movements.

Spotting: The spotters should stand on either side of the performer grasping the wrist and shoulders.

Suggested movements to follow side handstand:

    a. Half turn on low bar. (Note: If gymnast turns to the left she should have left hand in under grip.)

    b. Side handstand on high bar, half turn descent by giant swing to hang.

30.   CROSS HANDSTAND

M.   From a front support on the high bar, reach downward with the right hand and place it on the low bar. The right hand should be shoulder distance backward from the left hand and in reverse grip position on the high bar. Kick the legs upward to a handstand between the bars, turn the body to facing lengthwise.

Spotting: The spotter should stand with the left foot on the low bar, right leg hooked over the high bar grasping performer at thighs. A second spotter in front of the low bar grasps the wrist and shoulder of the right hand.

Steps in learning: a. Practice beside a stall bar, left hand on the bar 2-1/2 feet from the floor, the right hand on the floor. Kick up to a handstand.

    b. Right foot squat position on low bar, hands placed in position (left on high bar, right on low bar), kick up the left foot over the high bar and then follow with the right leg.

    c. Squat position on low bar. Kick up to a handstand, turning quarter turn to the right to place hips on the high bar.

29.   HANDSTAND STRADDLE TO STRADDLE SEAT

M.   From a front support on high bar, reach down and grasp the low bar. Swing the legs into a handstand with the legs spread in a wide straddle. Swing the legs through to a straddle hold position on the low bar.

Variations: a. Squat through between hands.

    b. Stoop through between hands.

    c. Straddle legs and pass under high bar, swing legs downward to backward hip circle to front support on low bar.

Circling Movements

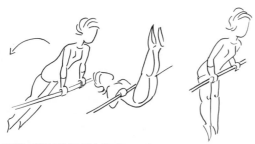

31.   HIP CIRCLE BACKWARD

M.   Hands in regular grip thumbs to the rear. Keeping the elbows straight, lift the weight onto the hands. Swing both legs from the hips forward then backward to a free front support (see Cast—Swinging Movements). Whip the legs from the hip forward under the bar. When in the inverted position pike the body sharply, keeping the bar in position at the groin.

Spotting: Stand to one side of the performer, hold the wrist with one hand, and with the other assist by boosting at the hips.

Steps in learning: Practice the hip lift (cast) and whip down under.

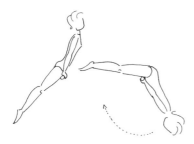

32.   HIP CIRCLE FORWARD

M.   (Note: There is an exception in the hand grasping position for this movement. The regular grip with thumbs to the rear is used here.) From a front support position on high or low bar, lift the weight onto the hands, arch the body and, leading with the chest, circle forward in a complete circle. The bar should be at the hip joint on the circling. End in a front support.

Variations: a. Free forward hip circle. This starts from hands over the head as in a swan balance (see Balance or Held Positions No. 23). The arms swing downward forcefully at the beginning of the movement and the hands grasp the bar in regular grip to finish the circle in front support.

b.   Free forward hip circle to catch high bar. Start on low bar facing out. This movement is the same as variation a except the hands will grasp the high bar at the

end of the hip circle and the movement is finished in long hang on high bar facing low bar (see sketch).

c.   Tuck forward hip circle. The same as free forward hip circle except after falling forward in extended body position the hips and knees forcefully bend into a tuck position, the hands may grasp lower legs to help the tuck. Complete a full circle forward arriving on top of the bar with body weight resting on hands.

Spotting: Same as hip circle backwards. In free forward hip circles the spotter stands behind the gymnast to one side. Place one arm back of the performer's legs to prevent any slipping off the bar. After the body bends, place the other hand under her low back and assist her in the turn.

Steps in learning: Practice lifting the weight on the hands and the body arch. Practice swan balance. Practice pulling the bar close into the groin on the turn.

Suggested movements to follow forward hip circle:

a.   Forward hip circle to handstand on the low bar or high bar.

b.   Any movement from the front support may be performed; e.g., stoop through (see Shoot Through—Connecting and Miscellaneous Movements).

33.   SINGLE-KNEE SWING UP

M.   Start in a stride position, hands in regular grip. Lift the weight off the bar with straight arms. Swing the rear leg backward and hang onto the bar with the bent forward knee. Drop backward and swing under the bar. As the momentum stops, swing the rear leg downward and backward to return to the stride support position.

Variation: Single-knee swing up catch high bar. Same as single-knee swing up, but on the return release the low bar and grasp the high bar in a regular grip.

Spotting: The spotter stands to one side behind the gymnast. Support the hips and assist her to return to the stride support position or to catch the high bar.

34.   SINGLE-KNEE CIRCLE BACKWARD

M.   Start in a stride support position, hands in regular grip. Lift the weight off the bar with straight arms. Swing the rear leg backward and hang onto the bar with the forward knee. Drop the trunk to the rear, keeping the head up and the trunk moderately arched. Continue the movement around the bar, ending in the starting position.

Variations: a. In a continuous movement from a long hang on the high bar, bring one leg over the low bar and continue the knee circle.
    b.   Single-knee circle backward, continue with a single-knee swing up to catch high bar.

Spotting: Spotter stands at the side of the gymnast in front of the low bar. Reach under the bar with inside hand (i.e., spotter's left hand grasps gymnast's right wrist) and grasp wrist with palm facing outward thumb outside of the gymnast's wrist so you are looking at the back of your hand. As the gymnast rotates, place the outside hand on the shoulder or upper arm to help the performer return to original position. A second spotter may be used at the beginning at the other side of the gymnast.

Steps in learning: Practice just lifting the body off the bar with the straight arms before trying to circle. Practice single-knee swing up.

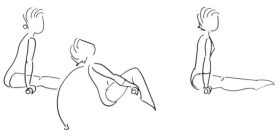

35.   DOUBLE-KNEE CIRCLE BACKWARD
    (HOCK SWING BACKWARD)

M.   From a rear support position or pike seat on low bar, hands in regular grip swing the trunk backwards, hooking the back of the knees on the bar. The arms remain stretched as the body swings downward. When the head and trunk reach slightly above the horizontal plane, pull with the arms, head to chest, and swing the body backward, returning to starting position.

Spotting: Stand in front of low bar to one side of the performer grasping her wrist and shoulder. On the upward lift, support the shoulder. See also spotting for Single-knee Circle Backward No. 34.

36.   MILL CIRCLE BACKWARD
    (BACK STRIDE CIRCLE)

M.   This may be performed on the low bar and on the high bar, and in each direction. From a crotch position lift the weight off the bars taking it on the hands. Hands in regular grip, thumbs to the rear. Lift the straight rear leg slightly and whip it backward and downward under the bar, keeping the crotch close to the bar. Lean the trunk slightly backward and keep the body in a slightly arched position.

Variation: From a long hang on the high bar, bring one leg over the low bar, grasp low bar and circle the low bar.

Spotting: Stand in front of the low bar, lift the rear leg with one hand and then push upward on the shoulder to return to the original position. See all spotting for No. 34.

Steps in learning: Practice dropping back to a single-knee swing up. Practice a single-knee circle backward.

37.   MILL CIRCLE FORWARD (FRONT STRIDE CIRCLE)

M.   This is similar to No. 36 except the movement is forward. The performer is in crotch or stride support position, hands in reverse grip (thumbs pointing in direction of the movement). Lift the weight off the bars with hands, keeping the legs rigid and holding the bar close to the crotch. The trunk is arched, with head back. Lead with the chest and let the bar rest on the rear thigh. Hold the arched position all the way around, keeping the bar close to the crotch.

Variation: Mill circle catch high bar. Perform a three-fourths mill circle forward and quickly release low bar and grasp high bar in a regular grip. The gymnast should first learn the mill circle forward and be able to perform it alone so that the spotter can stand between the bars and only help at the end of the circle supporting the hips with both hands to assist the catch of the high bar.

Spotting: Stand to one side behind the performer. Reach under the bar with inside hand (i.e., spotter's right hand, gymnast's right wrist), and grasp the gymnast's wrist with palm facing outward, thumb outside of the wrist so you are looking at the back of your hand. As the performer rotates, assist with outside hand at the hips to get the body up again to a stride support position.

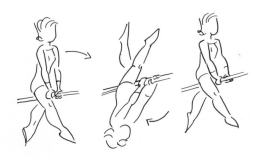

38.   CROTCH SEAT, SIDE CIRCLE

M.   In a crotch position, face the length of low bar, hands grasping the low bar in front of the body and close to the crotch in a mixed grip. Keeping the body rigid, circle

the body sideward around the low bar. Weight is taken on the hands which lift the body slightly off the bar. The movement must be performed quickly as the momentum assists in the return to the crotch position.

Spotting: Stand in front of low bar, in back of the performer. Assist on the up-rise, hands to shoulder. A second spotter may stand facing the performer between the bars and keep the performer from going past the point of balance in the crotch position.

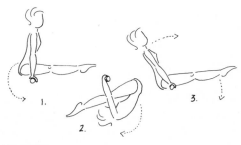

39.   SEAT RISE

M.   Sitting on the low bar or high bar facing out (rear support position), hands on either side of the bar in regular grip. Lift the seat from the bar taking weight on the hands. Keeping the body in a rigid pike position, let the body drop backward and swing under the bar, back of thighs close to bar. As momentum stops swing back to rear support by pulling with head and shoulders forcefully forward.

Variations: a. Seat rise catch high bar. Start from rear support on low bar facing out. Do a seat rise but on the return release the low bar and catch high bar in regular grip.

b.   From a rear support on high bar, swing down under the bar and back up to straddle cut catch high bar.

Spotting: Stand to one side behind the performer and assist at the hips.

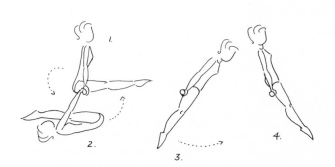

40.   SEAT CIRCLE BACKWARD

M.   Sitting on the low or high bar, legs forward, hands on either side of the body (rear support position), grasp with thumbs backward. Lift the seat from the bar taking the weight on the hands. Keeping the body in a rigid pike position, let the body drop backward and completely around the bar, ending in an open sitting position. Note that the arms are straight and the bar is kept under the seat throughout the movement.

Variations: a. Half back seat circle, disengage legs, kip to front support.

          b. Straddle seat circle backward. This is similar to the seat circle backward except the feet are in a straddle "L" support outside the hand grasp.

Spotting: Same as single-knee Circle Backward No. 34.

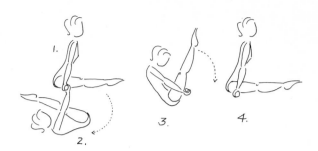

42.   SEAT CIRCLE FORWARD

M.   Sitting on the low bar or high bar, legs forward, hands on either side of the bar, reverse grip. Take the weight on the hands, keep knees close to the bar and hips high and circle the body forward, ending in a sitting position as at the start. The hands must slide around the bar for the movement to take place. Keep the back arched all the way around.

Variations: a. From a rear stand on low bar, hands on high bar in reverse grip, jump to a half seat circle forward and end in a rear support position on the high bar.

          b. Forward seat circle on high bar to straddle cut catch high bar.

          c. Straddle seat circle forward. This is similar to the seat circle forward except the feet are in a straddle "L" support outside the hand grasp.

Spotting: Same as Mill Circle Forward No. 37.

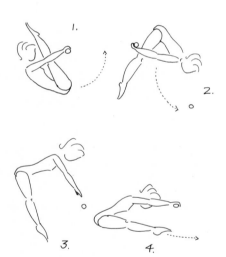

41.   SEAT CIRCLE BACKWARD TO DROP KIP

M.   Rear support on high bar facing low bar, hands in regular grip. Perform a 3/4 seat circle backward, then lift the head up so eyes can spot the low bar. Release high bar and slightly extend the hips (to approximately 90 degrees), drop to the low bar grasping the bar with regular grip. Continue the movement with a gliding kip on the low bar. The legs may be together or in a straddle position.

Spotting: Spotters stand between the bars at the side of the gymnast and support the upper thigh after the gymnast performs a partial back seat circle in order to help performer to catch the low bar in a right angle. (Note: The performer should be able to perform a seat circle backward without spotting.)

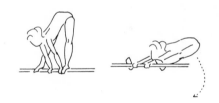

43.   STRADDLE SOLE CIRCLE BACKWARD

M.   Start from a straight arm support position. Flex body slightly and lift hips backward and upward and place feet (insteps) on the bar outside of the hands in a straddle position. (This movement may also start from standing on low bar facing the high bar with hands on high bar in a regular grip and jump into a straddle stand position on the high bar or reach down and grasp low bar to perform a straddle stand position.) From this position fall backward and circle completely around the bar ending in the original position. Keep a constant pressure on the bar with the feet.

Variations: See variations below in No. 44 Stoop Sole Circle Backward.

Spotting: Same as for Single-knee Circle Backward No. 34.

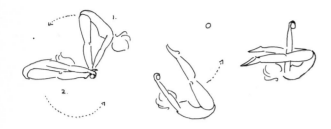

44.   STOOP SOLE CIRCLE BACKWARD

M.   This is similar to straddle sole circle backward except the feet are between the hand grasp.

Variations: a. Stoop sole circle backward (facing high bar), cast and catch high bar. (Note: Keep the stoop position until hips are above low bar, then extend the body and simultaneously release low bar and grasp high bar.)

b.   Stoop sole circle backward cast pike or straddle catch under high bar (see sketch). (Note: Ride hips high before feet leave the bar.)

Spotting: Same as for No. 43 or variations. Spotter stands between the bars at the side of the performer. As gymnast's feet leave the bar, support and lift at the back to help her catch high bar.

Spotting: Stand under the high bar to the right of the performer, grasp the wrist, then grasp the waist as she reaches the high bar.

46.   STRADDLE SOLE CIRCLE FORWARD

M.   Standing on low bar or high bar, legs in a stride position, hands between feet, hands in reverse grip. Keeping the hands and feet securely on the low bar, circle forward; on the up-rise of the movement, reach upward and grasp the high bar.

Variation: See variation in No. 47 below.

Spotting: Same as Mill Circle Forward No. 37.

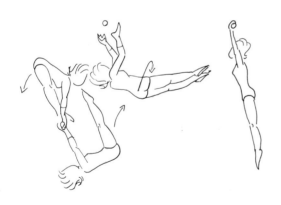

45.   STOOP SOLE CIRCLE BACKWARD WITH HALF TURN TO HIGH BAR

M.   Standing on the low bar facing high bar, hands on either side of straight legs. Three-quarter stoop sole circle backward, the arms and legs remaining extended. The legs extend forward and upward toward the high bar. Simultaneously the hands quickly grasp for the high bar with a mixed grip. The body makes a half turn to the left, ending in a long hang position facing the low bar.

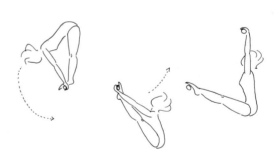

47.   STOOP SOLE CIRCLE FORWARD

M.   This is similar to straddle sole circle forward except the feet are between the hand grasp.

Variation: Stoop sole circle forward catch high bar. From a rear stand on low bar, bend forward and grasp low bar in a reverse grip. Perform a 3/4 stoop sole circle forward and quickly release low bar and grasp high bar in a regular grip (see sketch).

Spotting: Same as No. 45 above. For variation spotter stands between the bars at the side of the performer. As the gymnast is ready to release the low bar, support and lift at the back to help her to catch high bar.

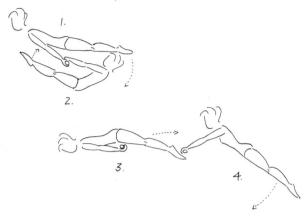

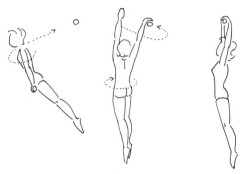

the waist). Step backward between the bars, continuing the grasp at the waist as the performer turns and reaches for the high bar.

48. FREE BACKWARD HIP CIRCLE

M.   This movement may be performed inward or outward, and on either the low or the high bar. From a front support position on the high bar facing low bar, hands in regular grip, swing legs forward and backward to get hips away from the bar into a free front support position (see Cast—Swinging Movements). Turn backward, keeping arms straight and body away from the bar and only slightly piked. At the finish of the turn direct the feet backward and push to a long hang on high bar. (Note: This movement is similar to the backward hip circle, the only difference being that the movement is more vigorous and the hips are a few inches away from the bar during the circling.)

Spotting: Practice this movement first on the low bar. Spotting similar to Hip Circle Backward No. 31.

50. FULL TURN FROM LOW BAR TO CATCH HIGH BAR

M.   Starting from a front support position on the low bar, or from any movement which finishes or goes through a front support position; e.g., front hip circle on low bar. Push off from the low bar turning to the right and immediately grasp the high bar with the right hand, right palm against the inside of the high bar, fingers over the top. Simultaneously bring left hand under the bar and grasp it in a regular grip. Continue the turn to the right, body slightly bent at the hips, and end in a mixed grip facing low bar, hanging on high bar.

Spotting: Stand between the bars to one side. Grasp at the waist to assist the gymnast if she fails to make the turn.

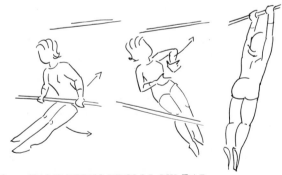

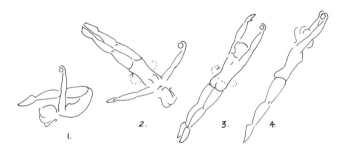

49. HALF TURN FROM LOW BAR TO CATCH HIGH BAR

M.   From a front support position on low bar, swing the legs underneath the low bar slightly, then whip the legs backward and at the same time push with the hands, executing a half turn to the left (or right). Finish by grasping the high bar with both hands in a hanging position.

Spotting: The spotter stands first in back of the performer as the legs are swung forward under the bar (grasping the performer at

51. CORKSCREW ON HIGH BAR

M.   Start from a rear support position on high bar facing low bar, hands in under or reverse grip. Fall forward and go into a bent inverted hang position. As soon as the body reaches the bent inverted hang position, thrust the legs to the rear and simultaneously release the left hand as body turns to the right. Regrasp the high bar with the left hand in a regular grip (now in a mixed grip) and complete the extension of the body, arching the back.

Spotting: Stand under the high bar to the right side of the gymnast in this case and prepare to assist at the waist.

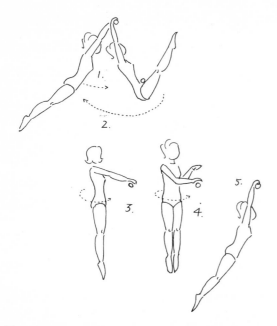

52. FULL TWIST FROM A LONG HANG

M. Start from a front support position on high bar, facing low bar. Hands in regular grip. Cast out and when coming into the low bar pike forcefully and swing legs upward and under low bar, then swing legs downward and to the rear. Simultaneously press down on bar hard to raise body upward. As the head is above the high bar, release grip and do a full turn to the left. Regrasp high bar in a regular grip and end the movement in a long hang.

Spotting: The spotter stands at the right side of the gymnast and supports and assists the turn by holding her thighs with both hands.

Swinging Movements

Nearly all of these movements may be performed facing inward or outward.

53. CAST

M. Start from a front support position on low bar with hands in regular grip. Flex the hips slightly and swing legs forward and under the bar, then extend the legs to the

rear upward with shoulders shifted well forward and lift the body away from the low bar to a free front support position. Then allow the legs to swing back to the bar while keeping the body in a fully extended position.

Spotting: The spotter stands to one side behind the performer. Grasp the arm with the inside hand to help push the shoulders forward. Assist to lift body away from the bar with the outside hand at the upper thigh.

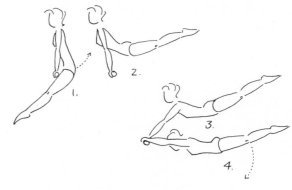

54. CAST OUT FROM FRONT SUPPORT ON HIGH BAR

M. Start from a front support position on high bar facing low bar. Flex the hips slightly and swing legs forward and under the bar. (Note: Beginner gymnasts will slightly bend arms while advance gymnasts will keep arms straight throughout the movement— see sketch.) Then extend the legs to the rear upward and push body away until you are completely extended. After the full extension the descent of the body should be smooth as the hips come forward toward the low bar.

Spotting: Stand to one side of the performer behind the bars. Put inside hand on the top of the thigh and outside hand back of the thigh and follow the whole movement to give support to the cast out.

Steps in learning: a. Practice first on low bar with a spotter to prevent hitting the legs on the mats.

b. From a front support position on high bar lower the body straight downward. (Note: This is done without the leg swing backward. This is a good grip check, since if the grip is weak the gymnast will release the grip and land on her feet.)

c. Next swing legs rearward just a little from a front support position on high bar and lower to hanging position.

d. Each time a beginner gymnast tries to cast she should swing her legs a little stronger and higher. A beginner cast should be low backward, at approximately a 45-degree angle or slightly above. Arms will bend and slowly straighten in the backward swing so that the body will be fully extended before the descent.

e. Only advanced gymnasts have the strength to cast above 90 degrees and keep the arm straight throughout the movement.

55. FLYING HIP CIRCLE

M. From a front support position on high bar, facing low bar, lift the hips upward and and slightly backward as the body swings into a hanging position. (Cast to long hang, see No. 54.) As the hips come forward and strike the low bar, whip the legs in a pike position around the low bar and instantly let go of the high bar, grasping the low bar; complete hip circle backward ending in a front support on the low bar.

Spotting: Stand to one side between the bars, one hand under the buttocks, the other at the back to assist the legs to whip around the low bar.

Steps in learning: a. Learn hip circle backward on low bar.

b. Hanging from the high bar, facing the low bar, practice swinging forward and letting the hips hit the low bar in the groin without letting go of the high bar. Later use a spotter on either side, assisting in maintaining the pike position around the bar after the swing.

c. Learn the cast out from the front support on high bar.

d. Then you are ready to put together the cast (c) and the hip circle (a).

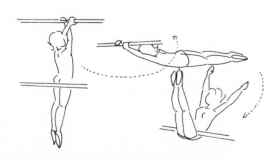

56. UNDERSWING WITH HALF TURN FROM LOW BAR TO BACK HIP CIRCLE

M. Sitting on the low bar facing the high bar, grasp the high bar with a mixed grip. (If turning to the left, left hand is in the over grip, right hand reverse crossed and under the high bar.) Swing the legs under the low bar slightly, then lift them forward away from the low bar until the body is in a hanging position on the high bar. At the peak of the forward swing, execute a half turn to the left and, facing the low bar, continue the body toward the low bar contacting the low bar at the groin. Pike, then release the high bar and quickly grasp the low bar and execute a backward hip circle.

Spotting: Stand between the bars, grasp the performer at the waist and assist in the turn and in the back swing before the hips touch the low bar.

Steps in learning: From a sitting position, grasp high bar with mixed grip, swing out, do a half turn, and swing back to low bar without the hip circle.

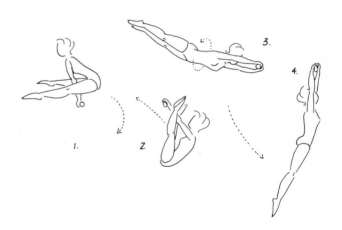

57. UNDERSWING WITH HALF TURN FROM HIGH BAR

M. This movement may be done from a front support on high bar facing out, straddle stand position on high bar, feet outside hands in a straddle, or from a straddle seat "L" hold (see sketch). Drop backward from the straddle "L" seat and disengage legs and extend them forward and upward until the body is fully extended, make a half turn and go into a long hang.

The most common skill following the underswing half-turn is a back hip circle.

Spotting: When turning to the left as shown in the sketch, the spotter stands between the bars to the right of the performer, grasping the waist when the hips underswing the bar to assist the forward swing and turn.

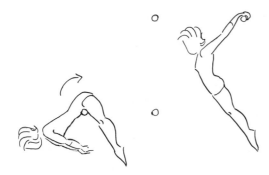

58.   EAGLE CATCH

M.   From a flying hip circle on the low bar the arms are swung up and backward to catch the high bar, both hands in an eagle grip on the high bar, facing the low bar.

Spotting: After the steps in learning have been taken, then on the complete movement the spotter should stand between the bars to one side, and step in to grasp the legs of the performer as the hip circle is completed and she reaches for the high bar. A second spotter should be in front of the low bar to grasp the performer in case she "opens up" too quickly.

Steps in learning: a. Practice a flying hip circle without using hands on the low bar.

b.   Get a feeling of casting back by having a spotter stand to the rear and step on her thigh as the arms are swung up and back to grasp the high bar.

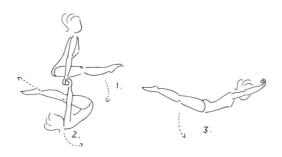

59.   DISLOCATE TO FLYING HIP CIRCLE

M.   Pike sitting on the high bar facing the low bar, arms in a spread position with under grip. Raise the hips and swing the body forward to an inverted pike position (partial forward seat circle), chin on the chest, arms and legs extended. Immediately extend the legs backward, dislocate the shoulders to an extended long hang with arms re-

maining in dislocate. Swing forward toward the low bar and as the hips contact the low bar, swing the legs upward and release the high bar and circle the low bar; end in a front support on the low bar with a regular grip, or do an eagle catch.

Variations: a. Do the same movement from standing on low bar, back to high bar, hands on high bar in wide reverse grip. Jump into dislocate (a pike position) under high bar. Assist this by raising the hips upward, tucking the head and rounding the back. Continue as described above.

b.   Dislocate to drop kip. Dislocate either from standing on low bar, or from an "L" position on high bar. Do not extend body fully as in the dislocate flying hip circle, only slightly extend hips, approximately to a 90-degree angle. Release the high bar, drop to the low bar, grasping bar with a regular grip. Continue the movement with a glide kip on low bar. The legs may be together or in a straddle position.

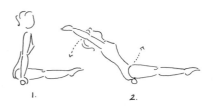

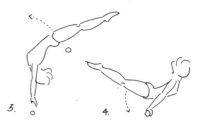

60.   THROW BACK

M.   Start in a rear seat on the high bar, back to low bar, hands in over grip. Swing arms upward and backward as body is arched. Let the body fall backwards in a deep arch, thighs still resting on the high bar. Continue the arch and grasp the low bar in an over grip, immediately shifting shoulders forward arms straight. Swing legs downward while forcing shoulders forward. Arch body until hips contact low bar. Continue with a backward hip circle.

Spotting: An overhead spotting belt should be used for this move, and control should be given as the hands reach the low bar.

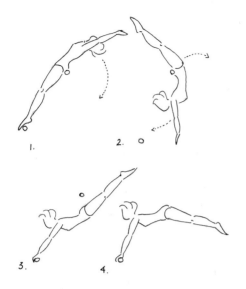

61. BACK LAYOUT OVER HIGH BAR TO CATCH LOW BAR

M. From a rear stand on low bar, move to rear support on high bar, simultaneously thrust the arms backward in order to turn backward to catch the low bar in regular grip. Keep an arched body position throughout the movement. Continue with a glide kip on low bar.

Spotting: An overhead spotting belt should be used for learning this move.

63. SINGLE-LEG STEM RISE (FALSE KIP)

M. May be performed with either leg. Start from a hanging position on the high bar, swing forward placing the right foot on the low bar. Lift the left leg, toe to the high bar, and whip down the left leg while simultaneously pushing with the right leg and pulling the body in close to the bar; pull the body to the rear, up and over the high bar to a front support position.

Spotting: Stand between the bars to one side of performer. Give a boost on the hips to help lift the body up and over the high bar.

Steps in learning: Learn to let the hands move loosely around the bar until the held position in front support. On the whip down of the straight leg, learn to pull the body upward at the same time as you push with the support foot.

Kipping Movements

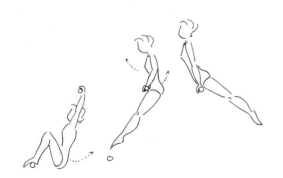

62. DOUBLE-LEG STEM RISE

M. Grasp the high bar with a regular grip, tuck the feet to the low bar. Push with the feet, forcing hips to high bar. Rotate grip and push downward with hands on high bar. Finish in a front support position on the high bar, facing the low bar.

Spotting: Spotter stand between the bars to one side of the gymnast. Assist by a boost at the hips.

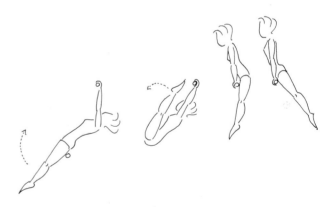

64. STATIONARY KIP (KIP FROM LOW BAR TO HIGH BAR)

M. From a sitting position on the low bar grasping high bar (rear lying position), swing both straight legs up, ankles close to the high bar, similar to a gliding kip mount. When the legs are up close to the high bar move them upward then downward and simultaneously pull with the arms, ending in a front support on the high bar.

Spotting: Stand between the bars to one side of the performer, and assist in giving the hips a boost upward.

Steps in learning: Practice the stem rise to both sides before learning the stationary kip.

65.   GLIDE KIP

M.   This movement is the same as the Glide Kip Mount No. 12, only the starting position is different, i.e., cast to free front support pike and glide kip.

Variations: a. Single-leg shoot through, glide kip.
    b.   Glide kip with legs in a straddle position.
    c.   Glide kip, catch high bar.
    d.   Glide kip, half turn catch high bar.

Spotting: Same as for Glide Kip Mount No. 12.

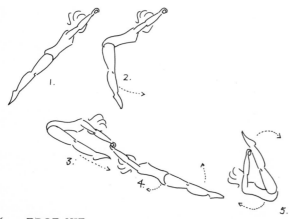

66.   DROP KIP

M.   Start from a long hang on high bar facing low bar. The movement may also start from seat circle backward on high bar (see No. 41) or from a dislocate on high bar (see No. 59, variation b). Swing legs backward then pike forcefully and release high bar, drop in this pike position to the low bar, grasping bar with regular grip. Continue with a glide kip. The legs may be together or in a straddle position.

Spotting: Spotter stands between the bars and supports the hips in order to help the gymnast to catch the low bar in a right angle.

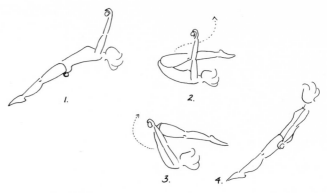

67.   REAR KIP

M.   This movement is the same as the Rear Kip Mount No. 15 if done with a glide. Here it will be explained from a rear lying position. From the rear lying position push forcefully and shoot both legs through the arms and swing under the high bar. At the end of this swing open the body slightly then close body position and allow the movement to reverse. This pumping action, the opening and closing in and out of kip position with the press down of the straight arms and grip rotation, will help the gymnast to end in a rear support position on the high bar facing low bar. Note that the arms are always straight and that the bar is kept under the seat throughout the movement.

Spotting: Spotter stands between the bars to one side of the gymnast. At first help to support the low back, then give assistance at the shoulders. This movement should be learned first on the low bar before attempting on the high bar.

68.   REAR KIP TO DROP KIP

M.   From a rear lying hang, perform a 3/4 rear kip as explained above in No. 67. Lift head up so eyes can spot the low bar. Release high bar and slightly extend hips (approximately to 90 degrees). Drop to low bar, grasping bar with regular grip. Continue movement with a glide kip on low bar. The legs may be together or in a straddle position.

Spotting: Spotters stand between the bars at the side of the gymnast and support the upper thigh after gymnast performs a partial rear kip, in order to help her to catch the low bar.

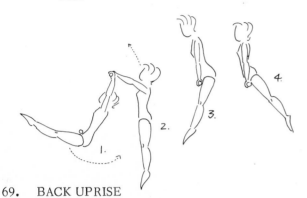

69.   BACK UPRISE

M.   Start from a front support position on high bar, facing low bar, hands in regular grip. Perform a high cast (see No. 54) and push outward until body is completely extended. Swing body forward completely extended to the low bar, then pike. As the hips swing backward straighten body, and as body gets under the high bar pike slightly at the hips and at the same time pull hard with the arms. This kipping action and pull should snap the body upward into a front support position on the high bar.

Spotting: Spotter stands between the bars to one side of the performer, and may push on the gymnast's near leg, just above the knee, in order to help the hips up over the high bar.

Connecting and Miscellaneous Movements

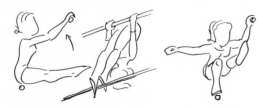

70.   BASKET

M.   (This may also be performed to the opposite side.) Sitting on the low bar and facing the high bar (inner seat), grasp the high bar with regular grip. Swing the legs in a pike position through the hands, touching the right foot to the low bar, bend knees and lower hips keeping left leg straight. Let go of the high bar with right hand and, holding on with the left hand, let the body naturally turn on the left, ending in a one-

leg squat on the right foot, left leg on the inside and extended.

Variation: Perform the same movement except place the insteps on the low bar.

Spotting: Stand to the right side of performer in this example between the bars. Support the hips as the performer turns under the arm, helping to keep the hips high.

Steps in learning: Practice the basket (skin-the-cat) movement on the low or horizontal bar.

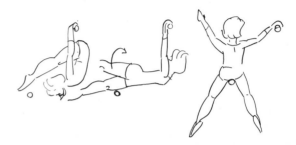

71.   BASKET WITH STRAIGHT LEGS

M.   The movement is the same as for the basket, but as the legs pike through the hands, continue keeping the legs straight as they slide over the top of the low bar. Arch the back and kick the right leg up and over the low bar, simultaneously let go high bar with the left hand. Continue the movement and end with the right leg near the high bar and right hand on the high bar.

Spotting: Stand between the bars and support the hips as in the basket.

72.   BACK HIP PULLOVER, LOW TO HIGH BAR

M.   From a rear lying hang, bend one knee placing the foot on low bar. Keep the other leg straight. Push from the foot and at the same time kick the straight leg up to the high bar and simultaneously pull the body close to the bar. The straight leg should rise up so that the high bar is at the hip. Continue the movement up and over the high bar, ending in a front support on the high bar.

Spotting: Stand between the bars, to the side of the performer. Assist by giving the hips a boost up and over the high bar.

Steps in learning: It is important that the push-off, and the kick-up of the straight leg, and pulling of the arms, occur simultaneously.

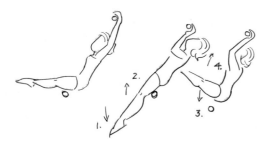

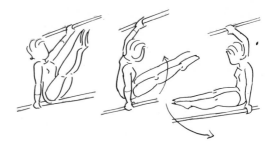

73.   DOUBLE-LEG BOUNCE, LOW TO HIGH BAR

M.   Sitting on the low bar facing forward, grasp the high bar with regular grip. Pulling on the arms, lift the straight legs upward and bounce on the middle of the thighs on the low bar. On the rebound of the legs, pull hard with the arms and continue the movement into a back hip pullover to the high bar. Finish with a straight arm support on the high bar. The timing of the rebound from the leg bounce and the pulling of the arms must be simultaneous.

Variation: Single leg bounce. Swing one straight leg upward and immediately follow with the other leg, taking the bounce on both thighs and continue as above.

Steps in learning: a. Learn first a single-leg bounce.
      b. The legs must be kept straight. The bounce should be taken on the middle of the thighs, never in back of the knees and never with bent hips.

75.   HORIZONTAL HIP CIRCLING ON LOW BAR

M.   This movement may be done in either direction. From a V seat on low bar, left shoulder to high bar and grasping high bar with left hand, swing legs to a side position, resting on the side of left hip, right hand to the rear, continue the movement around toward the high bar making a complete circle. Hands must be switched quickly as the body circles around; i.e., from the high bar, to low bar, and back to high bar again on the finish of the movement.

Spotting: Stand between the bars to the rear of the performer, holding the hips as she learns to switch hands on high bar.

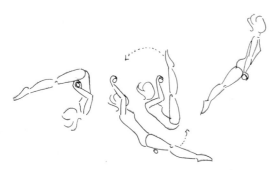

74.   FORWARD ROLL TO DOUBLE LEG BOUNCE

M.   Start from a front support position on high bar, facing low bar, hands in regular grip (thumbs grasping the bar in this movement at the same side with the fingers). Bend at hips, tuck head forward, and rotate hands around the bar. Swing straight legs over high bar, toward low bar and keep arms slightly bent. Bounce on the middle of the thighs on the low bar. On the rebound of the legs, pull hard with the arms and continue the movement into a back hip pullover to the high bar.

Spotting: Spotter stands between bars at side of gymnast. Help gymnast at the hips to slow down the forward roll and then help her with the bounce and pullover.

76.   HIGH ROLL FROM CROSS SEAT

M.   This movement may be performed on either side. From a cross sitting position on low bar on the left hip, left hand on the high bar in regular grip, right hand to the side. Swing the right leg straight to the side over the top of the low bar, face high bar, right hand under grip and crossed on high bar mixed grip. Continue the swing of the right leg around in a complete circle over the low bar, ending in a sitting position on the low bar, facing forward.

Spotting: Stand between the bars to one side of the performer and move into position in back of her after side swinging of the leg, catch the hips as the movement is finished in a sitting position on the low bar.

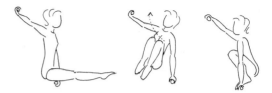

77. LEG SCISSORS ON LOW BAR

M. Start in a rear-lying position on the low bar grasping the high bar. Hands in mixed grip. Kick the left leg up into the air and pass the straight leg over the right leg, twisting the body as the weight is assumed on the left thigh and the performer faces the high bar. Continue the scissor movement turning the body back to original position by facing the end of the bar, left hand on the bar.

Spotting: Stand in front of the low bar and after the first swing of the left leg, grasp the performer's waist to help her to continue the the circle. Start the movement at the right end of the low bar.

79. REAR LYING, TURN TO SQUAT

M. From a rear lying position, hands in regular grip on high bar, release the left hand and grasp the low bar near the hip in a regular grip. Simultaneously bend the hips coming to a sitting position. Straighten the left arm and swing the legs to the right over the low bar. As soon as the legs cross the low bar, bend the knees coming to a squat position on the low bar, facing high bar. Release the grip on the low bar and come to a standing position.

Spotting: Stand outside the low bar grasping the left arm and assisting the gymnast to maintain the balance over the left arm.

78. DOUBLE-LEG CIRCLING SIDEWARD

M. From a hanging position on the high bar swing the legs up and over the low bar to a rear lying position. Swing the straight legs upward and to the right sideward between the bars, the right arm bending slightly.

The legs swing down to a long hanging, then bending the left arm slightly continue the swing, bringing the legs up to the left sideward and back to rear lying position.

Spotting: Stand in back of the high bar and grasp the waist of performer, assisting her in lifting the legs upward during the swinging of the legs over the bar.

80. FLANK VAULT OVER LOW BAR TO HALF TURN HANG

M. Start from a front lying position, hands in mixed grip on the high bar, right hand crossed under in reverse grip, left hand over in regular grip. Swing the legs forward and backward from the hips, moving under and in front of the low bar. Give a forceful backward swing of the legs and pull with the arms as the legs are swung to the right in a rear vault over the low bar. End in a long hang on the high bar facing the low bar and continue in a flying hip circle.

Spotting: Stand to the left side of performer between the bars; grasp the hips and help the turn.

back, lifting the head. Lower the left thigh to the low bar and release the right hand. The body will turn to the left making a 1/2 turn, then regrasp the high bar with the left hand in regular grip. The body rotates around the left thigh.

Spotting: The spotter stands between the bars to the right side of the gymnast and places her hands under the buttocks and around her waist to assist in the turn.

81.   UNDERSWING TO STRIDE SUPPORT ON LOW BAR

M.   From a front support position on high bar (facing low bar, hands in regular grip) drop backward and downward in a pike position keeping arm straight. As the body moves under the bar, slightly bend arms and separate legs, lifting right leg above the low bar. End in a stride support position on low bar, right leg in front.

Variation: Underswing to rear support on low bar. Underswing over low bar with both legs end in a rear support position.

Spotting: Stand between the bars to one side of the performer, assist at the hips as she lowers herself to the low bar.

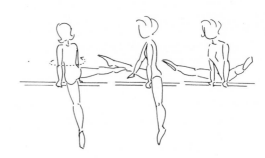

83.   STRADDLE "L" SUPPORT FROM HALF TURN

M.   Straight arm support on low bar facing high bar, right hand regular, left hand reverse grip. Lift right straight leg over the bar, letting go with right hand, placing it across left hand in regular grip, and turn to straddle seat on low bar. (Note: This movement may be performed facing inward or outward, and may be performed on the low or the high bar.)

Variations: a. Perform the same move on the high bar.
b.   Perform the same move from a standing position on the low bar facing the high bar.

Spotting: Stand to the outside of the low bar at the left side of the gymnast. Grasp the left arm to assist in keeping body weight over this arm. A second spotter may step between bars to assist in holding the straddle "L" position.

Spotting on high bar: Two spotters should be used standing between the bars to catch the gymnast if she loses balance forward. A third spotter may stand outside the high bar to support the back of the gymnast should she fall to the rear.

Suggested movement to follow this position: Straddle seat circle backward.

82.   VERTICAL OR NEEDLE SPLIT

M.   Hanging on the high bar in a bent inverted hanging position. As the body swings away from the bar, stride the legs by lowering the right leg and raising the left leg in a needle split. As the body swings inward toward the low bar, quickly complete the vertical split and at the same time arch the

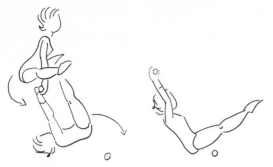

84. STRADDLE "L" ON HIGH BAR UNDERSWING TO LOW BAR

M. Start in the straddle "L" position on the high bar. Drop backward and as the body is in the inverted position, bring the legs together and end in a rear lying position on the low bar.

Spotting: Stand to one side to avoid being kicked by the legs. Grasp at the hips.

85. SHOOT THROUGH

M. (Note: This may be performed in either direction and on either bar.) From a front support position on the low bar, facing forward, lift the weight upward taking the weight on the hands. With a slight swing forward and backward at the hips to get them away from the bar (see Cast—Swinging Movements) shoot one leg through to crotch position. The knee may bend on the shoot through, or it may be held straight and, with a greater lifting of the hips, shoot the straight leg through to stride position. The weight should be above the shoulders which are pushed slightly forward on the shoot through. The arms must be straight.

Variations: a. The initial movement is the same as above, but squat both legs through to sit on the bar (see sketch).

b. The initial movement is the same, but stoop through with both legs.

c. Squat or stoop through on high bar to stand on low bar. Place a mat over the low bar when learning this skill. Do not attempt the skill until a control squat through is learned on the low bar. A spotter may stand on the low bar and hook one leg over the top bar to help to support the arm.

Spotting: Stand to one side and hold the wrist and arm of the performer. A second spotter may stand between the bars.

Suggested movements to follow: Single-leg circle forward or backward.

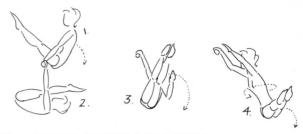

86. FLANK CUT TO LONG HANG

M. From a rear support on high bar, facing low bar, hands in regular grip, fall rearward to a bent inverted hang. As momentum stops swing back by pulling with head and shoulders forcefully. At the peak of the upward rise of the body, release the left hand and swing both legs to the left, immediately regrasping the high bar with the left hand, swinging legs downward and backward ending in a long hang position.

Spotting: Spotter should stand directly behind the gymnast placing hands on the hips helping her to control the cut and regrasp.

Movements to follow: This movement may be used prior to a flying hip circle.

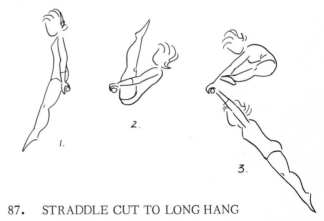

87. STRADDLE CUT TO LONG HANG

M. From a rear seat position on high bar, facing low bar, hands in regular grip (thumbs to the rear). Lift the legs forward in a pike position and swing the body backward under the high bar. The body will swing forward and backward. On the backswing when the shoulders reach the height of the high bar, the legs forcefully extend forward and upward and straddle sideward as the hands release the high bar momentarily while the legs cut past the arms. The hands quickly regrasp the high bar and the legs swing downward and backward into a long hanging position.

Spotting: The stunt should be learned on a low bar first. The spotter stands directly in back of the performer grasping her waist during the cutting action, and helps to lift the performer to regrasp the bar.

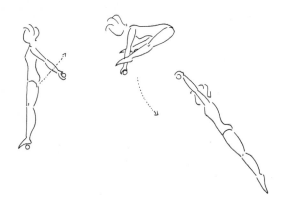

88. BACK STRADDLE JUMP OVER HIGH BAR TO LONG HANG

M. Standing on low bar with back to high bar, hands grasping the high bar in back. Jump into the air, legs in wide straddle, catching the high bar between the legs as they clear the bar. On the down swing bring the legs together and continue with a flying hip circle or any movement from a long hang.

Spotting: On the jump over the bar, spotter should be behind the performer, in back of the high bar. Grasp the waist of the gymnast and assist her to lift and pull the hips back. An overhead belt might be used at the beginning to assist in getting the jump and leg spread to the hanging position.

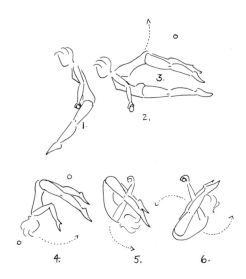

89. FRONT SOMERSAULT FROM LOW BAR TO CATCH HIGH BAR

M. Starting from a front support on low bar facing outward, hands in regular grip. Cast legs backward forcefully to a high free front support position. Then pike to lift seat close to high bar, simultaneously push with hands and release low bar, tuck head and somersault forward straddling legs. Catch

high bar between legs by bringing hands under the bar. Continue the front somersault and end facing low bar.

Spotting: Use an overhead belt. Later stand between bars to one side of gymnast. Assist by lifting at the hips to help gymnast catch high bar.

Dismounts

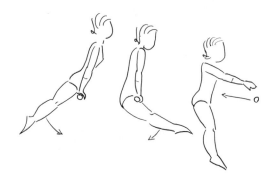

90. CAST OFF TO REAR

M. From a front support position on low bar facing high bar, swing both straight legs forward under the bar and backward. At the height of the backward swing, push with the arms and jump backward, end with bent knees.

The movement may be performed facing the opposite direction.

Variation: Cast off high bar.

Spotting: Stand to one side of performer in front of low bar. Grasp with one hand at the shoulder, and with the other hand assist in pushing the hips upward and backward away from the bar. When done on the high bar, stand behind high bar and be ready to catch gymnast at the waist to help the landing.

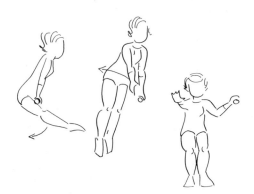

91. CAST OFF WITH QUARTER TURN

M. From a front support on the low bar facing high bar, swing the legs under the low bar, then backward. As the legs lift upward and backward and swing away from the bar, push with the hands turning the body a quarter turn and drop to the mat in a standing position, left side to the low bar, left hand on the low bar.

Variations: a. Cast off with half turn.
b. Cast off with full turn.
c. Cast off from high bar with quarter, half, or full turn.

Spotting: Stand to the left of performer, support the shoulder and then grasp the waist on the quarter turn.

92.   SINGLE-LEG FLANK QUARTER TURN DISMOUNT

M.   From a stride position on low bar facing outward, hands in reverse grip. Swing the right leg up and over the low bar as the body is supported momentarily on the left hand. Land on the mat with the left side to the low bar, left hand still on the bar.

Spotting: Stand in front of the bars, supporting the left wrist and shoulder.

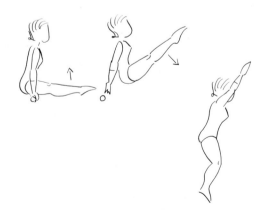

93.   PIKE POSITION SHOOT OFF DISMOUNT

M.   Sitting on the low bar, back to high bar, lift the feet into the air and cast the body away from the bar. Push with the hands and land on the feet a few feet away from low bar.

Spotting: Stand to one side of performer, supporting the wrist and shoulder.

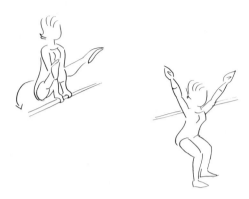

94.   STRADDLE SEAT CIRCLE DISMOUNT

M.   From a straddle seat on the low bar let the trunk fall backward. Simultaneously the legs lift up and over low bar and come together in an arched position as the arms push the body forward under the low bar.

Variation: Same movement on high bar. Start facing outward.

Spotting: Stand in front of the bars to one side of the gymnast, help her by grasping the waist.

95.   SKIN THE CAT FROM HIGH BAR

M.   From a front support on the high bar, reach to the low bar with a reverse grip; slowly slide down the bar until the hips are at the level of the low bar. In a controlled pike position bring the feet forward and push out with the hands to an arched position to standing, with back to low bar.

Spotting: Stand to one side in front of low bar, grasp the wrist and shoulder.

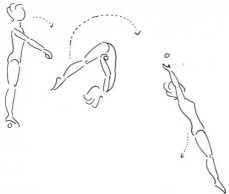

96.   FORWARD ROLL OFF HIGH BAR

M.   Standing on the low bar, facing the high bar, grasp high bar with regular grip. Lean into the high bar at the hip or groin and roll over the top of the bar simultaneously rotate hands around the bar. Come down to a straight hang position and then, with a small whip of the legs, snap outward to the mat.

Spotting: Stand between the bars and step in back of the performer, grasping the waist as the roll is completed over the high bar.

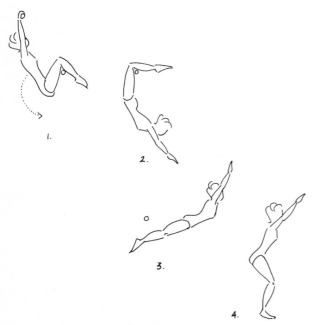

97.   HOCK DISMOUNT FROM LOW BAR (PENNY DROP)

M.   From a rear lying position, legs resting on low bar, body arched, hands grasping high bar in regular grip. Drop the hips downward and bend the knees. Let go the high bar and swing the arms backward and downward under the low bar, arching the body throughout this phase. At the height of the

upward swing, bring the feet under the body for a good landing.

Spotting: Stand to the outside of the low bar. As the grip from the high bar is released, place a hand on the ankles to control the knee bending. Then as the gymnast swings under the low bar, place a hand under her abdomen and immediately remove hand from ankles. Be prepared to lift the gymnast upward if the dismount is too low.

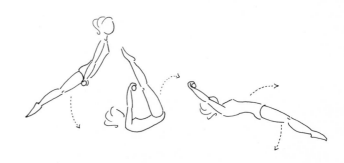

98.   UNDERSWING DISMOUNT FROM LOW BAR

M.   From a front support on low bar swing the legs under the bar, shifting the shoulders back to start the body falling backward, piking at hips. Keep the hips bent in a pike position, allow the body to swing forward under the low bar. As the feet come close to the low bar, quickly stretch the body and arch out as hands leave the bar.

Spotting: Stand to the outside close to the low bar. Place inside hand under low back, pressing back upward to assist in the arch off. Grasp the shoulder with the outside hand to steady the landing.

99.   UNDERSWING DISMOUNT FROM HIGH BAR

M.   Stand on the low bar facing high bar, hands in regular grip; jump into a pike position and swing the legs under and upwards under the high bar. Continue the swing to an underswing dismount.

This may also start from a one-leg squat.

Variations: a. Underswing dismount from high bar with half or full twist.

b. Underswing dismount from high bar over low bar. Start from a front support position facing low bar.

c. Underswing dismount from high bar with half or full twist over low bar.

Spotting: Stand between the bars, move in back of performer and grasp at waist if needed.

100. FLANK VAULT DISMOUNT

M.   From a straight arm support on low bar, back to high bar, swing the legs forward under the low bar, then backward and upward, over the low bar to the right side and flank vault over the bar. Land on the mat with the back toward the low bar.

Variations: a. Flank vault dismount from low bar with quarter turn. The movement is similar except the left hand grasps the low bar in reverse grip and the performer ends with the left side to the bar, left hand on bar.

b. Flank vault dismount over high bar with quarter turn. Start standing on low bar facing high bar, left hand in under grip, right hand in regular. Bend knees slightly and spring off low bar, swinging legs to the right over high bar. Release right hand grip and support body on straight left arm while performing the quarter turn. While the body descends let go with the left hand too and land with the side to the bars.

Spotting: Stand in front of the low bar, supporting the left wrist and shoulders.

101. SQUAT VAULT DISMOUNT

M.   From a straight arm support on the low bar swing the legs under the low bar, then lift the legs upward and immediately squat the legs through the arms and pass the feet over the low bar. Simultaneously push off with hands and raise upper body. Continue the movement toward the mat and land with the back to the low bar.

Variations: a. The legs may be straight, which is then a stoop vault dismount.

b. The legs may be spread or straddled, which is then a straddle vault dismount.

c. Squat, stoop, or straddle vault over high bar from straight arm support.

d. Squat, stoop, or straddle vault over high bar from standing on low bar facing high bar. See Flank Vault Dismount No. 100, variation b.

e. Squat, stoop, or straddle vault from high bar over low bar.

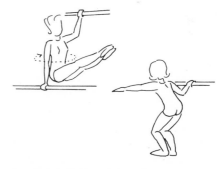

102. REAR VAULT WITH HALF TURN DISMOUNT

M.   Start from between the bars, grasping the low bar with right hand and the high bar with left hand in an over grip. Swing the legs forward between the bars and over the low bar in a rear vault with half turn. End with right hand on the bar, right side to the bar. Note the right hand must quickly change position from the original grip to an over grip again at the landing.

Spotting: Stand in front of the low bar, grasping the right wrist and shoulder.

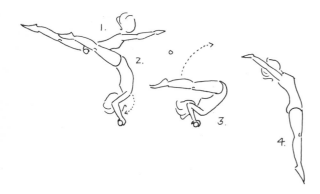

103. NECKSPRING FROM LOW BAR

M.   From a swan balance on the high bar reach downward, grasping the low bar in a regular grip. Bend the hips slightly sliding the legs down the high bar, and simultaneously bend the arms and tuck the head between the arms. Place the back of the neck on the low bar, sliding legs off from high bar and pike the body (body is in a hip-up position). With a thrust upward and outward with the legs, arch the body and let go of the low bar, landing in a vertical position in front of the low bar.

Variations: a. Neckspring from front support position. See No. 104.

b.   Neckspring with half or full twist.

Spotting: Stand outside of the low bar to the left of the gymnast. Grasp the gymnast's arm with the left hand, and use the right hand to push the hips upward and away from the bar.

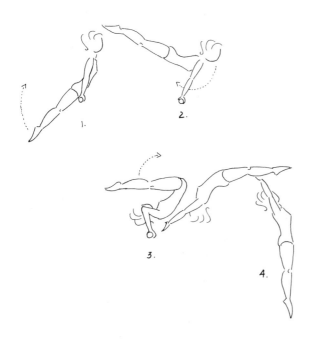

104. NECKSPRING FROM HIGH BAR

M.   Front support on high bar, facing out, hands in regular grip. Swing the legs to rear and upward to a free front support. Legs should be slightly above the horizontal. Immediately pike at the hips and tuck the head between the arms, chin to chest, and back of the neck on the high bar. The hips must shift forward and with a thrust extend the legs and arch the body. Release the hand grip, allowing the body to land.

Variations: a. Same movement but start from a standing on low bar facing high bar. Grasping high bar with regular grip, jump to a free front support on high bar and continue as described above.

b.   Neckspring from high bar over low bar. Start from a front support on high bar, facing in.

c.   Neckspring from high bar with half or full twist.

Spotting: Stand between the bars grasping the waist as the neckspring is initiated to help the landing.

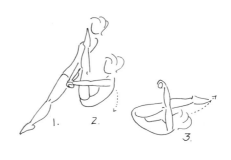

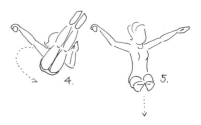

105. FLANK CUT DISMOUNT

M.   Standing on the low bar, back to high bar, hands on high bar in a regular grip. Spring upward, lifting hips high between arms to an "L" support on high bar. Swing the body in the pike position backward under the high bar. As movement starts upward, push downward on the high bar to allow body to rise upward. Release the right hand and turn the body 90 degrees to the right, release the left hand and land in upright position (left side to the bars).

Variations: a. A complete 180-degree turn may be made, ending with right side to the bar.

b.   Flank cut dismount over low bar. Start from a rear seat on high bar facing out.

Spotting: Stand to the outside of the high bar, facing

the back of the gymnast. Step in to assist the rise of the hips and the turn of the hips as the right hand is released. Grasp around waist should landing be incorrect.

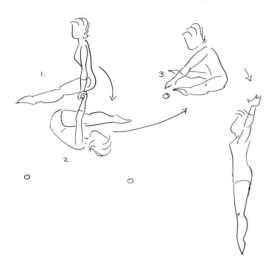

106. STRADDLE CUT DISMOUNT

M.   From a standing position on the low bar jump to a rear support on the high bar, legs in pike; turn rearward to bent inverted hang, then as movement upward starts, push downward with hands on high bar to allow body to rise above the bar. Then dismount releasing the grasp and executing a straddle cut-off, to end starting behind the high bar facing the low bar.

Variations: Straddle cut dismount over low bar. Start from a rear seat position on high bar, facing out.

Spotting: Lower the bar for practice. Also use overhead belt for the cut-off. The spotter should stand in back to catch the performer on the straddle cut-off. The spotter should also help at the waist to give height to the dismount.

107. CROSS HANDSTAND DISMOUNT

M.   From a front support position on the high bar reach down with the left hand to the low bar in a regular grip, right hand on the high bar, elbow bent. Extend the right elbow so that the handstand is at about a 120-degree angle; hold the position momentarily and then continue over to the floor. The right hand lets go of the high bar and grasps the low bar. End with the right side to the low bar.

Spotting: Stand in front of the low bar, grasping the left wrist and shoulder.

108. CARTWHEEL DISMOUNT

M.   From a front support on the high bar reach upward with the right hand and then place it on the low bar. Kick the legs upward to a handstand between the bars, facing lengthwise. The right hand should be shoulder distance backward from the left hand position on the high bar. Start to fall to the outside of the low bar, release left hand and continue to descend sideways. Land on the outside of low bar, right side of body to low bar.

Spotting: Stand in front of the low bar, supporting the right wrist and hip.

109. CROSS HANDSTAND WITH REAR VAULT AND HALF TURN

M.   From a front support position on high bar reach forward and grasp the low bar with right hand so that the hand is directly under the right shoulder. The left hand grasps the high bar. Kick the legs up to a momentary handstand, then let them swing between the bars and over the low bar in a rear vault, with a half turn. End with the right hand on the bar, right side to the bar. The right hand must quickly change position from the original grip with thumb toward the high bar on the handstand to an over grip with the thumb forward at the completion of the vault.

Spotting: Stand in front of the low bar and to the left of the performer; grasp the right wrist and shoulder.

110. FROM ARCH BACK TO SIDE HANDSTAND DISMOUNT

M.   From an inverted hang from double-knee position facing low bar reach down and grasp the low bar. Placing one foot on the high bar and extending the arms, lift upward to an arch back position. Then kick off the high bar to a handstand. Hold the

handstand for an instant, then continue the movement ending in a standing position facing the low bar.

Spotting: Stand between the bars to the side of performer; grasp the wrist and shoulder.

111. SIDE HANDSTAND DISMOUNT

M.   From a front support position on high bar raise the arms horizontally and reach forward grasping the low bar with a regular grip. Push the body off the high bar to a handstand position. Hold the handstand momentarily, then continue the arched position and turn over.

Spotting: The spotters should stand on either side of performer grasping the wrist and shoulder. They should stand in front of the low bar.

112. SIDE HANDSTAND QUARTER TURN

M.   From a front support position on high bar bend forward grasping the low bar with a mixed grip (right hand in an under grip, left in an over grip). Whip the legs out and over the low bar and hold handstand position momentarily. As the body slightly overbalances, do a quarter turn by releasing the left hand and shifting the weight over the straight right arm. Keep head up and body arched during the descent. Land on the mat right side to the low bar, right hand still on bar.

Spotting: Stand in front of the low bar, support the right wrist and shoulder.

113. SIDE HANDSTAND TO SHOOT THROUGH DISMOUNT

M.   From a front support on the high bar grasp the low bar with regular grip. From the leaning rest position on the high bar lift the feet off the high bar to a handstand, then tuck them and squat through; simultaneously the hands push off the low bar, landing with back to low bar.

Variations: a. The same movement with legs straight, side handstand stoop through dismount (see sketch).

        b. The same movement with legs spread—side handstand straddle through dismount.

Spotting: A spotter should stand on either side of performer in front of low bar, grasping the wrist and shoulder. For straddle through, stand in front of performer, put left hand on right shoulder and right hand on left shoulder to steady gymnast in handstand and to help lift the upper body.

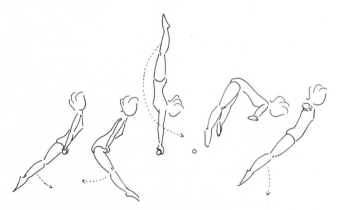

114. SIDE HANDSTAND DISMOUNT FROM HIGH BAR

M.   From support on the high bar, facing out, hands in regular grip. Swing legs forward under the high bar, then to the rear upward to a handstand. Or start from standing on low bar facing high bar, grasp high bar with regular grip and jump up to handstand on high bar. From handstand, turn over forward.

Variations: a. Handstand squat through.

        b. Handstand stoop through.

        c. Handstand straddle through (see sketch).

        d. Yogi handstand turn over.

        e. All the above may be done over the low bar —side handstand dismount from high bar over low bar.

Spotting: Use an overhead belt. Later spotter in front of the bar to control the gymnast landing. Use double mats for landing.

115. HECHT DISMOUNT FROM LOW BAR

M.   Start from a front support position on the high bar. Cast to the rear and whip legs forward in a hip circle without hands. The moment the hips touch the low bar, bend the hips and release the grip on the high bar. Keep the body in a piked position until a 3/4 hip circle is performed. Quickly force the arms upward, arching the body slightly above horizontal so that the straight legs will clear the low bar. The legs may be together or in a straddle position. After the legs have cleared the bar, bend at the hips and land with the knees slightly bent.

Variation: Hecht dismount with half or full twist.

Spotting: Stand to the outside of the low bar on the gymnast's right side. Place the left arm under the abdomen and place the right arm under the armpits or under the chest, helping to raise the body to clear the low bar.

Steps in learning: a. Learn first eagle catch.

        b. Hang over low bar in an upside down V position. Pop upwards several times, raising the upper body forcefully until you are able to perform the Hecht with a spotter.

        c. Then attempt the Hecht from a cast out from the high bar.

116. HECHT DISMOUNT WITH QUARTER TURN

M.   From a front support on high bar cast out and execute a back hip circle on low bar. As the upper body rises to the outside of the low bar, grasp the low bar with the left hand, arms slightly bent. Immediately swing the right arm forward and initiate a quarter turn; simultaneously the left arm is straightened. Arch the back to help the popping action over the bar. Keep the body arched during the descent. Land on mat with the left side to the low bar, left hand still on the bar.

Spotting: Stand in front of low bar; as gymnast places left hand on the bar assist by supporting the left arm. A second spotter may stand between the bars to the left side of the gymnast and can help to raise the body to clear the low bar.

Steps in learning: a. Before attempting this dismount a flying hip circle without hands must be learned.

b.   Hang over low bar in an upside down V position. Place left hand in under or reverse grip on low bar. Swing straight right arm upward and arch body. Practice this until you get the feeling of popping action and support of the left arm.

117. HECHT DISMOUNT WITH 3/4 TURN

M.   From front support on high bar cast out and execute a back hip circle on low bar. As the upper body rises to the outside of the low bar, grasp the low bar with the left hand and quickly arch the back, popping over the low bar. Immediately look over the left shoulder, swinging right arm to the left to grip the low bar. Release left hand and swing left arm to the left, opening the body. Dismount to floor with right side to low bar.

Spotting: Stand in front of low bar; as gymnast places the right hand on the bar assist by holding at hips and helping to rotate the body before the landing.

Steps in learning: Learn first the Hecht Dismount with Quarter Turn No. 116.

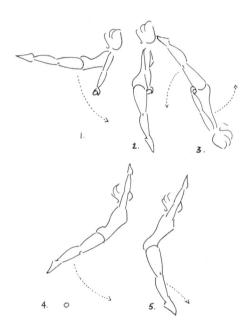

118. HECHT DISMOUNT FROM HIGH BAR

M.   From a front support on high bar facing out, hands in regular grip, cast to a high free front support position and continue with a partial hip circle backward, body only slightly piked. As the body is rising to the outside of the high bar, pull with the arms downward on the bar forcefully, then release grip and lift head and upper body to raise body to an above horizontal arch. This will cause a popping forward and over the bar. Land with back to the bars.

Variations: a. Hecht dismount from high bar with half or full twist.

b.   Hecht dismount from high bar over low bar (see sketch).

Spotting: Use an overhead belt. Hand spotting is the same as for the Hecht Dismount from Low Bar No. 115. Do not let go of the gymnast until she has landed on the mat. Use double mats for landing.

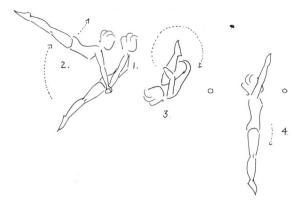

119. FRONT SOMERSAULT DISMOUNT

M.   From a front support on high bar, facing inward, hands in regular grip, cast legs
backward forcefully to a high free front
support position. As you move toward the
height of the cast, pike and lift seat as
high as possible. Immediately push with
the hands and release the high bar grip,
simultaneously tuck head, bend the knees
and grasp the shins, and pull as you do a
tucked somersault forward. As you spot
the bar, open up at the waist and straighten
knees, land facing high bar.

Variations: a. Piked front somersault dismount.

b.   Piked straddle front somersault dismount.

c.   Front somersault dismount over low bar.

Spotting: Use an overhead belt to learn this dismount. Then spot at the waist to help the
gymnast in the rotation and in landing.

Steps in learning: a. Practice only the cast and hip
lift first on low bar.

b.   Hands and knees drop on the trampoline
to front somersault.

120.   BACK SOMERSAULT DISMOUNT

M.   From a front support on high bar, facing low
bar, hands in regular grip, cast legs
backward to a free front support position.
At the height of the cast, bend at the hips
(pike) straddling the legs and raising the
hips, while shoulders are shifted forward.
As feet pass over the high bar, release
grip, simultaneously bring the legs together while lowering the hips, and bounce
on the middle of the thighs on high bar.
On the rebound of the legs, pull hard with
arms upward and somewhat backward, then
snap head back and perform a piked back
somersault for dismount.

Spotting: Use an overhead belt to learn this movement. Then spot at the waist to help the
gymnast in the rotation and in landing.

BEGINNING SKILLS AND COMBINATIONS

Selecting Skills

Usually the beginning gymnast will select from
the following skills for the beginning uneven bars
routine.

Mounts

Straight arm support
Shoot over low bar
Back hip pullover mount
Skin-the-cat to basket
Cross seat mount
Single-leg swing up
Crotch twist mount
Double leg stemrise mount

Balances or held positions

Seat balance
V seat
One-leg squat
Scale
Back pull away
Swan balance
Arch through
Rear arch
Arch back from knee hang
Squat stand

Circling movements

Hip circle forward or backward
Single-knee swing up
Single-knee circle backward
Mill circle backward or forward
Crotch seat, side circle

Swinging movements

Cast
Cast out from front support on high bar

Kipping movements

Double leg stemrise
Single leg stemrise

Connecting and miscellaneous movements

Basket
Basket with straight legs
Back hip pullover, low to high bar
Double-leg bounce, low to high bar
Forward roll to double-leg bounce
Hip roll on low bar
Thigh roll from cross seat
Leg scissors on low bar
Double-leg circling sideward
Rear lying, turn to squat
Underswing to stride support on low bar

Dismounts

Cast off to rear
Cast off with quarter turn
Single leg flank with quarter turn
Pike position shoot off dismount
Skin-the-cat from high bar
Forward roll off high bar
Hock dismount from low bar
Straddle seat circle dismount
Underswing dismount from low bar
Flank vault dismount
Squat vault dismount from low bar
Rear vault with half turn
From arch back to side handstand dismount
Underswing dismount from high bar

Beginning Combinations

1. Back hip pullover mount; single-leg cut to a
    stride support; single-knee swing up; single-
    leg flank with quarter turn dismount.

2. Cross seat mount; V seat; quarter turn facing
    high bar, basket; stand up and turn facing high
    bar; forward roll dismount.

3. Double leg stemrise mount; forward roll to
    double leg bounce; underswing to stride support
    on low bar, right leg in front; mill circle for-
    ward; quarter turn to left, placing left hand
    on high bar, swing legs between bars and do a
    rear vault with half-turn dismount.

4. Crotch twist mount (finish facing outward, back
    to high bar); single-knee circle backward; con-
    tinue without stopping to a single-knee swing up,
    catch high bar; back hip pullover from low to
    high bar; underswing to rear lying position on
    low bar; hock dismount from low bar.

INTERMEDIATE SKILLS AND COMBINATIONS

Selecting Skills

Usually an intermediate gymnast, in addition to
beginning movements, will select from the following
skills:

Mounts

Vault mounts
Glide kip mount
Glide kip on low bar, catch high bar
Glide kip double leg shoot through
Front hip circle mount

Balances or held positions

Arch back to backward hip circle
Cross handstand
Side handstand
Handstand straddle to straddle seat

1.

2.

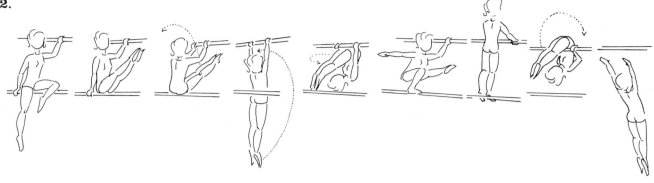

3.

4.

Circling movements

   Free hip circle forward
   Free hip circle forward, catch high bar
   Seat rise
   Double-knee circle backward
   Seat circle backward or forward
   Straddle sole circle backward or forward
   Stoop sole circle backward or forward
   Straddle seat circle backward or forward
   Half turn from low bar to catch high bar
   Stoop sole circle backward with
      half turn to catch high bar

Swinging movements

   Flying hip circle
   Underswing with half turn from low bar
      to back hip circle
   Underswing with half turn from high bar
   Eagle catch
   Dislocate to flying hip circle

Kipping movements

   Stationary kip
   Glide kip

Connecting and miscellaneous movements

   Flank vault over low bar to half turn
   Straddle "L" support from half turn
   Straddle "L" on high bar underswing
      to low bar
   Shoot through
   Flank cut to long hang
   Straddle cut to long hang
   Back straddle jump over high bar to long hang

Dismounts

   Cross handstand dismount
   Cartwheel dismount
   Cross handstand with rear vault and half turn
   Side handstand dismount
   Side handstand quarter turn
   Side handstand shoot through dismount
   Flank cut dismount
   Straddle cut dismount
   Neck spring from low bar
   Neck spring from high bar
   Hecht dismount from low bar
   Hecht dismount with quarter turn
   Squat, stoop, or straddle vault
      dismount from high bar

Intermediate Combinations

Note. The mounts and dismounts may be given just to get on and off the apparatus.

1. Jump to glide kip mount; hip circle forward; single-leg shoot through; single-leg flank with quarter turn dismount.

2. Jump to glide kip mount on low bar, catch high bar with regular grip; straddle legs over low bar to a rear lying position; stationary kip; cross handstand dismount.

3. Double-leg stemrise mount; flying hip circle to eagle catch; forward hip circle on low bar; flank vault dismount.

4. Flank vault mount; underswing with half turn from low bar to back hip circle; cast to squat stand on low bar, stand up and grasp high bar in regular grip; straddle cut dismount.

1.

2.

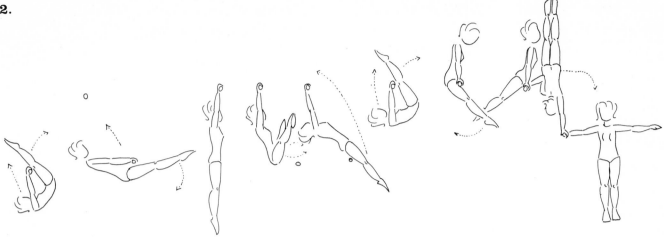

3.

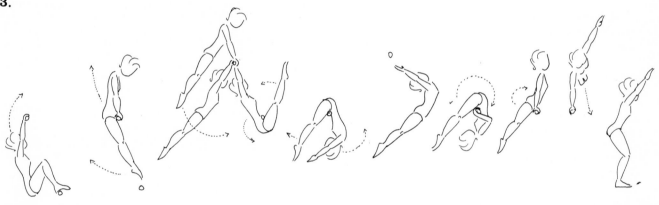

4.

ADVANCED SKILLS AND COMBINATIONS

Selecting Skills

Note: Many of the intermediate skills may be used in advanced routines, but sometimes they are used with variations. Either there is a greater twisting or more changing of grasping from bar to bar. Elegance and perfection of performance plus excellent timing and the unusual combination of skills makes for a more advanced exercise.

Mounts

> Glide kip on high bar
> Rear kip mount
> Handstand mount
> Glide kip double leg shoot through
>   straddle cut, catch low bar
> Full twist to front hip circle

Balances or held positions

> Side handstand on high bar, half turn,
>   descend to long hang
> (Any of the pauses may be used as connections in advanced exercises. Usually they are only done in preparation for a very difficult move.)

Circling movements

> Stoop sole circle backward cast pike or
>   straddle catch under high bar
> Full turn from low bar to catch high bar
> Corkscrew on high bar
> Seat circle backward to drop kip
> Seat circle forward on high bar
>   to straddle cut, catch high bar
> Forward hip circle to handstand
> Free backward hip circle
> Full twist from a long hang

Swinging movements

> Throw back
> Back layout over high bar to catch low bar

Kipping movements

> Stationary kip to handstand
> Drop kip
> Rear kip
> Rear kip to drop kip
> Back uprise

Connecting and miscellaneous movements

> Vertical or needle split
> Back straddle jump over high bar to
>   long hang drop to low bar and glide kip
> Front somersault from low bar
>   to catch high bar

Dismounts

> Straddle cut dismount over low bar
> Side handstand dismount from high bar
> Underswing dismount from high bar
>   over low bar with full twist
> From stand on low bar, kip or neck spring
>   from high bar with full twist to stand
> From front support on high bar, kip (neck
>   spring) with full twist to standing
> Hecht dismount with 3/4 turn
> Hecht dismount from low bar with
>   half or full twist
> Hecht dismount from high bar
> Front somersault dismount
> Back somersault dismount

Advanced Combinations

Note. The mounts and dismounts may be given just to get on and off the apparatus.

1. Straight arm support mount facing high bar; cast and stoop legs through; 3/4 seat circle forward to straddle cut, catch low bar; glide kip; immediately cast legs to squat stand on low bar; underswing dismount from high bar.

1.

2. Run squat vault mount to grasp high bar; immediately underswing with half turn to back hip circle without hands; half turn, catch high bar; half turn, catch low bar (drop kip); glide kip; cast off to rear dismount.

3. Jump to glide kip mount on low bar, catch high bar with dislocate or eagle grip; arch through to stand on low bar; back straddle jump over high bar to long hang; drop to low bar, glide kip, double-leg shoot through; pike position shoot off dismount.

2.

3.

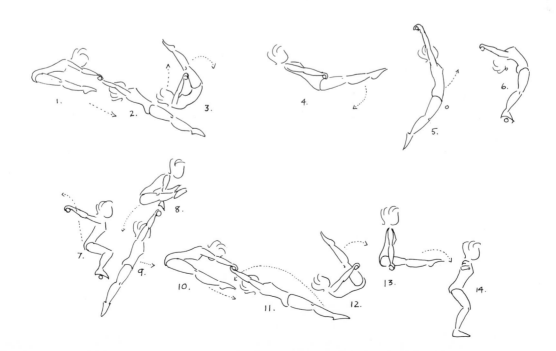

4.

4. Shoot over low bar from long hang on high bar mount; stationary kip; immediately forward hip circle on high bar; without stopping, cast to Hecht dismount from low bar with 3/4 turn.

BEGINNING EXERCISES

1. Double-leg stemrise mount.

2. Hip circle backward on high bar.

3. Underswing to stride support on low bar, right leg in front.

4. Single-knee circle backward, continue without stopping to a single-knee swing up, catch high bar.

5. Leg scissors on low bar to rear lying position with left foot on low bar.

6. Single-leg stemrise.

7. Forward roll to rear lying position.

8. Quarter turn to the right momentary V seat, turn to face high bar.

9. Basket-ending with right foot on low bar, stand up and turn to face high bar.

10. Underswing dismount from high bar with half twist. Land facing high bar and end routine standing in good posture.

INTERMEDIATE EXERCISES

1. Face high bar, gliding kip mount.

2. Hip circle forward.

3. Half turn from low bar to catch high bar.

4. Back hip pullover to straight arm support on high bar.

5. Straddle "L" support from half turn on high bar, underswing to low bar to rear lying position.

6. Stationary kip.

7. Flying hip circle, immediately go to eagle catch.

8. Shoot right leg over low bar to stride support position.

9. Mill circle forward, catch high bar.

10. Single leg stemrise, left foot on low bar.

11. Swan balance on high bar.

12. Side handstand straddle through dismount.

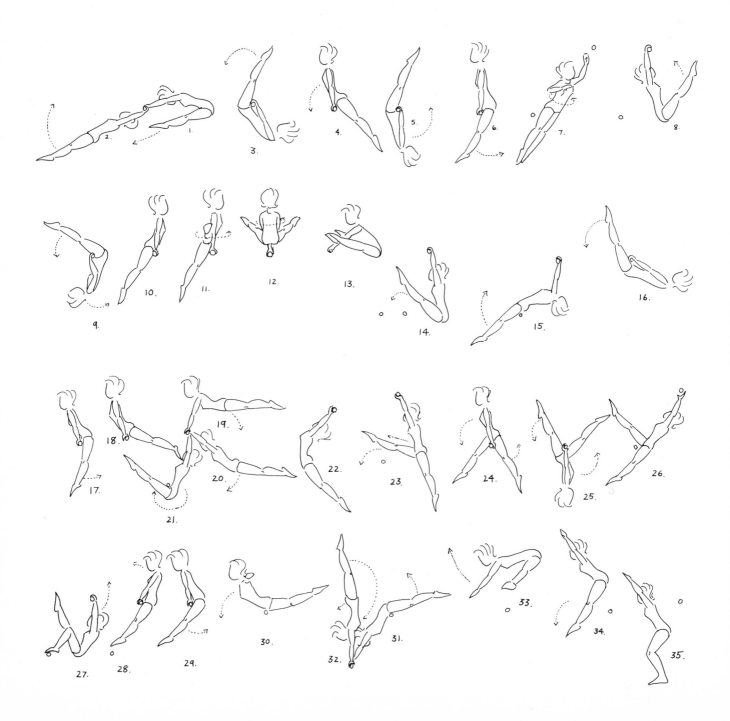

ADVANCED EXERCISES

1. Jump to glide kip mount, catch high bar with eagle or dislocate grip.

2. Whip to forward hip circle on low bar.

3. Immediately shoot through (stoop legs between arms).

4. Seat rise, catch high bar.

5. Rear kip to high bar.

6. Straddle cut to long hang, immediately release high bar and grasp low bar.

7. Glide kip double leg shoot through, catch high bar with regular grip.

8. Stationary kip.

9. Forward hip circle.

10. Immediately straddle "L" support from half turn (swing right foot over, left hand in reverse grip).

11. Underswing with half turn from high bar (turn toward the left).

12. Hecht dismount with 3/4 turn.

Chapter 14   Vaulting

Vaulting for women consists of movement over the side of the horse. There is a running approach, a take-off from a beat board, and momentary placing of the hands on the horse. The movement over the horse is varied and difficulty of the movement is rated on a 10-point scale in competition.

Fredrich Jahn is credited with devising the side horse with the pommels, in the early 1880's. The early German knights used it to improve their skills, and even suggested a head and tail for the horse. Men use the pommels on the horse for side horse competition, and remove them for long horse vaulting. Women originally used the side horse with the pommels, but later the pommels were removed. Vaulting was first introduced in 1828.

The exercises in vaulting are colorful, exciting, and can improve timing, balance, and coordination. Vaulting develops courage and confidence in the performer.

EQUIPMENT

Measurements of the horse for competition are 160 cm. (5 feet 3 inches) in length, and 40 cm. (15-3/4 inches) in width. The height from mat to the top of the horse, is 110 cm. (three feet 7 inches). A beat board or take-off board is used to assist in the spring. The beat board has standard measurements of 120 cm. (47-1/4 inches) in length, 60 cm. (23-5/8 inches) in width, and 12 cm. (4-3/4 inches) in height.

It is important that the elasticity of the board be even at the highest point. For women, the beat board should be covered with a layer of rubber. A regulation Reuther board is generally used in competition. The placing of the beat board with relationship to the horse depends upon the height of the individual performing, upon the type of vault to be performed, and upon the ability of the performer. Advanced performers place the board at greater distances from the horse than do beginners.

For competition, vaulting must be performed over the horse, but for school and developmental purposes a Swedish box is very effective. Vaulting may also be performed over a buck or a balance beam.

In the movements described in this chapter, the Swedish box is used both crosswise and lengthwise. Preliminary movements are suggested in which the horse is lowered and use is made of pommels.

Many of the preliminary activities lend themselves very well to class situations with large groups where the elements of fun and general fitness may be the major objectives. Pommels are occasionally used with beginning students, as will be noted in the following pages. Pommels are not used for competition.

TECHNIQUES

A vault consists of five main parts:

Run and take-off
Pre-flight
Arrival on the horse
After-flight
Landing

The five movements must be timed accurately, and coordinated so that each follows the other immediately without hesitation. In competition the vault is judged only from the take-off.

TEACHING SUGGESTIONS
Run and Take-off

1. To develop a good run and correct two-foot take-off from the beat board, practice without using the horse or Swedish box. Run, two-foot take-off on the beat board, and land on double thickness of mats.

2. Teach for a consistent run and approach. The run should not be slowed down as the performer approaches the beat board.

3. Focus so that the beat board and horse are seen with one glance at the start of the run. The beat board itself should not be watched, and about 10 feet from the board the focus should be on the horse.

4. The take-off should be executed with the feet parallel, and should be from the whole foot with a final push-off from the toes.

5. Measure the distance for the run by having each gymnast step off the distance and mark her starting point so that each run will be consistent.

6. The feet should hit half-way up the beat board. Mark the beat board if it is not already marked, so that the take-off is at the spot of greatest spring on the beat board.

7. At the take-off the knees are slightly bent and the body is in a vertical position. This type of landing on the beat board favors an upward as well as forward take-off.

8. At the take-off, the arms swing backward and then forward and upward.

9. The board take-off should be quick and sharp with a tightening of the hip and thigh muscles.

10. Placing the beat board with relationship to the horse will depend upon the height of the individual performer, and upon the ability of the performer. Advanced performers place the board at greater distances (a few inches more than their height), whereas beginners place the board closer to the horse.

11. The distance for vaulting, and the distance of the board from the horse, should be increased gradually, according to the ability of the gymnast.

Pre-flight

12. Students should study pictures of the correct position of the body as it goes over the horse. They should also observe fellow performers from the side, to get the best view of the vault. The beginner should strive for a good lift of the hips for a bent hip ascent, while the advanced performer should strive for the straight body ascent.

13. The center of gravity must rise and the body must rotate around it.

14. If the pre-flight is too high, there will not be enough horizontal speed left to get a good push-off, and a resultant good after-flight. Too high pre-flight results in riding the horse and a low after-flight.

15. Bent Hip Ascent
To develop a feeling of lifting the hips, the student may run to the horse or box and, with a two-foot take-off, just jump into the air. A feeling of pulling in with the abdominal muscles and lifting the hips as in a jackknife dive will help to get that feeling. At the same time, the performer must keep the head up. At no time should the chin be to the chest; rather, the neck should be arched backward so that the focus is on the mat three to five feet on the far side.

16. Straight Body Ascent
The straight body ascent is perhaps the most difficult movement to teach the performer, proportionately to the age of the student. Young children do not have fears, hence they are willing to run and "fly" through the air without inhibitions. The older student, however, just gradually builds security before she is willing to try this. To get a good take-off for the straight body ascent, there must be plenty of running space, the beat board must be far from the horse, and the speed of the run must be fast. Practice in using the horse lengthwise, or in using the box lengthwise, will assist in learning this technique. The body must be stretched, but not over-stretched.

Arrival on the Horse

17. The ideal position is with the arms straight, shoulders in line with the bands, and the hands flat and shoulder distance apart on the horse.

18. The hands are in line with the body, fingers always forward, and the position of the hands in relation to the body is always the same.

19. The weight is on the hands. The whole hand touches and the touch is very short and quick.

20. The function of the push-off is to bring the body obliquely upward.

21. The push-off from the horse is from the shoulders, with arms straight and it should be quick.

After-flight

22. The aim is height and distance which should equal the pre-flight, with the exceptions of the Hecht and Yamashita vaults.

23. The head should be up, with focus ahead and slightly upward. The push-off should be quick and forceful to propel the body diagonally upward.

24. If the after-flight does not equal the pre-flight, this usually indicates one of three things, or all of the following:
    a. The board is too far away for the gymnast's ability.
    b. The push-off of the horse is not strong enough.
    c. The push occurs not at the peak of the on-flight position, but later.

Landing

25. The landing is the final impression received by the observer. Therefore, a correct landing must be diligently practiced. The landing should be solidly in one spot which means that the shock is first absorbed by the toes, then heels, and finally the knees, which must bend. Balance must be acquired by a shifting of the trunk to a slightly forward position.

26. The arms may be spread forward, sideward, or diagonally upward, to assist in maintaining balance, but should be quickly placed to the sides as the erect position of attention is taken. Care should be taken to fall neither forward nor backward. Any excessive movement is an error, and for it points are subtracted.

27. Correct landing with no excessive movement is very difficult to accomplish, and even the best vaulters have difficulty with it. Therefor it should be taught from the very first vault, so that the gymnast learns good body control.

SAFETY

1. It is important to use gymnastic or tennis shoes for vaulting. Vaulting should not be done barefooted because the landing causes a great jar to the metatarsal heads and can have an adverse effect upon the arches of the feet.

2. In the beginning vaults, the performer should learn the proper run, the take-off, and the landing. Before actual vaulting is attempted, the correct running approach should be learned, with a jumping take-off from the floor, lifting the legs in the jump and landing correctly with the knees bending over the feet and the balance of the body slightly forward to avoid any backward fall.

3. The horse or box should be used at a lower height for the beginner and gradually raised as skill is perfected.

4. The beginner should have two spotters. The spotters should learn to hold the upper arm (near the armpit) with one hand, and grasp the performer's wrist with the other hand. Later on, one spotter is sufficient. The spotters must be careful not to stop or retard the momentum of the performer, but should move with the performer.

5. When pommels are removed as in regular vaulting, unless special equipment is available to fill the holes they should be covered with adhesive tape so that fingers will not slip into them.

6. At all times the vaulter must keep the elbows straight. A slightly bent elbow is very weak and cannot support the body weight.

SWEDISH BOX MOVEMENTS

The Swedish box, or vaulting box, is a four-section box so arranged that sections can be placed one upon another to increase the height. The base of the box is 36 inches wide by 60 inches long; the top section is 12 inches wide by 60 inches long. The box may be used at a height of 25, 33, 41, or 49 inches.

It is made of strong oak wood and has steel reinforcements, and the top is padded and upholstered.

Using the Box Sidewise

The following exercises will help the student to learn the approach, the spring, and the landing, all of which are necessary in vaulting. These activities are not difficult and usually are fun to perform, hence helpful in overcoming fear.

Even before using the box, students may play leap frog as a means of getting the feeling of vaulting over something. The base stands with trunk bent, knees straight, and hands braced on the knees. The performer places her hands on the upper back of the base and, with legs straddled, vaults over the base.

It is suggested that the box be lowered as far as possible and then gradually raised until the regulation height for the horse is obtained, which is 43 inches. The ingenuity of the instructor will undoubtedly add to the activities listed.

1. a. Spring to the top of the box and jump off.
        Take a running two-foot take-off, jump to
        the top of the box and jump off.
    b. Place several boxes at different places
        throughout the room and practice jumping
        from one to the other. Vary the heights of
        the boxes.

2. SWAN JUMP OFF

    The mount is the same as No. 1; jump off the
    box in a swan position.

3. STRADDLE JUMP OFF

    The mount is the same; jump off the box with
    legs in a wide straddle.

4. PIKE JUMP OFF

    The mount is the same; jump off the box with
    the legs in pike position, attempting to
    touch toes.

5. STAG LEAP TO SIDE

    The mount is the same; jump off the box, front
    leg bent and toe touching the knee of the
    other leg which is extended to the side.
    Land with feet together.

6. QUARTER, HALF AND WHOLE TURNS

    The mount is the same.
    a. Jump off the box with a quarter turn, end-
        ing with side to the box. Keep the body
        extended on the turn.
    b. Jump off the box with a half turn, ending
        with face to box.
    c. Jump off the box with a complete turn,
        end with back to box. Practice with turn
        to both sides.

7.   ARCH JUMP OFF WITH BOTH KNEES BENT

Jump from the box and arch backward, knees bending, feet to buttocks, arms over head.

8.   BATTEMENT TOURNEY

a.   Jump off the box, kicking the right leg forward and twisting the box in the air to the left; land on both feet facing the box.
b.   Reverse legs.

9.   KNEELING AND JUMP OFF

a.   Placing the hands on the box, land on both knees. Swing the arms backward and for-

ward and on the forward swing bring them up over the head and lift the legs and spring to the mat.

Note: This should be practiced on the floor first; i.e., from a kneeling position sit back on heels and with swing of arms forward and upward spring to the feet.

b.   Kneeling on horse or box (2 to 3 feet high), place hands down to the mat and forward roll off the box.

10.   SQUAT AND JUMP OFF

Spring from the beat board to a squat position on the box and swan jump off.

11.   DIVE ROLL OVER BOX

Dive over the box, placing hands on the far side of the box to catch weight; immediately tuck head and do a forward roll. This is a good exercise for learning a straight body ascent.

Using the Box Lengthwise

roll so that the hips just hit the end of the box and then swing the legs down with the feet to the mat.

b. Perform the above and immediately follow it with a forward roll on the mat.

12. JUMP TO SQUAT

From a regular take-off, jump to squat at the near end of the longwise box. Walk to the far end, step right, left, and as the right leg swings forward push off the left foot, and jump off landing on both feet.

13. SQUAT AND ROLL

Jump to a squat on the near end, and do a forward roll on the box, landing with the feet on the mat off the box.

15. FROG JUMP TO SWAN JUMP OFF

a. Spring to a squat position, reach forward placing the weight on the hands, spring again in a squat position (frog jump) to the end of the box; spring off the box with the body in an arched swan position.

b. Jump to a squat position, reach to the far end and straddle off.

c. Jump and immediately reach to the far end and straddle off. This is an excellent practice for the straight body ascent.

14. FORWARD ROLL

a. From a regular take-off place the hands on either side of the box about a foot from the near end. Catch the weight with the hands (do not take the weight on the head), lift the hips high and do a forward

16. STRADDLE AND TURN

Jump to a straddle position, do a half turn ending sitting on the box, back to the far end. Do a backward roll and dismount, hands on the box.

17. CARTWHEEL OFF (SWEDISH BOX)

Note: The cartwheel should be learned on the floor before attempting it on the box or horse.

Spring to a squat position on the near end, step forward placing hands at one side near to the end of the box. Kick up into a cartwheel but bring feet together above head so you land on both feet, knees bent. Spotter stands behind the performer and grasps the elbow of the second hand to be placed at the end of the box.

18. HANDSPRING ARCH OFF

Note: The handspring should be learned on the floor before attempting it on the box or horse.

a. Spring to a squat position on the near end, step forward placing hands near the end of the box. Kick up into a handspring, continue the arch and land on the mat, knees bent. Spotters should stand at either side of the box and grasp the performer at the wrist and shoulder, and should con-

trol the downward movement. This is an excellent preliminary to learning the handstand vault.

b. Step to one foot, step forward and handspring off.

c. Step up to one foot, at once handspring off.

d. Squat and handspring immediately (there is no stepping forward; push off with both feet).

SIDEHORSE MOVEMENTS

Vaulting may be performed across the Swedish box, the buck or the balance beam, though for competition all vaulting for women is across the horse. As mentioned previously, the five parts of the vault should be established at the very beginning. Also, adequate spotting should be used even for the beginning movements preliminary to actual vaulting.

To get the feeling of springing over something, a rolled mat may be placed in front of the beat board for the students to jump over. A regular springboard is quite effective in learning the technique of a two-foot take-off and correct landing with the knees bent.

Basic Skills

Note: Pommels are effective in learning the squat, straddle, stoop, and thief vaults; they should be removed as soon as the skill is mastered.

1. LANDING ON KNEES ON HORSE

a. After a correct take-off, land on the knees on the horse. The weight is caught by the hands which are placed on either side of the knees. Stand on the horse and jump down.

b. From the kneeling position, swing the arms backward and upward and spring from the knees to a standing position on the mat. (See sketch.)

Spotters stand on either side and grasp at the shoulder.

2.   LANDING IN SQUAT ON THE HORSE

Performed as the above, but land on the feet, hands on either side of the feet. Stand and jump down.

3.   LANDING IN STRADDLE ON THE HORSE

In this movement, spring to the horse, legs widely spread, hands between the legs. The head should be up and the focus forward. Push from hands and feet and lift arms over head, landing on both feet.

Spotting: One spotter stands on the far side facing the performer and grasps at the shoulders.

Bent Hip Ascent Vaults

4.   SQUAT VAULT—COMPETITIVE RATING 5.0 POINTS

After mastering No. 1 and No. 2, then the squat

vault should be attempted. The feet are brought through in a tucked position, toes pointed. There is a strong push-off with the hands and the feet do not touch the horse.

Spotting: Spotters on either side grasp upper arm of performer.

5.   STOOP VAULT—COMPETITIVE RATING 5.5 POINTS

From a two-foot take-off the hips are lifted high, head is up and eyes focus 3 to 5 feet past the horse. Legs remain straight as the body is in a pike position over the horse. A good push-off with the hands lifts the hips so that the legs can clear.

Spotting: Spotters stand on either side, grasping the shoulders.

6.   STRADDLE VAULT—COMPETITIVE RATING 5.5 POINTS

After mastering the straddle position with a stop on the horse, then the performer should straddle over the horse. The hips must be lifted high and the legs widely spread to clear the horse.

Spotting: Spotter stands in front facing the performer on the far side ready to grasp the shoulders.

7. FLANK VAULT (SIDE VAULT)—
COMPETITIVE RATING 5.0 POINTS

A flank vault may be performed to either side of the horse, depending upon the ability of the performer, but it should be practiced on both sides. The performer should designate whether it is to the right or left side of the horse, so that the spotter may change and not be struck by the legs as they clear the horse. Description is for one side; the reverse is true for the opposite side.

Flank vault to the left side.

a. Preliminary steps. Run and put right hand on the horse and right foot on the horse. Left leg is extended. Jump off.

b. Run and place both hands on top of the horse and vault over it—hips bent.

c. Flank vault.
With a run and two-foot take-off, place both hands on top of the horse, about the middle of the saddle. Lift the hips upward and sideways so that the left hip goes over the horse. As the whole body becomes parallel with the horse, lift the right hand. End with the back to the horse, arms spread on landing and to the sides for the finish posture.

Spotting: The spotter should stand on the far side of the horse and grasp the left shoulder.

Emphasis should be given to lift the body as high as possible so that it is almost horizontal, or above horizontal, as it clears the horse.

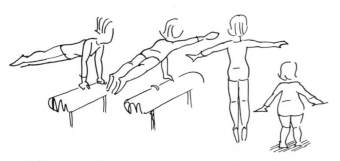

8. FRONT VAULT—COMPETITIVE
RATING 5.0 POINTS

From a two-foot take-off, place both hands on top of the saddle. The legs are lifted horizontally as the performer faces the horse. For a front vault over the right end, after both hands have been placed and the body is horizontal, the right hand should leave the horse for the landing. End with the left side to the horse.

Spotting: Same as for the flank vault.

Variations: a. Cross the hands on the horse, right on the far side; go over the horse in a tucked position.

b. Go over the horse in a piked position.

c. Go over with the body straight—horizontal.

d. Go over with a handstand position over the end.

e. Go over with a cartwheel position over the end.

9. REAR VAULT—COMPETITIVE
RATING 5.0 POINTS

From a two-foot take-off, place both hands on top of the horse at the saddle (middle). Lift the hips so that the buttocks are to the horse and the performer is looking upward. For a rear vault over the left side of the horse, after both hands have touched quickly lift the left hand, then the right hand is lifted as the hips clear the horse. End with the left hand on the horse, left side to the horse.

Spotting: The spotter should stand on the far side and grasp the right shoulder, but must be careful not to stop or retard the momentum of the performer. She should move with the performer.

Variations: a. Rear vault with 90-degree turn. After clearing the horse with the rear vault there is a 90-degree twist toward the horse, finishing the vault facing the horse. The hips should be high on the turn.

b. Rear vault with 180-degree turn. Turn toward the horse and end facing the opposite end of the original starting position. One hand supporting on landing.

10. THIEF OR WINDOW VAULT—
COMPETITIVE RATING 5.0 POINTS

Note: This vault can be learned more easily
if the pommels are on the horse for the
added height. Remove them as soon as
possible. Take off from one foot, passing
over the horse with one leg stretched,
the other flexed, without manual support.
Quickly join the legs placing hands on
horse after the legs have cleared the
horse. End standing rearways.

Spotting: Spotters should stand at each side.

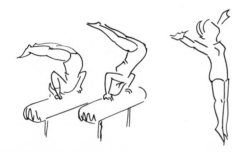

11. NECK- AND HEADSPRING VAULTS—
COMPETITIVE RATING 6.0 POINTS

a. Neckspring vault. After grasping the pommels, the back of the neck is placed on the
saddle; the body continues over the horse
in pike position. When the hips are past
the horse and the body feels off balance,
whip the legs sharply over head and down
to the mat.

b. Headspring. This is the same as neckspring except that the top of the head is
placed in the saddle instead of the neck.
The whipping action of the legs is delayed
until the hips are well past the horse.

As soon as the above are mastered with
use of the pommels, remove the pommels
and attempt to perform the movements
with hands placed flat on the saddle.

Spotting: Spotters on either side grasp upper arm
of performer.

12. BENT HIP ASCENT—HANDSPRING VAULT—
COMPETITIVE RATING NOT LISTED

Note: Deductions would be taken from straight
body ascent handspring for bent hips.

After mastering the various vaults under
No. 11, the handspring vault should be
performed. From a bent hip ascent, lift
the hips high as the straight arms are
placed on the saddle. As the hips reach the
off-balance position over the hands, whip
the legs over to the mat.

Spotting: Should be on either side at the shoulders.

13. STRADDLE VAULT WITH HALF TURN—
COMPETITIVE RATINGS 6.0 POINTS

This vault should not be attempted until No. 6
has been mastered.

The turn comes as the arms push off.
It is difficult to spot this vault, hence the
necessity of having complete mastery of
the straddle vault.

Spotting: Spotter may stand so that after the turn is
made she will be behind the performer to
catch her at the waist if her leg should be
caught.

Straight Body Ascent Vaults

The straight body ascent is important to master for all who are interested in competitive vaulting. In the preliminary discussion it was stated that using the horse or Swedish box lengthwise will help the performer to get the feeling of a straight body ascent. To accomplish this, the beat board must be 4 to 5 feet or more from the horse and the performer must get the feeling of "flying" through the air. If most of the previous vaults have been mastered, the performer should be ready to develop the straight body ascent.

To get the straight body ascent, run and take off and swing the arms forward and upward and simultaneously kick the legs up as though leading with the heels. The lifting of the heels is comparable to the emphasis of the lifting of the hips in the bent hip ascent.

A preliminary exercise for this position may be practiced on the floor. From a kneeling position, sit on the heels, place the hands on the floor and kick the legs straight up and back, then squat through between the hands to long sitting on the floor.

Most of the vaults may be performed at either side.

14.   LAYOUT SQUAT VAULT—8.5 POINTS

From a two-foot take-off with the beat board placed in front of the horse and 4 to 5 feet or more from the horse, the body is lifted so that the legs are above the horizontal position just as the hands touch the horse. From this position the knees are tucked to the chest while simultaneously pushing with the hands so that the upper body is lifted. As the feet reach toward the mat the arms are extended over the head and the body is arched slightly backward. Then the arms are brought to the sides on the landing.

Note: If the body is only horizontal at the pre-flight, the vault is worth only 6.5 points.

Spotting: The spotters should stand on the far side of the horse and grasp the shoulder and

wrist of the performer. A spotter should also stand between the beat board and the horse, pushing upward on the hips and thighs to assist the straight body position.

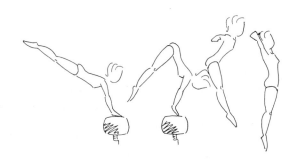

15.   LAYOUT STOOP VAULT—9 POINTS

With the same preparation as the squat vault, the hands are held only momentarily on the horse and as soon as the feet are brought down in a pike position the hands leave the horse and are swung sideward and upward and the body goes from a pike position to a slightly arched position on the landing.

Note: If the body is only horizontal at the pre-flight, the value of the vault is only 7.0 points.

Spotting: A spotter should stand on either side of the performer grasping the wrist and shoulders.

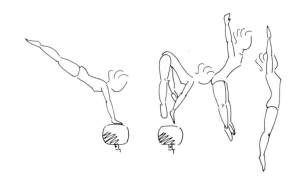

16.   LAYOUT STRADDLE VAULT—9.0 POINTS

The approach is the same as for the stoop vault. As the body assumes the layout position, the straight legs are swung to the side and straddled over the horse. Push hard with the hands and lift the upper body. Arch the body after the legs have cleared the horse.

Spotting: Same as for Straddle Vault No. 6.

17. HANDSPRING VAULT—9.7 POINTS

From a two-foot take-off the arms are held straight and the head is slightly lifted. From the handstand position on the horse the body continues over in an arch, the head remaining between the hands. The body continues the arch as the feet lead toward the mat. The weight rolls from the hand to the fingers, and the fingers push as the heels reach slightly past the vertical.

Variations: a. Handspring half turn.

b. Handspring full turn.

Spotting: A spotter should stand on each side of performer, supporting the wrist and shoulder. Also, a spotter should stand between the beat board and horse, and push upward on the hips to assist the straight body position.

Steps in learning: Lower the horse for the initial trials. Preliminary use of the box will give the feeling of handstand position and arch-off.

18. HANDSTAND QUARTER TURN—10 POINTS

The approach is the same as for the handspring vault, but as the body reaches the balanced inverted position the left arm is lifted and the body is arched and turned a quarter turn to the right in the vertical position. The performer lands with the right side to the horse.

Spotting: A spotter should stand on the far side and grasp the right wrist and shoulder. A second spotter may stand between the beat

board and the horse and push upward on the hips and thighs in the straight body ascent, if this is needed.

19. HANDSTAND QUARTER TURN PIVOT CARTWHEEL—10 POINTS

The approach is the same as for the handstand. When the inverted position is reached, lift the left hand and quarter turn to the right; put the left hand beside the right hand and continue to turn, lifting the right hand as in a cartwheel. End with the left side to the horse.

Spotting: A spotter should stand on the far side grasping the left wrist and shoulder to allow for the turn. A second spotter may stand between the beat board and the horse and push upward on the hips in the straight body ascent.

20. GIANT CARTWHEEL—9.8 POINTS

From a run and two-foot take-off the performer starts the cartwheel movement as soon as the body leaves the beat board by a quarter turn so that the left hand touches the horse first as the legs swing up to the vertical position. When the body is inverted and the weight is transferred to the right hand, the left hand then the right hand push off the horse to complete the cartwheel. The performer ends with the right side to the horse.

Spotting: Stand in back and on the far side; grasp the right shoulder and control the landing.

**21.   GIANT CARTWHEEL (HALF TURN)—
10 POINTS**

The approach, take-off, pre-flight, and arrival on the horse is the same as for No. 20 above. After leaving the horse do a half turn. Land sideways to the horse.

Variation: Giant cartwheel full turn.

Spotting: Spotter should stand so that after the initiation of the turn is made she will be behind the performer to catch her at the waist and help her to finish the turn.

**23.   HECHT-SWAN VAULT WITH
FULL TWIST—10 POINTS**

The approach is similar to No. 22, however as the Hecht is initiated, one arm swings down across the body as the body makes a full twist, landing with the back to the horse.

Spotting: Use first an overhead twisting belt. Then spot at the waist to help the twist.

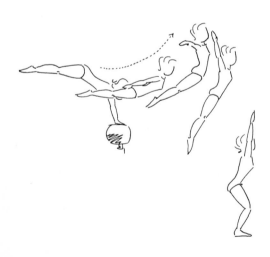

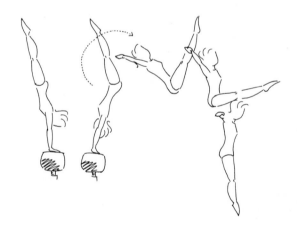

**22.   HECHT SWAN VAULT
(LEGS TOGETHER)—10 POINTS**

The approach is the same as for a stoop or squat vault, but do not straighten the body completely. Keep the hips slightly bent. A very forceful take-off is necessary, and a strong push with the hands and shoulders to clear the horse in the swan position. This position of the body is held until the performer passes over the horse in the swan position.

Spotting: Two spotters, one on each side. One should grasp the hand and shoulder and help the performer to go over the horse.

24.   YAMASHITA VAULT—10 POINTS

The approach is the same as for the handspring vault, however after the vertical position over the horse, give a push with the hands and bend at the hips and swing the arms and head upward, to achieve a free V seat position. Hold the pike for a second, then stretch legs forward and downward for landing. Land with back to the horse.

Note: The after flight in the Yamashita is higher and shorter than the pre-flight arc.

Spotting: Use an overhead belt first, then spot at the waist to help the gymnast to lift hips and arms to a V seat position and assist her in landing.

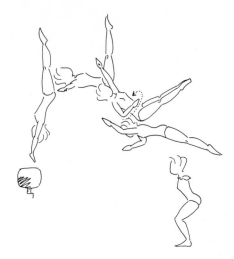

25.   YAMASHITA HALF TURN—10 POINTS

The approach is the same as for the handspring vault. From the vertical position the body pushes away from the horse as in No. 24, but the upper body stays in a horizontal position with a right angle at the hips, feet pointed upward. As the feet are lowered, one arm swings across the body, twisting the body in the lay-out position, end facing the horse.

Spotting: Use an overhead twisting belt first. Then spot at the waist to help the twist.

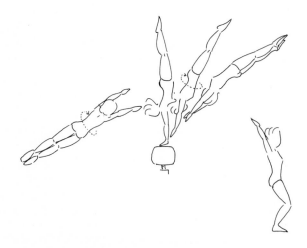

26.   HALF TURN INTO HANDSTAND, HALF TURN OUT—10 POINTS

From a two-foot take-off, the gymnast starts the half twist and lands on the horse in a handstand position facing the opposite direction. After the hands leave the horse the body continues to twist in the same direction, and the performer lands rearways to the horse.

Spotting: This should be learned with an overhead twisting belt.

COMPETITIVE EXERCISES

In advanced competition, the vaults are always performed with straight body ascent. For school work and for beginners the bent hip ascent is frequently used. The compulsory vaults are listed in the current Division for Girls' and Women's Sports Gymnastic Guide, the USGF Compulsory Guide, or the AAU Rule Book for each classification. The vaulter should perfect the compulsory vault, and then select one or two other vaults for the optional competition. It is advisable to select two vaults that have 10-point rating, and to work for perfection in them. Detailed attention must be given to the take-off, the position over the horse, and the landing. A controlled landing is difficult because of the momentum of the vault. Even in everyday practice and in school situations, good form should be emphasized throughout the vault so that it becomes second nature for the performer.

In compulsory vaulting the same vault is performed twice and the better performance is accepted. In voluntary vaulting the same vault may be performed twice, or two different vaults may be performed, and the better vault is accepted. In competition, aid by the coach or spotter during the vault will disqualify the vault. The presence of the spotter is acceptable for safety purposes, but she should refrain from touching the performer except in emergencies.

The following vaults are suggested for competition in the three classifications:

Beginning Vaults

The value of beginning vaults has been established by the Division for Girls' and Women's Sports of the American Association for Health, Physical Education, and Recreation, and by the United States Gymnastic Federation. These vaults are usually performed in school and club beginning meets. All the vaults are performed with a bent-hip ascent.

	Vault	Rating
1.	Flank vault	5.0
2.	Front vault	5.0
3.	Rear vault	5.0
4.	Thief vault	5.0
5.	Squat (bent-hip)	5.0
5.	Stoop (bent-hip)	5.5
7.	Straddle (bent-hip)	5.5
8.	Neck spring	6.0
9.	Headspring	6.0

Note: All the vaults listed above may be performed with a half twist during the after flight, which will increase the value by .5 point.

Intermediate Vaults

These vaults are performed with a straight body ascent, but are below 10 points.

1.	Squat (body horizontal)	7.5
2.	Stoop (body horizontal)	8.0
3.	Straddle (body horizontal)	8.0
4.	Layout squat (body above horizontal 45-degree angle)	8.5
5.	Layout stoop (body above horizontal 45-degree angle)	9.0
6.	Straddle layout (body above horizontal 45 degrees)	9.0
7.	Handspring	9.7
8.	Giant cartwheel	9.8

   (Note: The giant cartwheel is a difficult vault and is usually performed by advanced gymnasts.)

Advanced Vaults

These vaults are all 10 point rating by the F.I.G. (International Federation of Gymnastics). Most of the advanced vaults require turns, i.e., (a) vaults with turn during the pre-flight; (b) vaults with turn during the after-flight; and (c) vaults with turns in both flights. The turns may be quarter, half, or full turns. All of these vaults are performed with a straight body ascent.

1. Giant cartwheel with quarter, half, three-quarter, or full turn.
2. Handstand, quarter, half, or full turn.
3. Half turn on to the horse, handstand, half turn or full turn off.
4. Hecht vault.
5. Yamashita vault.

Chapter 15   Trampoline

The trampoline became a part of YMCA equipment about thirty years ago (around 1940), and has become popular in schools within the past 10 or more years. There are many conflicting reports as to the origin of the trampoline. Some say the Eskimos had a similar sport in that several persons held a large "bed" and tossed the performer into the air. It is also stated that a circus acrobat of the Middle Ages, whose name was "du Trampoline" may have been the originator of the trampoline. The modern trampoline as we know it today has been developed by the Nissen Trampoline Company, and has been gradually increasing in popularity since 1939.

The trampoline has been accepted as an official event in gymnastics meets in this country, but has not been accepted in the Olympic Games. World Trampoline Championship was initiated in 1964. Judy Wills of the United States won the first five World Championships.

EQUIPMENT

The size of the trampoline, or rebound tumbling unit, varies greatly although two sizes are commonly used: One, 9 x 15 feet with a bed of 6 x 12 feet, is commonly used in schools; a larger frame, 10 x 17 feet with a bed of 7 x 14 feet, is used in colleges and some high schools. There is a movement toward making the larger size the official trampoline for competition. Details of competition in trampoline for girls are given in Chapter 20, Judging.

TECHNIQUES
Positions

1. Layout—A position of the body in full extension, arms raised horizontally or over head.

2. Arch-out—A position of the body in hyperextension, back forming a concave bow, chest well out, arms raised horizontally.

3. Pike—A position of the body with hips well flexed, legs straight, knees locked, hands clasp-ing the under sides of the legs just below the knees. Arms may be extended to the sides for open pike position.

4. Tuck—A position of the body with hips and knees fully flexed, head tucked forward or tilted back, depending upon the direction of rotation; knees close to chest, heels close to buttocks, and hands clasping the shins.

Actions

5. Kick-out—Extending from tuck to pike position.

6. Somersault—A complete forward or backward rotation of the body on its transverse axis, performed in the air, from any take-off position.

7. Forward-turnover—Any fraction of a forward somersault from any take-off position.

8. Backover—Any fraction of a backward somersault from any take-off position.

9. Check, checking Slowing or halting rotation in side spins, twists, turnovers, or somersaults.

10. Come-out—Extending and checking preparatory to landing.

11. Break, breaking—Preventing or "killing" rebound by flexing the knees to absorb the recoil of the bed.

12. Spot, spotting—Executing a take-off and landing on the same spot on the bed unless specifically instructed otherwise.

13. Guard, guarding—Action of assistants stationed to aid the performer in maintaining control and position while learning new exercises.

14. Twists—Rotation of the body on its longitudinal axis.

15. Side-spin—Rotation of the body on its dorso-ventral axis.

16. Working the bed—The coordination of various actions required to obtain maximum lift from the bed without sacrifice of control.

17. Beat—Combination of techniques employed in executing the three phases of any given bounce; i.e., the drop during which the body is adjusted into position for landing; the landing and the take-off, during which the bed is "worked" to obtain maximum lift and control.

18. Cast—An off-balance take-off, resulting from unequal bed set, tilted bed, or faulty body mechanics.

19. The drop—During which movement is completed and the body assumes the proper position for landing.

20. Free bounce—Feet bounce, used for preparation.

21. The landing—During which various body actions are coordinated to work the bed.

22. Take-off—The lift and control necessary for recovery of the execution for the next movement to take place.

SAFETY

If carefully used and adequately supervised, the trampoline is not a dangerous piece of equipment. It should always be taught by a competent instructor, and should be kept locked except when supervised. Safety rules must be learned from the first lesson, and should be stressed repeatedly. Some of the basic safety principles are:

1. Use pads on the trampoline metal frame, both ends and sides.

2. Adequate instruction in opening and closing the trampoline should eliminate any unnecessary finger or hand injuries.

3. During instruction or practice periods, members of the class should be stationed around the trampoline to act as guards, ready to assist the performer should she lose control, and to prevent her landing on the springs or the frame. The minimum number of spotters is six, one on each end and two on each side.

4. Avoid fatigue by keeping practice periods short. This will also allow for greater rotation of students.

5. Tumbling shoes should be worn on the bed; socks may be permitted but they are slippery. A regulation tumbling shoe is best. The person should not be permitted to perform barefooted because of the chances of pulling a toe nail and for sanitary reasons.

6. The overhead belt should be used in learning all advanced skills such as somersaults and advanced twisting movements.

TEACHING SUGGESTIONS

Following are suggestions aimed at improving trampoline teaching. They are compiled from many sources and teaching experiences.

1. Mount. When mounting the trampoline for the first time, the student should be cautioned not to step on the suspension system (springs or shocks), but should place her weight on the frame while climbing up, and then transfer her weight to the bed itself. Do not step on the frame with both feet as it is slippery. At first, it might be simpler to use a small stool such as a stall bar stool until the beginner feels more at home.

2. Dismount. When dismounting the weight of the body is supported by the arm; as the performer dismounts, care should be used not to step on the springs or cables but to rest the hand on the steel railing and vault to the floor. A mat should be on the floor and care taken to alight upon the mat easily, since the legs will not be accustomed to the resistance of the floor after a session of bouncing.

3. Make a brief verbal explanation of each stunt prior to demonstrating it, emphasizing the more important aspects. Caution: Do not over-talk during the demonstration.

4. The technique of absorbing or killing the bounce or breaking by bending the knees to stop the bed, should be taught at the first lesson.

5. When possible, teach the positive approach; e.g., "Do it this way," not "Don't do this."

6. Don't delay the student's attempt to try the stunt after it has been discussed, demonstrated, and observed.

7. All new stunts should be learned at low elevation. Aim for control not height.

8. Teach the performer vertical bounce control so that the performer can "spot" her bounces before she is permitted to bounce high.

9. Teach balanced take-offs so that the performer will be moving vertically only and not horizontally when landing, thus reducing the chances of abrasions and strains.

10. Make on-the-spot corrections without stopping the activity of the group. Let class become

aware of the mistakes of others, through corrections given by the instructor while a student is performing.

11. Put individual stunts together in series as soon as each new stunt is learned.

12. Be alert and enforce all safety procedures.

13. Teach mastery of fundamentals before further progression. It is a good rule to have the student perform the same bounce three times in succession in good form before being permitted to go to the next skill. For example, she must do a seat drop to feet, to seat, to feet, to seat, with no bounces in between before she is ready to go on to the next skill.

14. Spotters should learn to reach out toward the performer, to keep her on the bed, but should not push her—simply act as a barrier so that the performer does not leave the bed.

15. At no time should the performer's eyes be shut during the execution of a stunt.

16. No bouncing from the trampoline bed to the floor should be allowed except for the more experienced and advanced persons. Mats should be on the floor at the point of leaving the bed.

17. No horseplay should be permitted; be very alert to fatigue. Students should not be allowed to continue if there are any signs of fatigue.

18. Somersaults should be learned through lead-up skills.

19. Backward and forward somersaults and their variations should be learned with a spotter's belt.

20. A progress chart will motivate students and will help the teacher to individualize the instruction. The student is allowed to check off each stunt as it is mastered. This will also remind them of the need for progression.

MOVEMENTS

Basic Skills

1. BASIC BOUNCE

   The basic bounce is a vertical movement from a two-foot take-off from the bed. The feet are about shoulder distance apart on the bed, and should be brought together with toes pointed in the air, and spread again for landing. The arms move from a low curved position in front to above shoulder level. The arms should always be in front of the body for vertical balance. The focus

should be about 5 or 6 feet in front of the performer at the edge of the bed. Focus at this point for all stunts unless otherwise stated.

2. THE BREAK

   The performer should learn to bend the knees upon landing on the bed, to stop the action of the bed. The performer must master the basic bounce and break before going on to variations of the basic bounce.

3. VARIATIONS OF THE BASIC BOUNCE

3.1 Swan bounce. When the body is in the air, it assumes a swan position, body is arched, arms above head and backward.

3.2 Tuck bounce. When the body is in the air, the knees are bent tightly to the chest, hands clasping the shins. The body should be vertical, head in line with body.

3.3 Jackknife. When the body is in the air, the hips are bent, legs extended, head to knees, arms to feet.

3.4 Open pike. When the body is in the air the hips are bent, legs extended, body slightly bent forward, arms horizontal.

3.5 Straddle pike position. When in the air the body is in a pike position with the legs spread, hands to feet.

3.6 Stag leap. When in the air the body is twisted slightly to the right as the left knee is in front knee bending and touching the right knee with the left foot. Right leg is extended.

3.7 Turns. The turns should be made with the body in a vertical plane, and should be controlled so that the feet return to the same spot. The turn may be a quarter, half, or full turn in the air.

3.8 Rope jumping. Jumping rope on the trampoline helps to gain a better rhythm in the bounce.

All of the basic bounces can be practiced with music, to get the feeling of a rhythmic bounce.

4. SEAT DROP

From a vertical position of the body in the air, lift the feet upward and land on the seat, legs extended forward, toes pointed. Hands are at the sides slightly behind the hips,

fingers pointed forward to feet. Hands and feet hit the bed simultaneously. Elbows may be slightly bent. There is a slight backward lean on the landing, then a forward lean for the rebound.

Have the beginner take the correct sitting position in the center of the bed. Have the guards around the trampoline start her bouncing by pushing the bed. When she feels capable she should come to her feet.

5. HANDS AND KNEES DROP (FOUR-POINT)

From a vertical position in the air, lift the hips, keep the trunk parallel to the bed, and drop on the knees and lower legs and on the hands. All four points hit simultaneously. Knees are about 18 inches apart, the hands shoulder distance apart, fingers forward. Head is in line with the trunk. Note: If the performer has difficulty keeping her trunk parallel to the bed, let her spot between her hands on the bed. This usually helps to correct the mistake.

6. KNEE DROP

From the vertical position in the air, bend at the knees only, keeping the back, shoulders, and head in correct alignment. Knees are about 12 to 18 inches apart, and the weight is evenly distributed on the knee and lower leg.

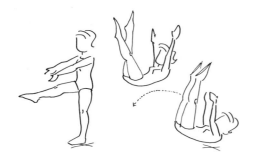

As soon as all the bounces described have been mastered they should be put into combinations; e.g., from a seat drop to four-point to front to standing. Seat, straddle through to front, to knee, to standing. Have the students make up various combinations of these skills. It might be advisable to establish a 5- or 6-point sequence for them to learn for testing purposes.

7. BACK DROPS

7.1 Straight knee back drop. Start standing on the bed, kick right foot upward as though kicking a ball held in front in the hands. Keep the back in this rounded position and fall backward to the bed as the other leg is also lifted. Keep the chin tucked to the chest by looking at the frame the whole way down. Land on the upper back, neck off the bed.

b. When the above is mastered try to take a small bounce and drop backward. The hands may be clasped in back of the head to help keep the head forward so there will not be a neck snap during the drop.

7.2 Kick-out back drop. From a tucked position in the air, kick the legs out forward as you land in the back drop position. Rebound again with the legs straight.

8. FRONT DROP

8.1 Front drop from four-point. Start from a four-point or hands-and-knees drop to learn the front drop. From the four-point extend the legs to the rear and the arms forward, bent at elbows; weight is taken on the forearms and thighs. The middle of the body (waist) should land where the feet were on the bed.

8.2 Front drop from standing. When the body is in the air the hips are lifted, body near to a horizontal position. The waist should land on the bed where the feet were placed. The performer may learn to do the front from a swan position or jackknife.

Combinations and Twists

9. HALF TWIST TO SEAT

The body is extended into the air, the arms stretched over the head. The turn should be initiated by the shoulders and body, rather than by the head. End in a seat drop facing the opposite direction.

10. SWIVEL HIPS (SEAT, HALF TWIST TO SEAT)

From a seat drop lift the body to an extension in the air, push with the arms and swing them up over the head and simultaneously swing the legs underneath the body, swing arms down and land in a seat drop again, facing the opposite direction.

11.   SEAT DROP TO FRONT

11.1   Piked. From a seat drop lift the hips in a pike position in the air, and land in a front drop.

11.2   Tucked. From the seat drop lift the hips and tuck the knees to the chest in the air. Land in a front drop. (See sketch.)

11.3   Straddle. From the seat drop swing the legs in a wide straddle in the air, swinging the legs to the rear and ending in a front drop.

12.   FRONT DROP TO SIT DROP

From front drop lift to a semi-pike position and land in a seat drop, facing the same direction.

13.   HALF TWIST TO BACK DROP

Explained for a twist to the left. On the take-off from the bed the body leans slightly forward and starts the twist as the right arm is swung low across the body near the knees, the head turning last. End in a back drop with the legs extended.

14.   BACK DROP TO FRONT DROP

14.1   Tucked. From the back drop come to a tucked position in the air, and drop into a front drop.

14.2   Piked. Try the same movement in a piked position.

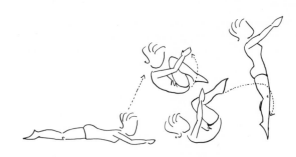

15.   FRONT DROP TO BACK DROP

After landing in a front drop, push off immediately so that the knees and body go into a tucked position. Do the back drop in the tucked position, and then kick out for rebound to standing.

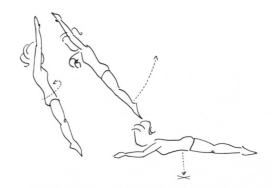

16.   HALF TWIST TO FRONT DROP (AIRPLANE)

From the take-off lean slightly backward, the arms going up over the head. As the body twists they lift upward and backward in a swan position. The twist is started by the hips followed by head and shoulders. End in a front drop.

17. HALF TWIST FROM BACK DROP

From a tucked back drop, kick out to an almost horizontal position. The body twists to the right. The head turns last. The arms drop to the sides, and the legs swing under to land on the bed.

18. HALF TURN TABLE

18.1 Half turn table tucked. From the front drop on the bed, push with the hands and knees and tuck the knees to the chest while in the air and twist. Land in a front drop facing the opposite direction.

18.2 Half turn table piked. From the front drop on the bed, push with the hands into a pike position as the body makes a half turn ending in a front drop facing the opposite direction (see sketch).

18.3 Full turn table. The body makes a complete turn, ending in the original position.

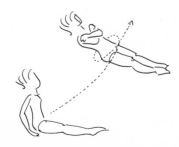

19. BARREL ROLL

From a seat drop lift the body straight into the air to about a 60-degree angle, twisting

completely around and using the hips to turn the body. Get the feeling of lifting with the mid-section of the body and twisting the body. Arms are crossed on the chest during the twist. End in original starting position.

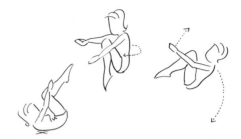

20. CRADLES

20.1 Twisting cradle simple in tucked position. From a back drop in tucked position, kick out the legs and twist the body as it comes to a full tucked position in the air. Land in a tucked back drop facing the opposite direction.

20.2 Try the same movement with a pike position.

Forward Somersaults

These are the advanced stunts and, except for the first few of them, they should be learned with assistance of the overhead safety belt. In some instances where the stunts are learned carefully in progression, the forward tucked somersault may be learned without the belt; however, for safety in most school situations the belt should be used.

21. FORWARD ROLL FROM SQUAT

Practice a regular forward roll on the bed. Practice a forward roll without the use of hands.

22. HANDS AND KNEES TURNTUCK

From a hands-and-knees (four-point) drop, tuck the head and turn over, extending the legs as the seat comes to the trampoline.

23. KNEE DROP, TURNPIKE

From a knee drop, tuck the head and turn over
to a seat drop.

24. TURNPIKE TO SEAT

From a feet bounce, turn over to a sitting
position. Start bending forward at the waist
by moving the hips backward and drop the
head and shoulders forward. The arms
move from over head to side horizontal
when the body is upside down, and to the
sides as the seat position is taken.

25. TURN TUCKED TO SEAT

From a regular bounce, shift the hips backward and the shoulders forward as you
leave the bed. The head is ducked at the
peak of the jump. Tuck the body and clasp
the knees. The legs straighten as you come
to a sit with a backward leaning position.
Rebound to standing.

26. TUCKED FORWARD SOMERSAULT

From a regular bounce, tucked forward turnover to feet. Reach up with the arms on
the take-off. At the height of the lift, bend
the waist and knees and hold onto the shins
with the hands. Hold the tucked position;
open out when the legs are almost under
the body. Keep the eyes open throughout.

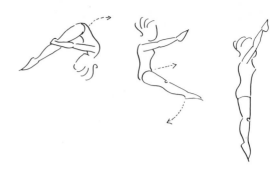

27. PIKED FORWARD SOMERSAULT

From the feet, pike forward turnover to feet.
As you are being lifted into the air, bend
sharply at the waist tucking the head and
grasping the legs behind the knees. Hold
the closed pike position until legs are
parallel to the bed, then open at the waist
without letting the knees bend.

28. FORWARD DIVE TO BACK DROP

This is a forward turnover, but with less
turnover than to a sit landing. The take-
off from the moderate bounce is with a
forward bend at the waist, as in the beginning of a turnpike sit. The head is not
tucked as the peak is reached, but the
performer continues to look at the bed.
When near the mat and descending in an
inverted position, she quickly ducks the
head and bends more at the waist, and
drops onto the back as in a straight knee
back drop.

29. TUCKED FORWARD ONE-AND-A-QUARTER
SOMERSAULT

A feet, tucked turn, to a front landing. Start
as for a forward tucked somersault; hold
the tuck a little longer, opening out to a
front drop when the body is horizontal.

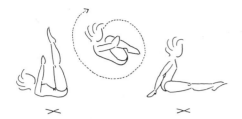

**30. FORWARD SOMERSAULT FROM
BACK DROP TO SIT DROP**

From a kick-out back drop, kick out forward
and upward to about a 45-degree angle with
the feet. Follow the kick-out by immediately ducking the head and doubling into a
hands-on-shins tuck. Open out of the tuck
to a straight seat landing.

Back Somersaults

These skills are best learned by an overhead
safety belt; a hand belt or hand spotting may be
used by experienced persons.

31. BACK PULLOVER

From a low bounce grasp underneath the knees
in the air, body in a pike position. Land
on the buttocks, holding the legs straight,
and turn over backward from a seat to a
feet landing.

This might be preceded by a regular
backward roll to get the feeling of the
mat.

32. TUCKED BACKWARD SOMERSAULT

Review the tucked position with a regular
bounce. After the regular bounce, push the
hips forward and pull the shoulders back
right after the take-off. At the height of
the bounce tuck and grasp the shins. The
head goes backward and the eyes are
focused on the trampoline bed. The body
is opened when the turn is about three-
fourths around.

33. SEMI-TUCKED BACK (TRAMP BACK)

This is a back somersault in a semi-tucked
position. It is designed to assist in moving
from one stunt to another. The movement
is like a skin-the-cat on the rings.

34. OPEN BACKWARD SOMERSAULT

At the beginning of the lift from the bed the
backward-bending action is started. This
gives the body rotation. The body remains
arched throughout most of the stunt, but
the knees bend to assist in the rotation.
Open up to a feet landing.

35. BACKWARD TUCKED ONE-AND-A-QUARTER SOMERSAULT

Do a backward somersault in a tucked position, continue holding the tucked position and finally release and straighten the legs to land in a sit position.

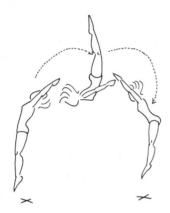

36. LAYOUT BACKWARD SOMERSAULT (BACKWARD SWAN)

At the beginning of the lift from the bed, the backward bending action is started. This gives the body rotation. The body remains arched throughout the stunt. The preliminary bounces should be high, with the arms thrown upward and backward as in a swan dive. The knees are kept straight as possible with as much body arch as possible.

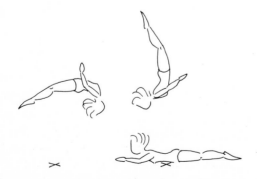

37. HALF-BACK SOMERSAULT

The take-off is the same as for the backward somersault in that the body is bent back-

ward and the arms are shoulder high. Turn and come forward, bending the knees slightly and bringing the arms forward in preparation for the front landing.

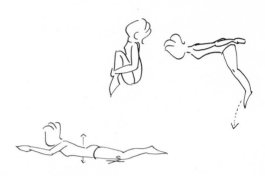

38. TUCKED CODY

A tucked backward somersault from a front landing. The front landing is slightly different in that there is a slight bending at the waist and the knees hit a little before the chest and arms. The knees start to bend at the contact, or slightly before. Push off with the hands, pull the head backward, and start the tuck. As the feet open out for landing, the arms are at the sides ready for the next swing into the following movement.

This stunt should always be learned with a safety belt, and started from a good take-off.

Twisting Somersaults

These are the most difficult stunts and, with the exception of the barani, should be learned with the aid of a "twisting" belt.

39. BARANI

Sequence in learning without a belt.

39.1 Knee barani. From a knee drop with arms raised, place the hands on the bed, arms straight, to a momentary handstand and with a half twist turn and land on the knees facing the opposite direction.

39.2 Perform a knee drop, half twist in the air in the inverted position without the hands on the mat; land in a knee drop.

39.3 Regular barani. (The barani is a half twisting piked forward somersault, done without ducking the head or looking away from the bed.)

From a take-off bend forward at the waist as in a piked forward somersault, except that the head is not ducked. Arms are spread sideways. If twisting to the left, swing the right arm across past the knees. The shoulders turn with the arm swing. Open at the waist from a pike to a straight position as the hips follow the shoulder twist. The arms drop close to the body. End on the feet facing the opposite direction.

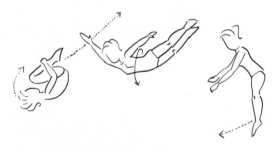

40. HALF TWISTING TUCKED FORWARD SOMERSAULT

The take-off is the same as for a tucked forward somersault, except that there should be an attempt to bend forward a little sooner and more forcefully, and to tuck earlier. When the tuck position is a little more than half-way over, straighten the knees and open at the waist with a hip-twisting action. The twist is from the hips with the head following; arms remain close to the body. Land in a standing position facing the opposite direction from starting.

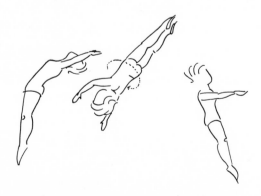

41. HALF TWISTING OPEN BACKWARD SOMERSAULT

The left twist is analyzed. Start as for layout somersault. When a little past half-way over, forcefully twist the lower body, hips, and legs to the left without bending at the waist. The shoulders and head follow the hips. End on the feet facing the opposite direction.

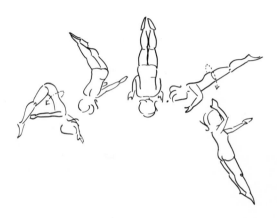

42. FULL TWISTING FORWARD SOMERSAULT

The first action of this stunt is a forward bend at the waist, with slightly twisting shoulders and trunk—much as in a barani. The shoulders initiate the twist, the arms remain close to the body, and the head follows the twist. End on the feet facing the same direction as at the start.

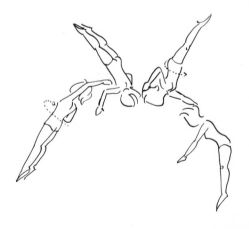

43. FULL TWISTING BACKWARD SOMERSAULT

The take-off is much the same as for a back layout somersault, except that the head is not pulled back all the way. The twist starts from the head and shoulders. When half of the twist has been completed the arms come in close to the body to finish the twist. The body is bent at the waist and the arms are spread to stop the spin.

BEGINNING SKILLS AND COMBINATIONS

Usually the beginning gymnast will select from skills No. 1 to No. 20 for her routine. These stunts can be put into various combinations.

Beginning Combinations

1. Knee drop; to seat drop; to hands and knees; to front drop; to feet.

2. Swivel hips; straddle through to front drop; half twist to back drop; to feet.

3. Turntable; half twist to back drop; to feet.

4. Cradle; from the second back drop go to front drop; half twist to seat drop; to feet.

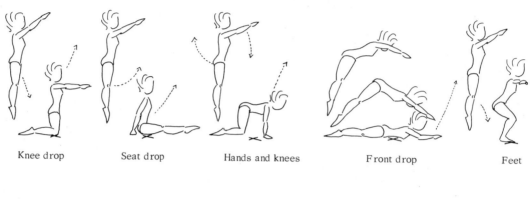

1.   Knee drop   Seat drop   Hands and knees   Front drop   Feet

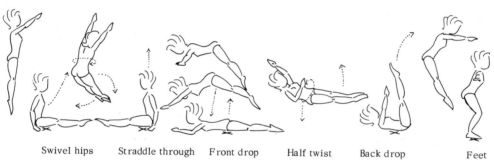

2.   Swivel hips   Straddle through   Front drop   Half twist   Back drop   Feet

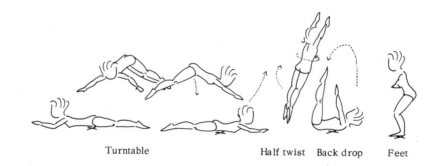

3.   Turntable   Half twist   Back drop   Feet

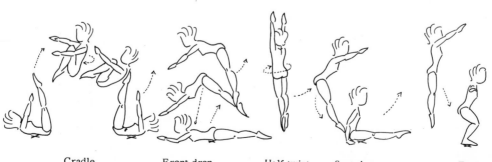

4.   Cradle   Front drop   Half twist   Seat drop   Feet

INTERMEDIATE SKILLS AND COMBINATIONS

Usually an intermediate gymnast in addition to beginning movements will select from skills No. 21 to No. 37 and No. 39.

Intermediate Combinations

1. Swivel hips; barrel roll; to feet; to tucked forward somersault to feet.

2. Forward somersault to back drop; cradle; to feet.

3. Barani; barani; forward somersault to feet.

4. Back tucked somersault to feet; front 1-1/4 somersault; half turntable; to feet.

1.   Swivel hips   Barrel roll   Feet   Tucked forward somersault   Feet   2.   Forward somersault   Back drop

Cradle   Feet   3.   Barani (repeat)   Forward somersault   Feet

4.   Back tucked somersault   Feet   Front somersault   Half turntable   Feet

*⚡ Change in direction

ADVANCED SKILLS AND COMBINATIONS

Usually an advanced gymnast, in addition to intermediate movements will select from skills No. 38 to No. 43.

Advanced Combinations

1. Back tucked 1-1/4 somersault to seat drop; barrel roll; to feet.

2. Cody (front drop, back tucked somersault to feet); back tucked somersault; barani.

3. Back pullover to feet; back piked somersault; back somersault with full twist.

4. Full twisting front somersault; back piked somersault; barani.

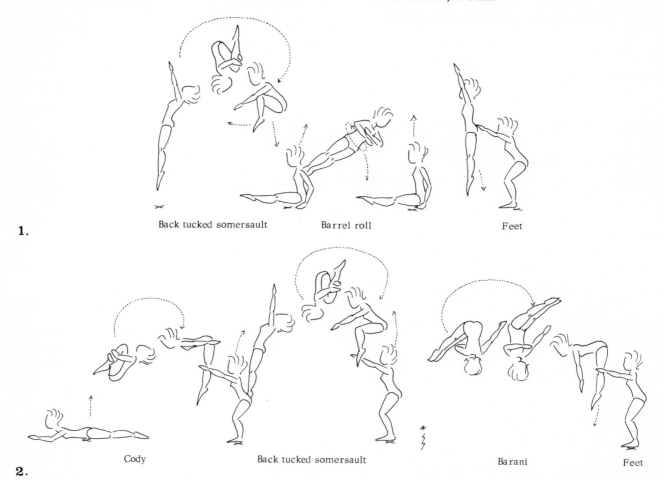

1.   Back tucked somersault   Barrel roll   Feet

2.   Cody   Back tucked somersault   Barani   Feet

---

* ⚡ Change in direction

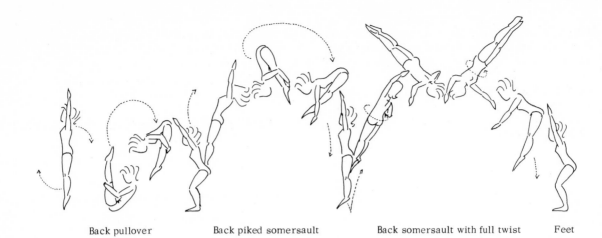

Back pullover   Back piked somersault   Back somersault with full twist   Feet

3.

Full twisting front somersault   Back piked somersault   Barani   Feet

4.

---

* ⚡ Change in direction

BEGINNING EXERCISES

Following are examples of routines for various levels of skill ability. The preliminary bounces taken to gain height do not count. The contacts are counted from the first contact with the bed on the first stunt. Each routine must end with a landing on the feet on the last count. These routines are geared for school use and are much easier than those used in trampoline competition.

		Contacts
1.	Straddle pike bounce	1
2.	Swivel hips (seat, twist to seat)	2-3
3.	Straddle the legs through to front drop	4
4.	Half turn table (in tucked position twist from front drop to face the opposite direction, end in front drop)	5
5.	Regular bounce (needed to gain height for beginner)	6
6.	Cradle (back, twist to back)	7-8
7.	Half twist from back drop to front drop	9
8.	To stand	10

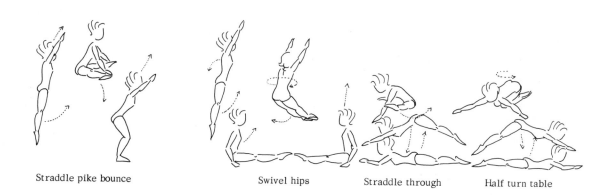

Straddle pike bounce   Swivel hips   Straddle through   Half turn table

Bounce   Cradle   Twist to front drop   Feet

INTERMEDIATE EXERCISES

		Contacts			Contacts
1.	Back tucked somersault	1	6. Barrel roll		6
2.	Back layout to front drop (3/4 back somersault)	2	7. Regular bounce		7
3.	Half turn table	3	8. Back somersault layout to feet		8
4.	To feet out of front drop	4	9. Barani		9
5.	Seat drop	5	10. Front somersault to feet		10

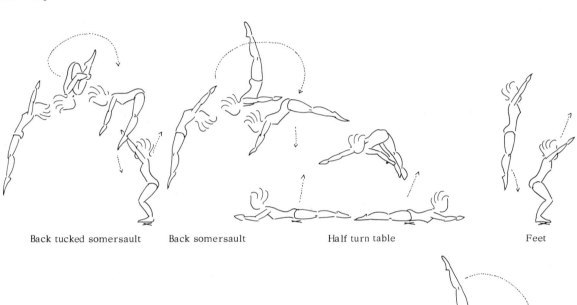

Back tucked somersault   Back somersault   Half turn table   Feet

Seat drop   Barrel roll   Bounce   Back somersault layout

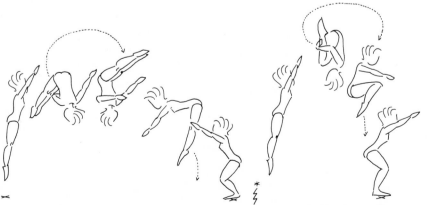

*⚡ Change in direction   Barani   Front somersault   Feet

ADVANCED EXERCISES

1. 1-1/4 back somersault to back   1
2. Cradle   2
3. Back pullover to feet   3
4. Back somersault, tucked   4
5. Full twisting front somersault   5
6. Back somersault, piked   6
7. Back somersault with full twist   7
8. Barani   8
9. 3/4 back somersault, layout   9
10. 1-1/4 cody to feet   10

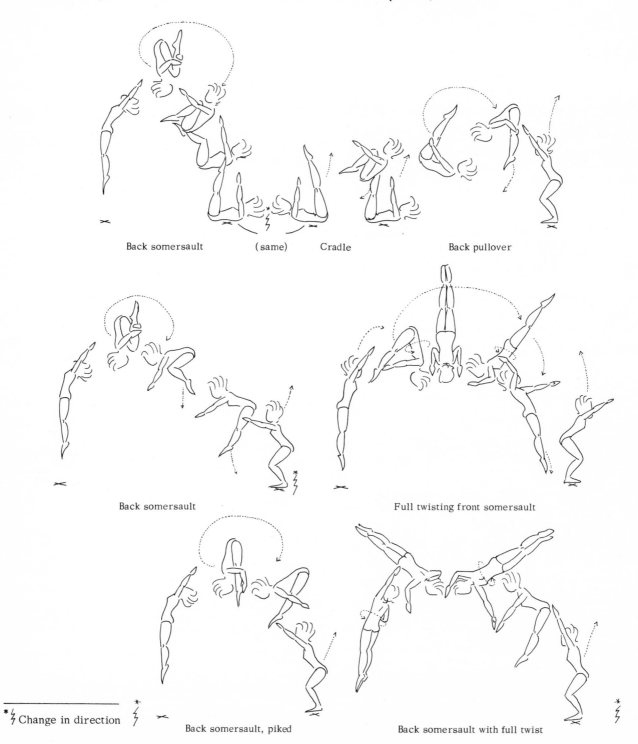

Back somersault   (same)   Cradle   Back pullover

Back somersault   Full twisting front somersault

Back somersault, piked   Back somersault with full twist

*⚡ Change in direction

Barani   Back somersault, layout   Cody   Feet

COMPETITION

There are 8 bounces in the beginning compulsory trampoline routine. Intermediate and advanced compulsory routines are 10 bounces. The optional routine calls for 10 to 12 bounces, including at least one superior difficult movement (C), three difficult movements (B), and the rest being intermediate or class (A) skills. The routine shall have both front and back rotating skills with at least two front rotating skills.*

The USGF Compulsory Routines for special events in Trampoline are given below.** These are the current routines, and will undoubtedly be adopted by DGWS for their meets.

Point Value	Contact	Stunt

BEGINNER LEVEL

2.0	1	Back tuck somersault
3.0	2	Front 1-1/4 somersault
1.5	3 & 4	Swivel hips
	5	Feet
2.5	6 & 7	Cradle
1.0	8	Arch out to feet

LOW INTERMEDIATE

1.5	1	Back tuck somersault
2.0	2	Back 3/4 somersault
	3	1/2 turntable
	4	Feet
1.5	5	Barani
1.5	6	Back tuck somersault
1.5	7	Barani
2.0	8	Front somersault

---

* Information courtesy Mr. Jeff Hennessy, AAU Technical Committee of Federation of International Trampoline, University of Southwestern Louisiana, Lafayette, La. 70501.

** Mrs. Ledford, Fresno, Calif., USGF Representative.

HIGH INTERMEDIATE

1.5	1	Back layout somersault
1.0	2	Barani
1.0	3	Back somersault
	4	Back 3/4 somersault
2.0	5	Cody
1.0	6	Barani
1.0	7	Back tuck somersault
2.5	8	Back layout with full twist

ELITE DIVISION

2.0	1	Front somersault with 1-1/2 twist (Rudolph)
.5	2	Back tuck somersault
1.5	3	3/4 back somersault, layout
	4	Cody, tucked position
1.5	5	Barani
2.0	6	Back somersault with full twist
.5	7	Barani
.5	8	Back somersault, piked position
1.5	9	Swan dive, layout, to back
1.0	10	Ball out, tucked, with 1/2 twist (ball out-barani)

The AAU Junior Olympic Trampoline exercises are as follows:

Contact	Stunt

GIRLS 9 YEARS AND UNDER

1	Back drop
2	1/2 twist from back to feet
3	Straddle jump
4	Tuck jump
5	Seat drop
6	1/2 twist to seat drop (swivel hips)
7	Bounce to feet
8	Back somersault tuck

GIRLS 10 to 12 YEARS

1	3/4 front dive to back
2	1/2 twist from back to feet
3	Straddle jump
4	Back somersault tuck
5	Barani
6	Tuck jump
7	Back somersault tuck
8	Back somersault pike

GIRLS 13 to 14 YEARS

1	Back somersault pike
2	Back somersault tuck
3	Tuck jump
4	Straddle jump
5	Barani
6	Back somersault tuck
7	3/4 back somersault layout
8	Cody tuck
9	Barani
10	Back somersault layout

GIRLS 15 to 18 YEARS AND OVER

1	Full twisting back somersault
2	Barani
3	Back somersault tuck
4	3/4 back somersault layout
5	Cody tuck
6	Barani
7	Back somersault tuck
8	Back somersault pike
9	Front 1-3/4 somersault tuck
10	Barani ball out tuck (barani from the back to feet)

The National AAU Trampoline Championships for men and women held at Sarasota, Florida, in December, 1969, listed the following required routine for both men and women.

1	Barani to back	pike
2	Back pullover	free
3	Barani	pike
4	3/4 back somersault	layout
5	Cody	tuck
6	Full twisting back	free
7	3/4 front dive	layout
8	Barani ball out	tuck
9	Back somersault	layout
10	1-1/2 twisting front somersault	free

The following are the Compulsory Exercises for the 6th World Championships, 1970, and 2nd European Championships, 1971, as developed by the International Trampoline Association.*

Point Value	Contact	Stunt
CLASS A		
6	1	1-1/4 piked forward somersault with 1/2 twist
3	2	3/4 back somersault, free style
5	3	Barani piked
3	4	3/4 backward somersault, stretched
5	5	Back cody, tucked
6	6	Backward somersault with full twist
3	7	3/4 forward somersault, stretched
6	8	1-1/4 forward somersault tucked with 1/2 twist
5	9	Backward somersault, stretched
7	10	Rudolph
49		
CLASS B		
3	1	3/4 forward somersault, stretched
2	2	1/2 twist (into standing position)
4	3	Backward somersault, tucked
2	4	Full twisting, foot bounce
5	5	1 forward somersault with 1/2 twist piked, into seat bounce
1	6	1/2 twist into standing position
0	7	Pike straddle jump
5	8	Backward somersault, piked
3	9	3/4 backward somersault, stretched
5	10	Back cody, tucked
30		

* Courtesy Mr. MacDuff, E. P. Finigan Co., San Francisco.

Chapter 16   Tumbling

Tumbling is one of the basic skills that the gymnast should master because many of the tumbling movements are used on apparatus. Tumbling should be preliminary to apparatus work, although in many instances it will need to be learned at the same time. Ideally, tumbling should be learned when the child is in the elementary grades since it is at this age that the child is flexible and has little fear.

The purpose of this chapter is to acquaint the student and teacher with the tumbling movements commonly used in competition. Numerous excellent texts give the preliminary background in stunts and tumbling; but it is very important that tumbling skills be taught and learned in progression, from simple to difficult movements. Spotting is very essential, and each student should learn to spot the tumbling movement as well as to perform it.

TEACHING SUGGESTIONS

1. All tumbling must be performed on mats; if aerial movements are being performed, a double thickness of mats should be used. Most mats are 5 x 10 feet in size, and the newer light-weight mats are very easy for girls to handle. Some of the newer mats come with an adhesive edge which allows them to be placed together without their sliding apart. The newer extra thick mats are effective for the more difficult stunts.

2. Form in tumbling is of utmost importance, from the very first roll learned. The student should start from a position of attention and finish in the same position.

3. In teaching the more difficult aerial skills an overhead belt is desirable. A belt that moves along ceiling cables permits the performer to run and perform several skills in succession. Hand belts are a good substitute, however, and if a hand belt is not available two towels, one in front and one in back of the performer and twisted and held at either end by good spotters, may be used.

4. As soon as each stunt is mastered the student should attempt to perform two or more in a series. As soon as other stunts are added, simple sequences should be practiced so that the student learns to complete one movement and immediately go into the next.

5. In all tumbling movements the fingers should point in the direction of the movement.

MOVEMENTS

Forward Rolls

1.   SQUAT ROLL TO STAND

S.P. Squat on the mat, knees between the hands, fingers pointing forward.
M.   Tuck the head downward to the mat as the hips are lifted. The shoulders should feel the mat. Roll over and immediately come to standing.
Spotting: The spotter kneels to one side and places one hand under the back, tucking the head; and places the other hand at the hips and helps to give a boost over.

2.   STAND, ROLL TO STAND

S.P. Standing at attention.
M.   In one continuous movement squat down, tuck head and roll and come up to standing.
Spotting: Same as for No. 1.

S.P. = Starting Position   M. = Movement

3.   DIVE FORWARD ROLL, TUCKED

S.P.   Standing at attention.

M.   Spring forward, or run a few steps and take off from both feet. For a slight time fly in the air in a small pike position. Take the weight on both hands, elbows slightly bent, and quickly tuck the head and roll to standing.

It is easier to teach this by having the performer do a dive roll over a student crouched on all fours, or over a low Swedish box.

Spotting: Stand forward where the roll will take place, be ready to tuck the head.

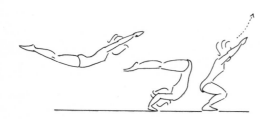

4.   SWAN DIVE FORWARD ROLL

S.P.   Standing at attention.

M.   Run a few steps and take off from both feet to a swan position of flying in the air. Take the weight on the hands, tuck the head and roll into a pike position, come to standing. The regular dive forward roll should be well done before attempting the swan. The swan is a spectacular stunt when well performed.

Spotting: Same as No. 3.

5.   STRADDLE FORWARD ROLL

S.P.   Standing in a wide straddle position.

M.   Place hands on the floor between the legs as far to the rear as possible. Tuck the head and shoulders, roll forward, the legs remaining in spread position. As the performer comes out of the roll, reach forward with the body from the hips and place the hands close to the crotch to give a boost to the straddle position again. Shoulders should be far in front of the hands, head up, arms straight.

Spotting: Stand to one side of the performer so as not to be hit by the legs. Move in quickly and give a boost on the buttocks to help lift the performer to straddle position.

Backward Rolls

6.   LONG SITTING, ROLL TO SQUAT POSITION

S.P.   Sitting in long sitting position on mat.

M.   Bend forward over the knees, roll backward bringing the knees to the chest, hands placed at the shoulders and thumbs near the neck. Keep the piked position and roll over ending in a squat position.

Spotting: a. Kneel to one side and after the hands reach backward, place one hand under the shoulder and lift the head through.

b.   Stand to one side and as the knees come to the chest, move into position in back of performer, lifting the hips and helping to lift the head through.

7.   SQUAT TO STAND

S.P.   In squat position.

M.   Roll back to the hips and back as the hands are placed by the shoulders as in No. 1. Keep the tucked position and roll and come to a standing position.

Spotting: Same as 6b.

8.   STAND, TUCKED, TO STAND

S.P.   Standing.

M.   Lean backward in a pike position until coming to long sitting position on the mat for a second. Take the weight on the hands, fingers pointed forward. Immediately tuck the legs to the chest and roll backward ending in a standing position.

Spotting: Same as for No. 6b.

9.   STAND, PIKE, TO STAND

S.P.   Standing.

M.   From a pike position, lean backward to a long sitting position on the mat, for a second. Then swing the legs up over the head as the hands are placed at the shoulders. Roll over keeping the legs straight, and come to a standing position.

Spotting: Same as for No. 6b.

10.   BACK STRADDLE

S.P.   Standing in a wide straddle position.

M.   Lean backward in a piked position with hips to the rear. Place the hands on the floor between the legs momentarily as the weight falls backward, then shift the hands to the shoulders on the roll and end in a straddle position.

Spotting: Stand to one side in back of the performer. As the hands are placed by the shoulders and the buttocks are in the air, grasp the hips and pull the performer through to a straddle standing position.

11.   BACKWARD ROLL TO HEADSTAND

S.P.   Standing.

M.   Do a tucked or piked backward roll, but at the instant the legs are over the head stretch them upward, taking the weight on the hands and head in a headstand. Snap the legs down and come to standing position.

Spotting: For beginners, have a spotter on each side. Spotters grasp the legs as they are extended upward and help to lift the person to the headstand position. Then let go as the snap-down takes place.

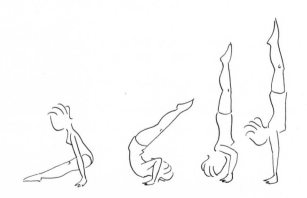

12.   BACKWARD ROLL TO HANDSTAND (BACK EXTENSION)

S.P.   Standing.

M.   Do a tucked or piked backward roll, but at the instant the legs are over the head stretch them upward and push with the hands to a momentary handstand. Snap the legs down to standing.

Spotting: Same as No. 11.

Inverted Tumbling Stunts and Springs

13.   MULE KICK

This is not a tumbling stunt, but a preliminary skill to correct performance of many stunts.

S.P.   Standing.

M.   Bend forward placing the hands on the mat shoulder distance apart and at the same time kick up the right foot, followed by the left. As the left leg goes upward the right returns to the floor.

Spotting: Stand to the side of the performer, helping her at the waist.

14.   HANDSTAND, SNAP DOWN

S.P.   Standing.

M.   Placing the hands on the mat shoulder distance apart and about a foot in front of the feet, kick one leg upward, followed by the other, into a momentary handstand. Push off with the hands and snap down from the hips to the standing position.

Spotting: Stand to the side of the performer, grasping the waist at the snap-down.

15.   CARTWHEEL

S.P.   Standing, side to the mat.

M.   (Cartwheel to the left side.) Kick the left leg upward and place it forward on the mat, bending forward as the weight is taken on the left hand, then on the right. Arms are straight and shoulder distance apart. Legs are split in the air. Land on the right, then on the left foot as the body ends facing the original position. There should be an even 4-count rhythm; i.e., left hand count 1, right hand count 2, right foot count 3, left foot count 4. The cartwheel should be learned to both sides.

Variations: a.   Cartwheel from a run.

        b.   Dive cartwheel—run and dive into the cartwheel.

        c.   One-arm cartwheel.

Spotting: Stand on the opposite side to the kick-up, hands crossed, left hand crosses over the right and grasps right waist of the performer, and assists the performer through the movement by lifting at the waist.

16.   ROUND-OFF

S.P.   Standing, facing forward.

M.   Take a run, skip on the right foot lifting the left leg. Place the left foot on the mat followed by the left arm as in a cartwheel. As the legs reach the overhead position hold them for an instant in a handstand, then snap the legs down to the mat with a quarter turn and end facing the opposite direction from the starting position.

Practice landing with the knees slightly bent so that you will be ready to push off into another stunt. The round-off is frequently followed by a back handspring or somersault.

Spotting: This movement should not be attempted until the performer has mastered a handstand snap-down and the cartwheel, as the spotter is usually a hindrance rather than a help.

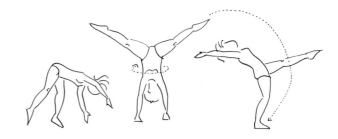

17.   TINSICA

The student should learn the forward walkover before performing a tinsica. Refer to Floor Exercise, since the walkover is not a true tumbling skill.

S.P.   Standing, left side to the mat.

M.   A tinsica is a combination of a cartwheel and forward walkover. The beginning of the tinsica is like a cartwheel in that the tinsica to the left would be started with a run. Place the left foot to the mat on a fast take-off. Place the left hand to the mat, then the right. The legs are in a split position over head. As the left leg comes down, give a slight twist to the body so that you are ending by facing forward as in a walkover.

Spotting: The spotter stands to the left side of the gymnast, grasping at the hips to help her in the twist and lift to the standing position.

18.   TWO-FOOT LIMBER

This is not a tumbling movement, but is a preliminary skill to learning the springs.

S.P. Standing, facing the mat.

M. Placing the hands on the mat, kick the legs up in a momentary handstand; let both legs drop forward to a momentary arch, and pull up to standing. (An arch should be practiced before this stunt; see conditioning exercises.)

Variations: a. Do a run and spring into the limber by diving forward and taking the weight on the hands.

      b. Two-foot limber backward. This is preliminary to the back handspring.

Spotting: Stand to one side, grasping the performer near the shoulders and waist and assisting her to stand. Also, two spotters may use a wrist grasp holding the performer at the waist and lifting at the shoulders with the free hand. The spotters may either stand or kneel.

20. NECKSPRING

The neckspring may be learned in the same sequence as for the headspring. However, when the spring is from the neck the head must be tucked under. This is more difficult to perform than the headspring since the hips are lower.

19. HEADSPRING FROM A ROLLED MAT

S.P. Standing on one side of a rolled mat.

M. a. Place hands and head on top of the rolled mat as for a headstand (see Floor Exercises). Push off with the legs to a piked headstand and let the hips move forward way over the head; then whip the legs from the hips up and over the head, landing on the feet in a squat position. From the squat position the performer is ready to continue on to another movement.

      b. Headspring on flat mats. Perform the same movement as above, on the mat.

      c. Headspring from a run. With a slight run, bend forward placing the hands and head on the mat (weight is primarily on the hands); whip the legs over to a squat position.

      d. Headspring arch out. This is performed the same as c, but land in an arched position instead of a squat. This usually ends a sequence of movements.

Spotting: A spotter should be on either side and assist by lifting the shoulders and waist.

21. FORWARD HANDSPRING

This should be first learned with a rolled mat as for the headspring, then on the mat.

S.P. Standing in front of a rolled mat.

M. From a few running steps place the hands in front of the rolled mat and roll on it; end in a standing position. The weight is taken on the arms which remain straight throughout the movement, and a strong push is made from the shoulders.

Spotting: a. With two spotters, they should hold hands in a wrist grasp under the performer's waist, and should assist at the shoulder with the free hand.

      b. With only one spotter, the assistance should be given under the shoulder with one hand and at the waist with the other hand.

22.   WALKOVER HANDSPRING

S.P.   Standing, facing the mat.

M.   Take off with a run and spring as for an ordinary handspring, but keep the legs in a split. Push off from the mat with the hands, landing on one foot; then step forward with the other foot. The body is in a greater arch than for the handspring.

Spotting: Same as for No. 21.

23.   DIVE TINSICA (MOUNTER)

S.P.   Perform a tinsica or a walkover handspring to get momentum.

M.   Land on the left foot, place both feet on the mat in a two-foot take-off. Spring into the air as for a forward somersault, but open the body reaching forward with the arms. Place the hands at a slight angle, left forward as in a cartwheel or regular tinsica. The legs are in a split position over the head. The left leg comes down to the mat first, followed by the right as in a forward walkover.

Spotting: Use an overhead belt, or spot as for No. 17.

24.   BACK HANDSPRING (FLIP-FLOP)

S.P.   Standing, back to mat.

M.   From a standing position with the feet slightly apart and parallel, swing the arms downward bending the knees as though sitting on a chair. As the body falls off balance backward, vigorously swing the arms upward over head and then throw the head backward. Push off the mat by straightening the legs. As the hands touch the floor the body is in a momentary handstand position, arms straight. From this position, snap the legs down to a standing position.

Variations: a. Handsprings. Several done in succession.

b. Round-off—handspring. The round-off is usually done to give momentum. On the round-off the feet snap down close to the hands, to give the necessary backward momentum. The push-off is from the heels.

Spotting: An overhead belt or hand belt is preferred when learning this stunt. If hand spotting is used, place the right hand under the performer's low back and use the left hand to assist her in turning over. This is difficult for most women, hence a belt is preferred.

Aerial Somersaults

All aerial stunts are advanced stunts, and should be attempted only after all previous skills have been learned. They should be learned with the use of an overhead or a hand belt. Most women find the overhead belt more desirable. The stunt should be mastered from a standing position before it is done with a running start or in a series of movements.

25.   FORWARD SOMERSAULT

Some of the basic skills for this movement may be learned on the trampoline. A preliminary movement is to run, do a forward roll over a stack of rolled mats.

S.P. Standing, facing a long mat.

M. Run and two-foot take-off. The take-off is a vertical movement as high as possible from a strong push-off from the balls of both feet. Throw the arms forward and upward, and at the height of the spring bring the arms downward and simultaneously come to a tight tucked position grasping the shins. After completing the somersault, shoot out of the tucked position and land in a standing position.

Variation: Handspring to a forward somersault.

Spotting: Use an overhead or a hand belt. The spotter holding the belt runs with the performer and is thus able to give a lift at the right instant. Later hand spot—near hand in front of hips to aid lift up, far hand under upper back to aid rotation.

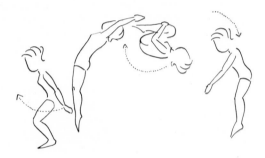

26.   BACK SOMERSAULT

a. Standing back tuck. This is a preliminary movement in learning the back somersault.

S.P. Standing.

M. From a standing position swing the arms down and bend the knees; jump into the air lifting the arms upward. At the height of the spring bring the arms downward grasping the knees to the chest. Shoot out of the tuck and land on the feet.

b. Standing back somersault.

S.P. Standing, feet slightly apart, arms at sides.

M. The push-off is from the balls of the feet, not from the heels as in a flip-flop. Swing the arms downward and bend the knees. Jump into the air lifting the arms upward. At the height of the spring bring the arms downward grasping the knees to the chest. Snap the head backward and pull the knees over. When you see the ground again, shoot out of the tuck and land on the feet in a standing position. (See sketch.)

Variation: Back somersault from a round-off. Perform a round-off and go into the back somersault. Note that the push-off is from the ball of the feet, thus from the round-off the feet are kicked backward from the

hands. In this way the backward motion is checked and the push is directed upward for the somersault.

Spotting: a. Stand behind the performer and place a hand at her upper back to prevent over-springing, or help at the waist to get the necessary height by a lift upward.

b. Use an overhead belt or hand belt. Later hand spot at the back and thighs to aid rotation.

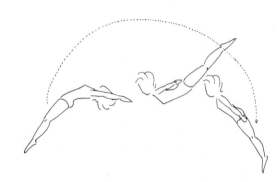

27.   BACK LAYOUT SOMERSAULT

S.P. Perform a round-off and flip-flop to get momentum.

M. After a forceful take-off, reach upward with the arms. Arms are usually thrown out into a swan position. Lift the chest, head, and hips upward, body arched throughout the movement. The head lifts and the arms drop toward the body slightly for landing.

Spotting: Use an overhead belt or hand belt. Later hand spot at back and thighs to aid rotation.

28.   AERIAL CARTWHEEL

S.P. Standing at one end, facing a long mat.

M. With a running start and good hurdle take-off, push hard against the mat as the back leg whips up. Perform a cartwheel without the use of the hands. Pull the hands close to the body as the legs swing over the head.

Spotting: Use a hand belt with single sash. Later hand spot under hip of lead leg.

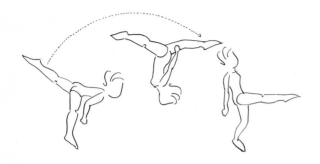
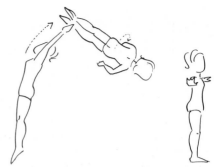

29.   AERIAL WALKOVER

See No. 42 Floor Exercise.

S.P. Standing at one end, facing a long mat.

M.   With a run and a take-off from one foot, bend forward swinging the arms downward and backward as the head is pulled strongly backward. Kick the leading leg strongly to the rear. Continue the movement of a walkover, but keep the body extremely arched, elbows pulled close to the body.

Spotting: Use an overhead belt or hand belt. Later hand spot, with the lead hand spot at the hip and with the other hand under back on whip-over.

Aerial Twisting Somersaults

All of these movements are advanced, and should be learned only after previous skills have been mastered. They should be learned with an overhead twisting belt to ensure adequate safety.

30.   HALF TWISTING FORWARD LAYOUT SOMERSAULT

S.P. Standing, facing a long mat.

M.   Run and two-foot take-off. Simultaneously throw the arms forward and upward to a swan position of flying in the air, body almost horizontal to mat. Half twist to the right (or left), body slightly piked. Throw head and hand upward and backward, tuck forcefully and do a back somersault. Land on feet facing the opposite direction.

Spotting: Use an overhead or hand belt. Later hand spot by facing the performer and after the take-off place hands on hips to aid the lift, twist, and rotation.

31.   HALF TWISTING BACKWARD SOMERSAULT

S.P. Perform a round-off, and flip-flop or back handspring to get momentum.

M.   Go up and back as for a back layout as you land from the handspring. After almost half of the back turn-over is finished (to perform to the right), first throw back the head, then to the right side as the right shoulder is dropped and the left arm comes across the body. Bring the arms close in to the chest as the twist is performed while in the inverted position, then lift the arms forward and swing the legs down under the hips for an erect landing.

It is very important that there be a great build-up of backward momentum for this stunt, and that the throw is at the maximum height.

Spotting: This should be learned only with an overhead twisting belt.

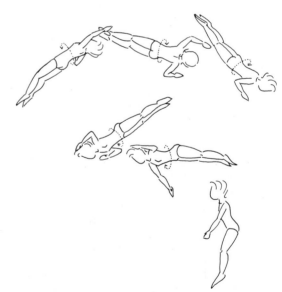

32.   FULL TWISTING BACK SOMERSAULT

S.P. Perform a round-off, and flip-flop to get the necessary momentum.

M.   Throw and spring upward for maximum height. Fling the head to the right and look over the right shoulder. Bring the left arm to the right shoulder. In the vertical position, spin around to the right drawing the arms close to the body; release the arms as the body passes through the reverse vertical position, and swing the legs down to land in the same position as for the take-off.

Spotting: This should be learned only with an overhead twisting belt.

BEGINNING SKILLS AND COMBINATIONS

Usually the beginning gymnast will select from skills No. 1 to No. 16 for her routine. These stunts can be put into various combinations. See Tumbling Competition, beginner routines.

INTERMEDIATE SKILLS AND COMBINATIONS

Usually an intermediate gymnast in addition to beginning movements, will select from skills No. 17 to No. 24 for her routine. For combinations, see Tumbling Competition, intermediate routines.

ADVANCED SKILLS AND COMBINATIONS

Usually an advanced gymnast, in addition to intermediate movements, will select from skills No. 25 to No. 32 for her routine. For combinations, see Tumbling Competition, advanced routines.

BEGINNING EXERCISES

The following trips are suggested for school tumbling units. Each trip should start and finish in the erect standing posture. For current USGF-DGWS routines, see end of chapter.

1. Dive forward roll, straddle forward roll, tucked forward roll, straddle forward roll, tucked forward roll to standing.

2. Cartwheel, cartwheel, round-off, back tucked roll to standing.

1.

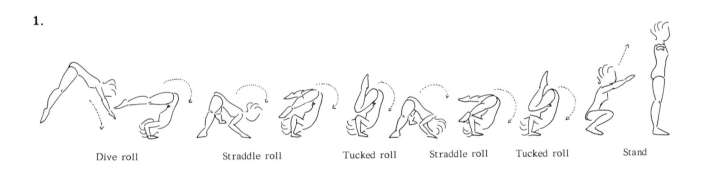

Dive roll   Straddle roll   Tucked roll   Straddle roll   Tucked roll   Stand

2.

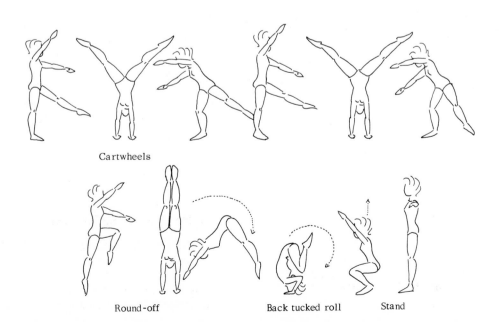

Cartwheels

Round-off   Back tucked roll   Stand

3.

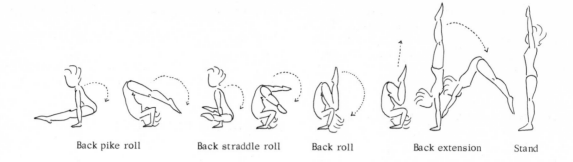

Back pike roll   Back straddle roll   Back roll   Back extension   Stand

4.

Running cartwheel   Round-off   Rebound half-turn

Cartwheel   Back roll   Back extension   Stand

3. Back pike roll, back straddle roll, back roll, back extension to standing.

4. Running cartwheel, round-off, rebound half-turn, cartwheel, back roll, back extension, end standing.

INTERMEDIATE EXERCISES

1. Handspring, headspring, forward roll, cartwheel, tinsica.

2. Running cartwheel, round-off, rebound, backward roll, back extension.

1.

Handspring   Headspring   Forward roll   Cartwheel

Tinsica   Stand

2.

Running cartwheel   Round-off

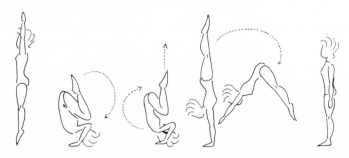

Rebound back roll   Back extension   Stand

3.

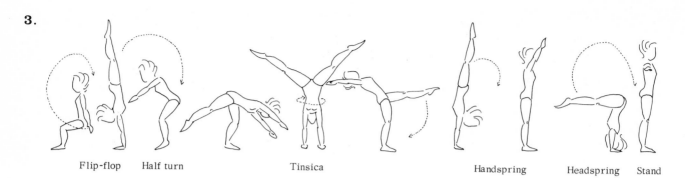

Flip-flop   Half turn   Tinsica   Handspring   Headspring   Stand

---

4.

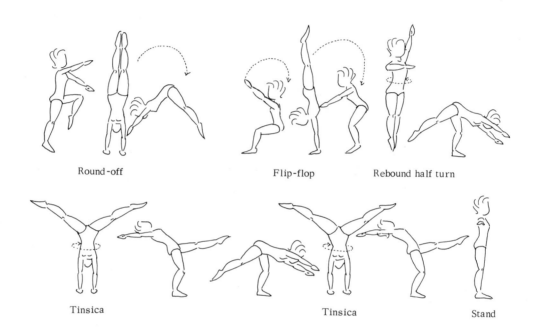

Round-off   Flip-flop   Rebound half turn

Tinsica   Tinsica   Stand

3. Standing flip-flop, half turn to step out, tinsica, handspring, headspring.

4. Round-off, flip-flop, rebound half turn, step out to tinsica, tinsica.

ADVANCED EXERCISES

1. Round-off and three flip-flops.

2. Round-off, flip-flop, flip-flop, back layout somersault.

3. Aerial cartwheel, tinsica, aerial walkover.

4. Round-off, flip-flop, full twisting back somersault.

1.

Round-off   Flip-flops   Stand

2.

Round-off   Flip-flops   Back layout somersault   Stand

3.

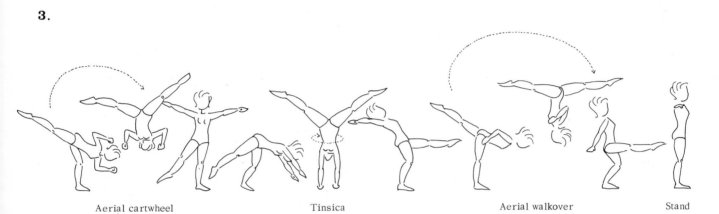

Aerial cartwheel   Tinsica   Aerial walkover   Stand

4.

Round-off   Flip-flop

Full twisting back somersault   Stand

COMPETITION

Tumbling is considered a special event in district and national meets. It consists of a maximum of four trips down the 60-foot mat in a two-minute duration, including the rests between lengths tumbled. As a rule, the tumbling trips consist of a forward trip down the mat, a backward trip, and a combination of forward and backward movements. The movements must be continuous, and it is therefore very important that the students learn to perform several movements in succession as the individual skills are learned. Contortional or acrobatic movements are not considered tumbling; however, some of the dance movements and floor exercise movements are helpful in development of the tumbling skills.

The current USGF-DGWS Compulsory Tumbling routines are listed as follows:

Point Value   Trip Description

BEGINNER

1.5   1   Dive forward roll to straddle, forward roll without hands, dive forward roll.

2.5   2   Backward roll to straddle, backward roll, backward roll extension, roll backward to kip position and kip-up (neckspring) to stand.

3.0   3   Cartwheel left, cartwheel right, forward roll with a walkout, round-off, backward roll, jump with 1/2 turn to stand, dive forward roll.

3.0   4   Handspring to forward roll, dive forward roll, round-off, backward roll, backward roll extension to stand.

LOW INTERMEDIATE

2.0   1   Handspring, dive forward roll, handspring, dive forward roll, handspring to arched landing.

2.5   2   Standing backward handspring, walkout with 1/2 turn, round-off, backward roll to extension, backward roll, backward roll extension.

2.5   3   Cartwheel, tinsica, round-off, jump with 1/2 turn to feet, dive forward roll and then handspring forward to arched landing.

3.0   4   Round-off backward handspring, walkout with 1/2 turn, tinsica, front handspring to headspring.

HIGH INTERMEDIATE

2.5   1   Round-off, three backward handsprings.

2.5   2   Tinsica, flying tinsica mounter, tinsica, round-off, backward handspring to backward somersault tucked position to stand.

2.5   3   Front handspring with a walkout, front somersault, dive forward roll, tinsica to a front handspring to stand.

2.5   4   Round-off, backward handspring, back tucked somersault, backward handspring to backward tucked somersault.

ELITE DIVISION
(For use in USGF National Championships)

2.5   1   Round-off, two backward handsprings, full twisting backward somersault.

2.5   2   Front handspring, front somersault (tucked), forward roll to front somersault.

2.5   3   Forward somersault, dive forward roll with walkout, round-off to backward handspring, backward tucked somersault.

2.5   4   Round-off, backward handspring to back layout somersault.

Part IV   CURRICULUM, DEMONSTRATIONS, MEETS, JUDGING

Chapter 17 Planning the School Curriculum in Gymnastics

Gymnastics should be included in the physical education curriculum, from elementary through college level. This statement is predicated by the belief in potential values of the activity. Let us examine some of these values.

Many activities in the physical education curriculum are group or team games. It is therefore important that we have some activities which appeal to the individual, and which allow her to develop according to her own desires. Gymnastics is such an activity.

The physical fitness values of gymnastics have been mentioned many times, both in this book and in other literature. In addition to these physical factors, gymnastics develops mental alertness, courage, self-confidence, perseverance, and self-discipline. Creative ability is also given unlimited opportunity in gymnastics. The challenge to perform a given stunt or skill makes gymnastics a self-motivating activity. Gymnastics helps to develop a beautifully poised feminine body which is the aim of most girls.

With these values in mind, it is obvious that gymnastics should be included as part of the school physical education program on a progressive basis from the first grade. The content of this book is primarily planned for secondary level, but many skills can be taught at the elementary school level.

The very nature of gymnastics means that competition is a necessary part of the activity. The beginner wonders if she can do a roll as well as someone else; the advanced performer wants to compete with the advanced gymnast. In sports, the team game is the culminating purpose for learning skills; in dance, the performance is the ultimate purpose for learning dance steps; while in gymnastics, the meet is the opportunity for the student to match her abilities against those of others. Competition is part of our life, and a chance to experience it on a continuum will help the student to adjust to adult life. Thus competition in gymnastics tends to become a valuable experience toward future development.

TEACHING METHODS

It is essential that the teacher have complete control of the gymnastics class. This does not mean autocratic control, but she must know what each student is doing at all times. She will find it necessary to keep the group under her personal supervision if they are young, inexperienced, or irresponsible. Safety is of utmost importance and if students have not learned to be responsible spotters for their fellow classmates, they should not be permitted to participate in that capacity. In many situations, students are eager to learn and they wish to progress faster than they should. Good judgment on the part of the teacher is necessary in such matters. Skill charts showing progression may be used as incentives for students to develop their skills. These charts can be marked as the student masters each new skill, and in that way both student and teacher can keep track of the progress.

Each skill should be learned with all safety factors considered; i.e., the student should know where the mats should be placed, what the spotter should do, etc. The buddy method is usually the best, with each girl taking turns as performer and spotter.

When students are sufficiently mature and can be trusted to work independently the teacher should organize the class into groups, each with a leader. She should so organize the class activity that she can teach new skills to at least one group per day while the others are working independently. This allows for much practice and hence quick mastery of skills. When the class is divided into groups, it is of utmost importance that the teacher place herself in a position such that she can supervise all the activity. Also, it should be understood that new skills are not tried until they have been thoroughly demonstrated and analyzed.

The correct organization of the gymnastics class contributes greatly in the learning process. Before planning a class schedule the following must be considered: the age of the gymnast, her background, the available time, and the competition schedule. If optional exercises are to be learned, time should be allowed for individual instruction.

The lessons should be planned at least two weeks in advance; however, it is necessary to be flexible since it is impossible to anticipate how quickly the group may learn. Plan all of the material in progression. If the gymnast does not know the basic exercises, she might learn a more difficult skill, but it will take much longer and her form will not be as fluent as though she had gone through the correct progression.

The class period should be divided into five parts, as follows:

a. Roll call, and information given to the whole group. (3-5 min.)

b. Warm-up (5-10 min.). Mass exercises, the whole group performing with instruction from the teacher. Rhythmic gymnastics, and tumbling or free exercise are good for this part of the lesson. There are disadvantages in having the whole group together since the slow learners and the fast learners are together; but the advantage is that the teacher herself is giving the proper instruction.

c. Day's lesson (dependent upon available class period time). Much can be accomplished if the class is organized into groups or squads. Select the groups according to ability, and plan the activity for each ability group. The disadvantage of such a plan is that students are leaders since the instructor can be with only one group at a time. The advantage is that much more activity is possible for each student. The instructor should take time to train the student leaders.

d. Individual teaching. This must be done with one student or a very small group. This is very essential when putting together voluntary exercises; also, it allows for individual attention to the slow as well as the fast learners.

e. Conclusion (5 to 10 min.). Finish the lesson with a game or discussion, to reaffirm what has been learned during the lesson.

TEACHING SUGGESTIONS

1. In teaching a skill, the instructor should demonstrate and explain it, immediately bringing out the correct form and techniques of each movement. After the demonstration, let the students try the movement. Correct only the major mistakes at first, and later go into the details of perfecting the movement. Many details will correct themselves as the skill is practiced.

2. Safety is of utmost importance. The teacher should always be the first person in the gymnasium, and the last to leave. Be sure to check the equipment and to place the mats for greatest safety.

3. It is helpful to teach beginners on low apparatus first; e.g., the beam and horse, because fear interferes with learning. When they have confidence gradually lift the equipment to the proper height. Do not tell the students that the equipment is being lifted; gradually lifting it will

maintain their self-confidence and not bother them psychologically.

4. It is helpful to teach the same movement on different apparatus at the same time; e.g., teach the V seat and scale on the floor, balance beam, and unevens. Thus the gymnast learns the movement quickly and it has greater meaning for her.

5. Put the exercises together after the individual has mastered separate skills. It is important to teach spotting not only for the safety factor, but because it helps in getting a feeling of the movement and aids in the performance.

OBJECTIVES OF A SECONDARY SCHOOL GYMNASTICS PROGRAM

The objectives listed below are general; more specific purposes should be planned by the individual teacher for the specific situation. Definite objectives must be planned by the teacher for the specific unit to be taught, according to the needs of the class. Objectives or purposes of any activity should be understood by the students and if this is a new experience for them, time should be taken to explain what gymnastics is and what it can do and accomplish for the girls.

1. To develop a poised, graceful, and physically fit body.

2. To develop coordination, timing, speed, endurance, and agility.

3. To develop a sense of rhythm.

4. To develop creativity through freedom to evolve new and different movements in floor exercise and on the apparatus.

5. To develop courage, initiative, and perseverance.

6. To stimulate interest and enjoyment in gymnastics.

7. To learn to work with a partner and with a group.

8. To learn to organize and produce a gymnastic demonstration or meet.

Probably the best application of objectives is through the development of a sample resource unit. The following are good examples; the teacher should make adjustments to fit her situation.

SIX-WEEK RESOURCE UNIT USING APPARATUS

Activities include: Floor Exercise, Tumbling, Trampoline, Balance Beam, Vaulting, Uneven Parallel Bars.

Unit Objectives

Physical objectives

1. To develop good posture, and a skilled body capable of performing most of the activities of the unit.

2. To develop coordination, agility, speed, strength, and balance.

3. To develop rhythmic skills.

Psychological and social objectives

1. To strive for individual perfection.

2. To learn to work for group unity and cooperation.

3. To develop qualities of courage, self-confidence, perseverance, and originality.

4. To develop a spirit of play and fun in accomplishment.

5. To assume leadership and "followship" roles when needed.

6. To observe safety precautions at all times.

Intellectual objectives

1. To develop knowledge of history, terminology, judging, and general understanding of the activity.

2. To develop appreciation for women's gymnastics.

Class Organization

For the most effective use of class time, divide the group into three or four smaller groups, each with a student leader selected for her skill and leadership ability. Each skill should be demonstrated and analyzed by the teacher, and safety methods of spotting stressed. Generally, it is well to have the group together as a whole for some part of the lesson. This is perhaps best accomplished by having a warm-up for the entire class, or some other skills taught en masse such as tumbling or floor exercise.

Unit Content

WEEK 1

Monday   Orientation to the gymnastic unit. Short history of gymnastics. Explain the purposes, desired outcomes, methods of instruction, evaluation, costume, etc. Discuss safety and perhaps introduce them to the various pieces of equipment. A brief demonstration would be very desirable.

Activity.   Warm-up exercises for developing
See Ch. 2   strength, flexibility, and endurance.

Tuesday   Organize class into squads; assign each squad to a mat or area.

Activity.   Warm-up exercises, particularly for trunk
See Ch. 2   flexion.
Tumbling. Forward and backward rolls
See Ch. 16   and, if possible, dive and straddle rolls.

Wednesday   Warm-up, flexibility and balance exer-
See Ch. 2   cises. Introduce class to balance beam, go over general spotting, demonstrate the skills.
See Ch. 11   Group 1 - At balance beam.
Front support to crotch seat mount.
Swing legs to crouch to standing.
Walk to the end and jump off. Those not on the beam, practice walking in a line on the floor.

Group 2 - Practice rolls and all variations.
See Ch. 16   Group 3 - Learn headstand, handstand.

Thursday   Warm-up, strength exercises for shoul-
See Ch. 2   ders and back; balance exercises. Teach all of the following movements to the entire group on the floor: balance beam—
See Ch. 11   walk forward, crouch turn, walk forward scale, walk backward, crouch turn, plié walk to center of beam and jump dismount.
Group 3 - To balance beam.
See Ch. 16   Groups 1 and 2 - Practice tumbling, the handstand, and headstand.

WEEK 1 cont.
Friday   Warm-up, particularly of feet and legs. Go
See Ch. 14   over jumping and correct landing. Introduce the entire class to vaulting. Teach spotting with each vault. Use Swedish box sequence if possible; otherwise, use the vaulting sequence.
See Ch. 14   a. Jump to squat on horse, stand, jump off.
b. Jump to straddle on horse, jump off.
c. Squat vault.
Group 1 - Practice vaulting.
Group 2 - On balance beam.
Group 3 - Tumbling.

WEEK 2
Monday   Warm-up, including stretching for low back
See Ch. 3   and preparation for splits. Also select some of the dance skills for warm-up. Combine some of the dance skills with the tumbling learned thus far into a floor exercise sequence which all in the class

See Ch. 12   may perform. All of the class (in squad formation) learn cartwheel, snap down from mule kick, round-off.

Tuesday   Warm-up. Review the floor exercise sequences taught Monday.
Group 1 - To tumbling.
Group 2 - To vaulting.
Group 3 - To balance beam.
Review the activities learned thus far, then rotate to the next station.

Wednesday   Introduction to the trampoline.
See Ch. 2, 3   Warm-up. Include feet and leg exercises, jumping, ballet arm positions.
See Ch. 15   Teach regular bounce, break, and seat drop. After a demonstration and analysis, divide the class. Student leaders at balance beam, tumbling, and vaulting. After performing the trampoline, rotate to the other apparatus for practice. Teacher stays with the trampoline.

Thursday   Warm-up, for strength and flexibility of
See Ch. 13   the shoulder girdle. Introduction to uneven parallel bars. Emphasize safety and spotting. Select a mount, one held position, one swinging movement, a dismount.
After the demonstration:
Group 1 - To uneven bars.
Group 2 - To trampoline.
Group 3 - To vaulting.
Review the activities learned thus far, then rotate to the next station.

Friday   Warm-up general exercises.
Practice day. Teacher may select the activities which the students need to practice, or students may elect to work on a given apparatus. (Teacher should note individual progress and perhaps reorganize the groups into ability groups.)

WEEK 3
Monday   Warm-up; select exercises according to
See Ch. 2   class needs.
All of class review headstand with vari-
See Ch. 16   ations, handstand, and roll out of handstand, and cartwheel and round-off.
Practice in groups:
Group 1 - Trampoline ... add four point and front drop.
Group 2 - Uneven parallel bars ... add another held position.
Group 3 - Balance beam ... add a low balance, a high balance, and turn.

Tuesday   Warm-up with general exercises.
See Ch. 14   Group 1 - Vaulting. Learn flank and straddle vaults. Review squat vault.
See Ch. 11   Group 2 - Balance beam. Same as Monday.

See Ch. 15   Group 3 - Trampoline. Work on four point and front.

Wednesday   Warm-up; select exercises according
See Ch. 2   to class needs.
Group 1 - Balance beam. Learn new activities from Tuesday's lesson.
Group 2 - Vaulting. Same as Tuesday.
Group 3 - Unevens. Same as Monday.

WEEK 3 cont.
Thursday   Warm-up; tumbling and floor exercise skills.
Group 1 - Uneven parallel bars ... learn Monday's sequence.
Group 2 - Trampoline ... four point and front drop.
Group 3 - Vaulting ... flank and squat vaults.

Friday   Skills evaluation.
A check list should be prepared, and student leaders at each of the five stations. The girls will rotate from one activity to another as soon as completed.
Station 1 - Cartwheel, headstand.
Station 2 - Flank vault, squat vault.
Station 3 - Trampoline: seat drop, four point, front drop.
Station 4 - Balance beam A sequence of a mount, walk, 1 low balance, 1 high balance, and dismount previously learned.
Station 5 - Uneven parallel bars: 1 mount, 1 held position, 1 swinging movement, 1 dismount.

WEEK 4   As an outcome of the skills test on Friday, regroup the class into ability groups. New skills should be taught in all the activities, rotating the groups from one station to another. The selection of skills to be according to the progress made by the class and which are included in the compulsory routines.
Use new tumbling skills and floor exercise skills for warm-up activities with all the class participating.
Divide the class into four groups, a group on each piece of apparatus.
Analyze and demonstrate a new skill on each apparatus each day, then have the groups rotate to practice.

WEEK 5   The teacher should hand out written compulsory exercises for the class meet to be held the middle of the sixth week. Each student may select either floor exercise or tumbling, and one apparatus for the meet.

Monday   Have all the class go over the floor exercise compulsory sequence, then divide into groups for practice.

Tuesday   Have all the class go over the tumbling trips, then divide into groups for practice on apparatus.

Wednesday   Have all the class go over the balance beam sequence on the floor, then divide into groups for practice on apparatus.

Thursday   Go over the trampoline sequence (a 6-bounce sequence is sufficient for beginners). Go over the required vaults. Practice on apparatus.

Friday   Go over the uneven parallel bar sequence to correct any errors. Have class practice selected activities.

WEEK 6

Monday   Discuss judging and the organization of the class meet. Any remaining time, students may practice on selected activities.

Tuesday   Allow practice for the meet.

Wednesday   Gymnastics meet - Events; balance beam, vaulting, floor exercise.

Friday   Short written test on gymnastics. Student evaluation of the meet and of the unit.

THREE-WEEK RESOURCE UNIT IN MODERN RHYTHMIC GYMNASTICS

This unit may be longer, although a three-week sequence will give sufficient suggestions for a longer unit. The length will depend upon the age of the participants and the individual school situation. On the other hand, it might not be possible to complete all of the suggested material for each day and the teacher will then have to make adjustments accordingly.

Unit Objectives

Physical Objectives

1.   To develop a more flexible, graceful body.

2.   To develop agility and coordination.

3.   To learn the skills of rope jumping, ball handling, wands, clubs, and hoops.

4.   To learn to move rhythmically.

Psychological and Social Objectives

1.   To find enjoyment in the rhythmic use of the body.

2.   To learn to plan activities with others.

3.   To develop creativity through the development of original sequences of skills.

Intellectual Objectives

1.   To gain appreciation for line and movement.

2.   To develop knowledge of history, terminology, and judging.

3.   To learn compulsory routines and be able to execute them for audience participation.

Unit Content

Start with a percussion instrument and use music as soon as possible.

WEEK 1

Monday   Introduction to the unit. Short history of
See Ch. 2   Modern Rhythmic Gymnastics. Explain
See Ch. 5   the content, evaluation, and class organization.*

Tuesday   Warm-up using wand.
See Ch. 9,5   Ball exercises.

Wednesday   Warm-up using wands.
See Ch. 9,5   Teach a group exercise with balls to music.

Thursday   Warm-up — stretching exercises using
See Ch. 7   ropes.
Rope swinging.
Rope jumping.

Friday   Warm-up—stretching exercises using ropes.
See Ch. 7   Review rope jumping.
Practice partner jumping.

WEEK 2

Monday   Warm-up exercises to music, emphasizing
See Ch. 7   dance steps.
Start a group rope jumping routine to music, let class complete it.

---

*   Records with music especially selected for use by students and teachers in junior and senior high school have been directed by the authors. (Rhythmic Gymnastics, Balls and Ropes No. 4010-1; and Rhythmic Gymnastics, Clubs and Hoops, No. 4010-2, Hoctor Dance Records, Inc., Waldwick, New Jersey.) These records describe movements using various hand apparatus. Individual skills are explained and performed to original music. There are also series of movements or short routines with each of the hand apparatus, which demonstrate how the skills may be combined choreographically.

Tuesday   Warm-up exercises—swinging movements
See Ch. 8   using hoops.
                  Hoop exercises.

Thursday   Warm-up exercises to music.
See Ch. 6   Exercises with one club.

Friday   Warm-up exercises to music.
See Ch. 6   Teach a group exercise using one club.
                  Set the routine to music.

WEEK 3
Monday   Warm-up exercises with two clubs.
See Ch. 6   Make a class routine using two clubs and
                  set it to music.

Tuesday   Organize the class into groups according to
                  preference. The groups would work with
                  hoops, clubs, balls, ropes. Each group
                  should prepare an original exercise to
                  show the rest of the class on Friday.
                  Discuss evaluation of routines.

Wednesday   Groups practice their routines.

Thursday   Groups practice their routines.

Friday   Presentation of creative routines. Teacher
                and student evaluation of the routines.

Chapter 18   Gymnastic Demonstrations

Gymnastics lends itself well to demonstrations of all types, whether for a school open house, a school rally, recreation hi jinx, or for a simple class program. Rhythmic gymnastics lends itself well to large group demonstrations, as does tumbling and special arrangement of floor exercise movements. Apparatus, however, is more difficult to use in the demonstration because its use requires more time for performance and fewer persons can perform. Apparatus can certainly be used in the gymnasium for an open house program, and can be used on some stages.

Sample exercises have been given in all of the activities and these could be used or—better yet—the students might create their own exercises.

One of the purposes of a demonstration is to give the students a goal in perfecting their skills, and the opportunity to show their improvement to others. It also allows an opportunity for students to learn to plan together, to organize details, and to work as a harmonious group. Individual duties and responsibilities should be worked out well in advance, with each person knowing what is expected of her. If there are members of the class who are unable to perform, they may assist by being the mistress of ceremonies, music manager, equipment manager, or they may be in charge of advertising and printing the program. If everyone in the group is performing, then these must be extra responsibilities and worked into the practice time, so that the final program runs smoothly.

The following is a suggested outline for a gymnastics program to be given in a school gymnasium.

A TYPICAL HIGH SCHOOL GYMNASTIC PROGRAM

1. Introduction
   Have music playing while the audience assembles. It will make the time pass more pleasantly, and will drown out any distracting noises.

2. Greetings
   The mistress of ceremonies should greet the audience and introduce the activities, explaining briefly what each one is.

3. Entrance
   The students should march into the gymnasium in some attractive manner. If they have had instruction in marching and fancy drills, they may want to use this for an entrance; otherwise, they should walk in by twos or fours.

4. Mass Exercise
   The entire group should perform mass exercises of a floor exercise nature, done to music. It is well to have a large group to open the program and to close it.

5. Tumbling
   Groups should go immediately to the mats for tumbling. The mats might be arranged in a spread U, with students of different abilities on different mats, as indicated below:

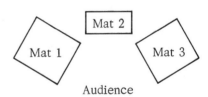

Audience

Follow-the-leader stunts and tumbling may be performed, or a planned movement for each mat, such as:

a. Four students per mat. Two students start at either end of the mat doing a diving forward roll, and a forward roll to the center of the mat.

b. Form a simple pyramid. The bases are on all fours facing each other. The tops place one foot on the bases' hips and one on the shoulders, placing their hands together in a triangle.

c. From the pyramid the tops jump off and the bases do a forward roll, everyone finishing in a straight line at the side of the mats.

Other similar movements may be made across the mat by fours and by groups. Start with simple movements and finish with the advanced students showing a regular tumbling trip across the mats which are placed together.

6. Rope Jumping

   While the mats are being put to one side, have a small group perform a rope jumping exercise to music.

7. Balance Beam and Vaulting

   Use short balance beam routines so that many girls can perform in a brief time. Start with less difficult and end with the more difficult movements. Vaulting may be going on simultaneously. Show a progression of vaulting skills by having the group follow the leader. As the vaults increase in difficulty, the less skilled may drop out.

   Time these two activities so that they are not over 8 to 10 minutes long.

8. Hoops or Clubs

   While the balance beam and horse are being removed and the trampoline and uneven parallel bars are being put into correct position, have a small group perform a hoop routine or club routine to music.

9. Uneven Parallel Bars and Trampoline

   A progression of skills should be shown. Each person should be on the apparatus very briefly, to allow for many performers. Alternate uneven bars and trampoline exercises.

   The time should not be more than 8 to 10 minutes.

10. Ball Exercises

    Have the entire group participate in a ball exercise, with music.

The mistress of ceremonies should keep the show going by using any break to acquaint the audience with gymnastics, or to explain what is being done. The entire program should not be longer than one hour.

The gymnastics program could be the outcome of a regular class or gymnastics unit, or could be the culminating activity of a Girls' Athletic Association gymnastics club. The students should create as much of the program as possible, and committees should work out the details for each number on the program. Every girl should be given an opportunity to participate in the program. Even though she is a beginner, the experience is as valuable to her as to the highly skilled student.

CHECK LIST FOR PLANNING A DEMONSTRATION

The following suggestions will help in planning a gymnastics demonstration:

1. Plan the time, place, and program well in advance.

2. Plan a budget for all expenses.

3. Advertise the demonstration in the school paper, community papers, posters, fliers, invitations, programs. If tickets are to be sold, plan for ticket sellers. This is a good way to make money for school functions.

4. In planning the program, have a mass exercise or group exercise first, such as marching, calisthenics, tumbling, balls, ropes, clubs, etc.

5. Plan to give opportunity for individuals to demonstrate their talent in optional exercises.

6. Have demonstrations on as many pieces of apparatus as possible, to give variety to the program.

7. Include folk dancing to add color to the program.

8. Include a fun event; e.g., clown tumbling or floor exercise.

9. Include boys in the program, perhaps alternating the girls' and the boys' activities.

10. Vary the program by having a group followed by individual events.

11. Have musical background or musical accompaniment for as many numbers as possible.

12. None of the events should be longer than 6 to 8 minutes.

13. The total program should last no longer than 1-1/2 to 2 hours.

14. Plan a rehearsal for everyone two days before the performance.

15. Have a mistress of ceremonies to explain the events and to keep the program going.

16. Plan for the organization of equipment so that little time will be lost in setting it up or removing it.

17. Each of the events should follow smoothly, with no interims.

18. Use a different costume for rhythmic exercises than used for other exercises.

19. Plan suitable decorations, particularly if the performance is on stage.

20. If the performance is on stage, special attention must be paid to safety because of the many hazards on most stages, such as lights, curtains, etc.

21. Evaluate the demonstration, and record the information for planning the next program.

Chapter 19   The Gymnastic Meet

A list of approved events for women in which local, national, and international competition is held are listed below:

a. Individual events
1. Floor exercise
2. Uneven parallel bars
3. Balance beam
4. Side horse vaulting
5. All-around (consisting of 1, 2, 3, and 4)

b. Special events
6. Trampoline
7. Tumbling

The gymnastic meet is the culminating activity in this sport. Guidelines are important if the meet is to be run smoothly. From the novice club meet, or inter-class meet, to state, national, or international meets, the organization and conduct of the event needs special attention. Frequently the school or club conducting a novice meet attempts to pattern the organization after the Olympic competition, rather than making ground rules covering the specific situation. The following suggestions should assist in organizing and running the meet.

COMPULSORY MEET

The compulsory meet has been established in some areas as the best way for the beginning performer and coach to get started. Most secondary schools and many clubs are now using the compulsory routines developed by the Division of Girls' and Women's Sports (DGWS) of the American Association for Health, Physical Education and Recreation, the United States Gymnastic Federation (USGF), and the Amateur Athletic Union (AAU). In the latter meets the international rules are usually adopted.

If compulsory routines are to be used, adequate understanding of the execution of each movement must be established, either through prior clinics or written and visual aids. Judges must also be acquainted with the routines to adequately serve at a compulsory meet.

OPTIONAL MEET

The optional meet does allow for greater creativity of the performers and is much more interesting to spectators and judges alike. However, some classification should be made of the performers, i.e., beginning, intermediate, or advanced. Otherwise, performers in each category may be entered in the same competition, which is unfair for the participants and very difficult to judge fairly.

COMBINATION OF COMPULSORY AND OPTIONAL MEETS

Sometimes it is desirable to combine a compulsory meet followed by an optional meet. For example, a compulsory meet may be held on Friday night, followed by an optional meet on Saturday. Or the two meets may be held at separate times, a week or more apart.

In some areas, the gymnasts who place in the first 10 places in a compulsory meet are invited to participate in the optional meet. This method will eliminate those not ready for competition, and will bring the performers to a more homogeneous grouping.

OPEN VS. LIMITED MEET

An open meet without any restrictions might be the best way to start the sport in some situations; however, restrictions of some kind are usually necessary to avoid a large, unmanageable meet. Sometimes the "open" refers to no geographical limitations. Generally it is important to place some restrictions on the number of participants in a meet, hence the host club or school might designate a specific number of entries from each school or club. It is hoped that meets should progress from an intramural situation to an interschool or interclub, to state, regional, and national. In this way the gymnast may increase her competition as success occurs.

PLANNING THE MEET

The host school or club must be responsible for many details if the meet is to run smoothly. There is much organization necessary prior to the meet, at the meet, and following the meet. Each of these will be discussed separately.

1. The Invitation

   The host school or club should send an invitation to all partipants a month in advance, and preferably earlier. In some areas, meets are planned a year in advance on a league basis. The notice should state the type of meet (compulsory or optional), the time, the place, and any special information pertinent to the meet, as well as the number of entries to be accepted and the entry deadline date. If there are to be any special changes made in an event, this should be stated in the letter. An entry blank should accompany the invitational letter.

2. The Entry Blank

   The following entry blank is based upon the premise that:

   a. The compulsory exercises have been established by the participating schools, or they use the DGWA-USGF Compulsory Routines.

   b. The schools have copies, or copies are sent out by the host school.

3. The Entry Fee

   The entry fee should cover all necessary expenses of the meet. Usual expenses are for ribbons or medals for the winners, trophies if a team award is given, janitorial services, services of a registered nurse during the meet, and incidental expenses such as paper and postage. Whenever possible, it is desirable that an honorarium be given the judges. The size of this fee might be established by agreement of the participating schools or clubs.

4. Letter to Judges

   As soon as the date and type of meet have been established and the entry blanks have been sent out, a letter should be sent to the judges. The letter should allow the person to check her preference of events to be judged. If there are too few judges available, she might be asked to judge two events. Copies of the compulsory routines or pertinent information regarding the optional meet should be included so that the judges are prepared.

   In many communities the judges are paid an honorarium. This amount may be small, sufficient to defray expense, or it may be larger, depending upon the size and type of meet. Monies to cover this expense should be considered in planning the amount of the entry fee.

Entry Blank

Compulsory Gymnastic Meet for High School Girls in
Stanyan School District

April 1, 1970

Entry deadline: March 20, 1970
Mail to: Miss Sue Jones, Instructor
Scott High School
Stanyan, Calif.

School _____

Address _____

Teacher _____

Enclose an entry fee of $1.00 per gymnast with this form.

Contestant	School	Classification			Events						
		Beg.	Low Inter.	High Inter.	Floor Ex.	Uneven Bars	Bal. Beam	Vaulting	All-around	Tumbling	Trampoline
1. Sue Smith	Hamilton		X		X	X	X	X	X		
2. Mary Green	Hamilton	X						X			X
3. Ida Perkins	Hamilton			X						X	X

5. Timing the Events

It is very important in running the meet to consider the time element in planning. Floor exercise usually takes the longest time because of music changes, time of the performance, and judging. A good estimate is about 5 minutes per person. Of the apparatus, the balance beam usually takes the longest.

It is preferable to run all the events simultaneously in a large meet, with the performers rotating to events. This will cut down the length of the meet and will eliminate unnecessary fatigue of both performers and judges. In a smaller meet, it may be possible to run two or three events at a time. This will all depend upon the number of entrants, but the total time of the meet should be limited to three or four hours.

6. Facilities and Equipment

A floor plan should be made showing where each event is to be held. Consideration must be given to natural traffic problems, placing of judges and audience. Adequate free space must be around each piece of apparatus so that there will be no obstructions or possibilities of accident. All apparatus should be in place before the meet starts. If it is necessary to move apparatus during the meet, plans should be made for the placing of it by persons other than the performers, and with the least possible confusion and loss of time.

The equipment should be checked for safety and for regulation height. If possible adjacent equipment for practice should be available. This might be in another gymnasium, and the area should be adequately supervised.

7. Audio-visual Equipment

It is important that a good loud-speaking system be used for the meet. The meet chairman should see that this is working well before the meet and should practice ahead of time if unfamiliar with the equipment.

Several tape recorders should be available so that tapes used for floor exercise may be placed ahead of time. It is well to ask gymnasts to have a leader tape before the actual music to minimize operation. Small individual tape recorders which have little volume should not be used, as usually they cannot be heard over the confusion of a big meet. The host school might suggest the type of tape to be used for the meet.

Several phonographs with speed and sound regulators should be available. All equipment should be supervised by several persons in charge of music. Frequently meets fail to run smoothly because of inadequate sound equipment and poor control of it.

8. Scorers' Table

There should be a scorers' table with at least three persons (preferably teachers, although students may be used) who will handle the last minute changes in contestants, such as scratching names of those originally entered but now unable to perform. Additions should not be made to the original list unless a mistake has been made. Last-minute entries should not be permitted.

The scorers should have the official scoring sheets upon which they will record scores and figure the placing of the contestants. These should be reproduced several days before the actual meet, and the master copies kept for the final report to the partipants. If runners are to be used to bring the scores from each event, it might be well to have one person in charge of the final sheet for each event, so that the averages and placings can be figured almost immediately upon completion of the event.

The placing of the scorers' table should be such that traffic flow will be adequate, and so that the contestants will not be hampering the duties of the scorers.

If team scoring is to be used as well as individual scoring, there are different methods of handling it. The Olympic method has six girls on each team. Every competitor goes all-around, and the five best averages out of the six in each event are counted as the total team score in that event. The team score is the total of the event scores.

In areas where the team size may be limited, four girls per team may compete in each event, and the three best averages are scored for the event. The team score is the total of the event scores for that team. In this method, a girl can compete in as many events as she is ready for. One girl or more from each of the competing teams may go all-around.

9. Flashing of Scores

In the new FIG guidelines, the scores of individual judges are not flashed any more. Only the average is shown to the public. However, in school and club meets, and where the public is to be considered, the flashing of the individual scores may still be more acceptable. The host school or club should establish the number of judges per event, the method of scoring, and how the scores will be flashed and recorded, as international rules may not be applicable for minor meets.

10. Gymnastic Score Sheets

Below are two samples of score sheets. The type of score sheet to be used will depend upon the type of meet and number of judges. The first example is a gymnastic score sheet using three judges. The high and low scores are scratched and the middle score is the final score. This is a quick way of scoring. Another way when using three judges is to average all three scores and divide by three for the final score. The latter method takes longer, though some think it is a fairer method.

Gymnastic Score Sheet (Three Judges)

Event   FLOOR EXERCISE

Classification   BEGINNER

Judges: 1. Mary Goldman
2. Dorothy Parent
3. Virginia Pitman

Gymnastics Meet
Scott High School
April 1, 1970

Scorer: Susan Jones

Contestant	School	Scores			Official	Place
		1	2	3	Score	
1. Florence Richard	Lowell	6.5	7.2	7.1	7.1	1
2. Mae Colline	Hamilton	6.3	7.0	6.8	6.8	3
3. Jan Wallace	Scott	6.6	6.9	7.0	6.9	2

In the international rules, each event is judged by four judges and one superior judge. The score of the head judge does not count unless there is severe disagreement among the four judges. (For details, see chapter on Judging.) In this method the high and low scores are scratched and the middle two scores are averaged, and the average or final score is the only score flashed. The following is a sample of the score sheet using the four judges.

Gymnastic Score Sheet (Four Judges)

Event   BALANCE BEAM

Classification   INTERMEDIATE

Judges: 1. Mary Jones
2. Sylvia Smith
3. Marie Green
4. Edith Johnson

Gymnastic Meet
Solano High School
April 1, 1970

Head judge: Susan Brown

Contestant	School	Scores				Official	Place
		1	2	3	4	Score	
1. Nancy Collins	Solano	6.1	6.4	7.0	6.5	6.45	2
2. Mae Marks	Smith	7.0	6.5	6.8	6.6	6.7	1
3. Janice Jones	Kennedy	5.9	6.0	6.2	6.4	6.1	3

11. Scoring Slips

Prior to the meet slips should be prepared for the use of the judges. These should contain the following information, though the form of the slip or the detail may be minimized.

OPTIONAL EXERCISES

EVENT _____

Name or Number of Contestant _____

Scratch Area	Value	Breakdown	Deductions
	4.0	Value of Difficulty	
	1.5	Originality-Combinations	
	0.5	Value of Composition	
	1.5	Technical Execution	
	1.5	Amplitude	
	1.0	General Impression	
		Interference	
		Falls	
		TOTAL DEDUCTIONS	
		FINAL SCORE	

OPTIONAL VAULTING

Name or Number of Contestant _____

Scratch Area	Phases	Deductions First Attempt Value	Deductions Second Attempt Value
	Preflight		
	On Horse-Repulsion		
	After-Flight		
	General Balance		
	Interference-Spotting		
	TOTAL DEDUCTIONS		
	FINAL SCORE		

COMPULSORY EXERCISES

EVENT _____   _____
                                     Name or Number of
                                     Contestant

Scratch Area	Value	Breakdown	Deductions
	2.0	Exactness of parts	
	0.5	Precision of Direction and Floor Pattern	
	1.5	Exactness of Rhythm	
	1.0 1.0 1.0	Elegance Coordination Lightness	
	1.5 1.5	Amplitude Sureness	
		Falls	
		Interference-Spotting	
		TOTAL DEDUCTIONS	
		FINAL SCORE	

COMPULSORY VAULTING

HIGH INTERMEDIATE—Layout Stoop—10 points   _____
                                                Name or Number of
                                                Contestant

Scratch Area	Value	Phases	Deductions First Attempt	Deductions Second Attempt
	2.0	Pre-flight		
	2.0	Repulsion		
	2.0	After-flight		
	2.0	Stretch of Body		
	0.5	Direction		
	1.5	General Balance		
		Interference-Spotting		
		TOTAL DEDUCTIONS		
		FINAL SCORE		

If the optional vault is not a 10-point vault, it is advisable for the judge to indicate the value of the vault on the score sheet.

These individual slips may be picked up from each judge and given to a head judge, who checks them then sends them to the scorer; or they may be sent directly to the scorer in a small meet. The scorer will place the final score of each judge on the official score sheet and flash the official score.

Drawing for All-around

It is necessary to draw for the first event, then divide the number of performers by the number of apparatus; e.g., 20 performers, each on the four apparatus or four events: 20 divided by four equals five. Then:

The first event would be uneven parallel bars and No. 1 would start.
The second event, balance beam and No. 6 would start.
The third event, free exercise and No. 11 would start.
The fourth event, vaulting and No. 16 would start.

This establishes equality in placement and in judging.

PROCEDURE IN THE MEET

1. The meet should start with a march of all the contestants and should be led by flag bearers. A suitable march should be played. This should be followed by a salute to the flag.

2. The gymnastic chairman or manager of the meet should briefly welcome the audience and participants.

3. A statement regarding the procedures for the meet; i.e., where the warm-up area is; which events are to be called and in what sequence; where each squad or group is to start. This information should also be posted in strategic areas for all to see.

4. The designated first aid station should be pointed out, as well as the scorers' table.

5. All pertinent information regarding the running of the meet should be stated including intermissions.

CHECK LIST FOR THE MEET

The following check list of duties and suggestions are helpful in planning the gymnastics meet:

Duties of gymnastics chairman or manager

1. Assume responsibility for the whole overall organization of the meet.

2. Decide upon the place and time.
3. Set up the apparatus—preferably two sets.
4. Obtain a loud speaker, record player, tape recorder, and piano.
5. Obtain magnesium (gymnastic) chalk.
6. Decide upon the audience space, judges' space; arrangement of chairs, tables, and flash cards.
7. Establish the main scorekeepers' table.
8. Have the dressing rooms ready for performers.
9. Have a place for the performers to sit when not active.
10. Have a nurse and first aid equipment available.

Duties of vice chairman or assistant manager
(If there is no vice chairman, these duties are performed by the chairman.)

1. Organize scorekeepers so that there is one for each event.
2. Have official scorers at the scorekeepers' table.
3. Notify schools, clubs of the time, place, and send an entry blank.
4. Organize the order of the meet; i.e., the sequence of events and contestants.
5. Obtain judges for each event—at least three judges for each event, and preferably five.
6. Explain responsibilities to scorekeepers and judges.

Scorekeeper

1. Call the performers and call the next person; e.g., "Sue Green performing, Mary Smith up."

2. Calculate the results and flash the official score. Send the scores to the main scorers' table so that the all-around can be calculated.

ANNOUNCING THE AWARDS

The results of each event should be announced as soon as possible, reading the results starting with the fifth place. Actual awards may be withheld until the end of the meet if that is desirable.

At the conclusion of the meet, the meet chairman should thank the judges, and should announce the awards. Ribbons or awards should be given to the 1st, 2nd, and 3rd places in each event, and to 1st, 2nd, and 3rd places in the all-around. Team scores may also be announced with awards or trophies for the first three teams. The awards should be prepared while the meet is in progress, so that at the completion of the last event the awards will be ready and only the final all-around and team awards need to be figured. One or more persons should be in charge of the awards and should work directly with the scorers. The giving out of the awards to the contestants should be announced over the loud speaker, and should be done with dignity and good sportsmanship.

POST-MEET DUTIES

Within a reasonable time, the host school should send the written results of the meet to the participating schools or clubs. If the original score sheet has been dittoed or mimeographed and the masters kept, it is not difficult to place the figures alongside the contestant's name, and to make copies of the final scores.

A thank-you letter should be sent to the judges, including the honorarium for the meet.

If there is a rotation of the host school or club each year, it might be valuable for the present chairman to make a list of any problems or suggestions for the future running of the meets. These notes should assist the next chairman so that gradually the caliber of meets will be improved.

The chairman of the meet should see that adequate publicity is given to the local papers and magazines, giving the results and a general statement regarding the meet.

Chapter 20   Judging

The growth of gymnastics depends in part upon the development not only of good teachers and coaches, but upon the development of adequate judges. Whether it is a local, regional, national, or international meet, the efficiency and perfection of the judges will do much to enhance the learning situation. The need is for impartial judges, well-versed in rules and routines, who are able to give unbiased opinions. Whenever the human element is brought into judging, rather than objective means such as a stop watch, there is bound to be some error. The present development of judging rules has been an attempt to eliminate unfairness as much as possible, and to develop unbiased and exact individual judging.

The judge must learn the compulsory exercises and know all the detailed deductions. She should be prepared to make her evaluations rapidly and without being influenced by the reputation of the gymnast. She should not talk to the gymnasts, coaches, nor the public while judging. At all meets she must remain in her seat as long as contestants are on the floor area.

The judge must write her scores legibly and must initial any erasures. Her conduct should be dignified, and she must not smoke in the hall of competition.

The attire for the judges for all important meets should be a grey skirt, while blouse, and blue jacket. For novice and school meets, normal street wear is acceptable.

The list of approved events for women in which district, national, and international competition is held are listed below:

A. Individual events
1. Balance beam
2. Floor exercise
3. Uneven parallel bars
4. Side horse vaulting
5. All-around—consisting of the above four events

B. Special events
6. Trampoline
7. Tumbling

In many local and regional meets, all six events may be included, though there seems to be a greater trend to have meets of only the four individual events and all-around, with separate meets being held for the special events.

Rules for the events are established after each Olympiad by the International Federation of Gymnastics (FIG). The international rules are used by all groups, i.e., the Amateur Athletic Union of the United States (AAU), the United States Gymnastic Federation (USGF), and the Division of Girls' and Women's Sports of the American Association of Health, Physical Education and Recreation (DGWS). Frequently these groups may modify routines and rules to comply with local needs. Such changes are in the interest of assisting performers and teachers alike who are at a lower level of accomplishment. However, for final judgments, the FIG should be the criteria. Therefore, the following information will be based on the current FIG Rules.*

GENERAL RULES OF JUDGING

All judging, whether compulsory or optional exercises, will be evaluated by four women judges and one woman superior or head judge. The four judges give their scores independently, and each score is given to the head judge for verification. It is the duty of the head judge to score all the exercises, but not to communicate her score except in case of a conference, when the difference between the two middle scores is greater than what is allowed. The individual scores are not flashed; instead, the average of the two middle scores is made known to the gymnast and the public.

Except for finals on each apparatus and floor exercise, the four judges shall consult after the first exercise in order to find a starting point. Thereafter, the differences between the highest and the lowest of the four scores shall not be greater than listed below:

0.30 point for scores between 9.50 and 10.0
0.50 point for scores between 8.50 and 9.45
1.00 point in all other cases

---

*   For details consult the FIG Code of Points which is available through the United States Gymnastic Federation, Box 4699, Tucson, Arizona 85717.

In the finals on each apparatus, the entire difference between scores shall not be greater than listed below:

0.20 point for scores between 9.50 and 10.0
0.30 point for scores between 8.50 and 9.45
0.50 point for scores between 7.00 and 8.45
1.00 point for all other cases

In most school or novice meets, five judges are usually not available; for such meets three judges may be acceptable. The scores may then be figured in either of the following ways:

a. All three scores are considered, and averaged.
b. The high and low scores are scratched, and the middle score becomes the official score.

The latter method is common practice in many European meets, and a practice which is certainly acceptable for school meets. Whichever plan is used, it should be fully publicized with the information given to the competitors regarding the meet so that misunderstandings do not occur.

In school meets, where there are only three judges, one of the three should be designated as the head judge, and it should be her duty to make final decision in all cases of disagreement. It is desirable that all judges be DGWS-USGF or AAU rated officials.

Judging the Compulsory Exercises

The compulsory exercises are evaluated from 0 to 10 points by tenths of a point. Only one execution of the compulsory exercise is allowed, except in vaulting, when two attempts are authorized. In order for compulsory exercises to be judged correctly, there must be established a list of general faults with corresponding penalties. The compulsory exercise may be reversed, but only in total, except where indicated otherwise.

The 10 points for the compulsory exercise in floor exercise, uneven bars, and balance beam are divided as follows:

Composition

Exactness and correctness of the parts of the exercise	2.00
Exactness and precision of the direction and floor pattern	0.50
Exactness of the rhythm of the exercise	1.50
Total points	4.00

Execution

Elegance of the gymnast	1.00
Sureness of execution	1.50
Amplitude of the movements	1.50
Coordination of the movements	1.00
Lightness of the jumps and acrobatics	1.00
Total points	6.00

If the gymnast does not execute one difficulty in the exercise, the penalty will be 1.0 point for a superior element, and 0.50 for a medium element. Small changes which do not facilitate the execution are 0.10. (For more details consult the FIG Code of Points.)

The compulsory horse vault is evaluated in a different manner, and the listing of points will show how each part of the vault is rated. Each vault must be evaluated separately, and the best execution becomes the official score. The 10 points for the vault are divided as follows:

Pre-flight	2.00
Push-off	2.00
After-flight	2.00
Extension of the body	2.00
Direction of the vault	0.50
General balance (landing)	1.50

Judging the Optional Exercises

The optional exercises are evaluated from 0 to 10 points by tenths of a point as are the compulsory exercises. The optional exercise should differ from the compulsory exercise, though some elements of the compulsory may be included on condition that the combination is totally different. If the same mount or dismount is used in the optional routine as is required for the compulsory, there is a 0.30 point deduction. When there is team competition, team members must have different mounts and dismounts, or a team penalty is given of 1.00 to 1.50 points.

The elements should not be repeated, as every difficulty repeated in the course of the routine will only be considered as a total of one difficulty. However, it is understood that some element of medium difficulty repeated several times in succession may make it a superior difficulty. For example, two backward walkovers or several different leaps having the same amplitude on the beam are not considered as repetitious, but rather as superior difficulty because of the combination.

The optional exercise should contain four elements of medium difficulty and two elements of superior difficulty. The judging is based on the following:

Composition

Value of the different elements		
4 elements of medium difficulty	0.50 each	2.00
2 elements of superior difficulty	1.00 each	2.00
Total points		4.00
Originality and value of connections and combinations		1.50
The general structure of the composition		0.50
Total points for composition		6.00

Execution

Execution	1.50
Amplitude	1.50
General impression	1.00
Total points for execution	4.00

General faults are bad position of the feet, legs, body, head, etc., and are divided as follows (for details consult the FIG Code of Points):

Small faults   penalty 0.10 to 0.20 point
Medium faults penalty 0.30 to 0.40 point
Serious faults penalty 0.50 point

Specific faults and penalties on the different apparatus will be considered under each event.

BALANCE BEAM

The balance beam exercise is primarily one of balance, showing excellent body control. All turns, jumps and leaps, running steps, steps, and difficulties must be performed with amplitude and with complete control. The complete length of the beam must be used, and the elements of difficulty must be logically distributed throughout the exercise, and should be placed at different parts of the beam rather than entirely at one end. The mount and dismount should be in accord with the difficulty of the complete exercise. Variations in the use of elevation are necessary, and the gymnast should avoid excess lying or sitting positions.

For details of beam measurements, see Chapter 11. The Reuther board is allowed for mounts, and it may be placed on the mat. For safety purposes, it should be removed immediately, unless such removal will interfere with the judging of the event.

Duration of the Exercise

The balance beam exercise is from 1 minute 20 seconds to 1 minute 15 seconds. The timers will start at the moment that the feet of the gymnast leave the floor or board, and will stop at the moment the gymnast's feet touch the floor upon completion of the exercise. A warning signal is given at 1 minute 40 seconds and a second signal at 1 minute 45 seconds. If the exercise is too long, i.e., longer than the 1 minute 45 seconds, a deduction of 0.30 point is made. If the exercise is too short, terminating before the minimum of 1 minute 20 seconds, the deduction is 0.05 point for each second short. In novice and school meets one timer should be sufficient.

Rhythm

Rhythm is very important in the balance beam exercise. The aim is to show variety of rhythm, emphasis on vigorous execution where needed, in contrast with fluency and smoothness at other times. In other words the exercise should be dynamic and continuously moving. If there is monotony throughout the duration of the exercise, a deduction of 0.50 point is made. If there is monotony of rhythm in a given passage, a deduction of 0.20 point is taken. Thus monotony of rhythm must be avoided, and the sustained positions should be held briefly.

Execution

As has been emphasized, the balance beam is a continuous exercise, with a maximum of three stops allowed. If there are more than three stops, without reason, a deduction of 0.20 point is taken for each stop.

In both the compulsory and optional exercise, an additional run or take-off is allowed providing the gymnast does not touch the beam. If the gymnast does touch the beam, but does not mount, a penalty of 0.50 point is noted.

A fall from the beam is penalized 0.50 point, and if the gymnast does not remount the beam within 10 seconds, the exercise is considered terminated. Other penalties found in execution are: support of the hands on the beam to maintain balance, a penalty of 0.50 point; touching the hands on the beam for purposes of maintaining balance, a penalty of 0.30 point; unnecessary movements of the trunk in order to maintain balance, a penalty of 0.30 point. If one leg is used on the side of the beam for support, a penalty of 0.40 is deducted. Unnecessary movement of the arms or legs to maintain balance is penalized 0.20 point every time it occurs. All jumps or leaps must have amplitude or a deduction of 0.20 point is made; and all turns must be with sureness, or 0.20 point deduction is made.

Table of Difficulties

At the end of Chapter 11, there are combinations and exercise routines for the various levels for the balance beam. For national and international competition, medium and superior difficulties are specifically listed in the FIG Code of Points. A brief summary of these is mentioned below. The advanced gymnast should refer to the rule book for ratings.

Many of the mounts are similar in the first movement, but it is the combination of movements which follows that makes it more difficult, and hence rated as a superior mount. For instance a jump on the end of the beam on one foot, the other leg free or in moderate arabesque, would be a medium difficult; whereas a jump on the end of the beam on one foot, the other leg in scale position above the horizontal, would be a superior mount.

In turns the medium difficulty calls for a complete turn on one leg. The leaps and jumps of superior difficulty are done with a half turn, i.e., stag leap with half-turn. In the area of limbers, a forward or backward walkover is of medium difficulty, whereas a one-arm walkover, or a series of walkovers, is of superior value.

All handsprings, aerials, and flip-flops are superior moves. All rolls are of medium difficulty except free forward roll without use of hands. Likewise, handstand forward roll is medium difficulty.

All aerial somersaults, flip-flops, aerial cartwheels are superior difficulty dismounts; whereas walkover, cartwheels, handsprings, and tinsica dismounts are of medium difficulty.

In balance beam there are innumerable combinations, and it is up to the gymnast to use creativity and uniqueness in combining moves to make them interesting and of superior quality.

FLOOR EXERCISE

The floor exercise must be original. There are innumerable combinations and the gymnast must be creative in combining dance and tumbling movements. She must perform her routine with liveliness, grace, elegance, change of space and expression.

The area for floor exercise is 12 meters by 12 meters (39-1/3 square feet). The gymnast must perform within this area, and should she go outside of it, there is a penalty of 0.10 point for each occurrence. In national and international meets, line judges will raise a flag when the feet of the gymnast are completely outside of the lines. In less technical meets, the head judge will penalize for such errors without having a specific line judge. Such a penalty is deducted from the total score.

Duration of the Exercise

The length of the floor exercise is 1 minute to 1 minute 30 seconds. The clock starts as soon as the gymnast begins a movement of the exercise, and stops with her final pose. A warning signal is given at 1 minute 25 seconds, and a second signal at 1 minute 30 seconds. If the exercise is not finished by the second signal, 0.30 point is deducted. If the exercise is too short, i.e., less than 1 minute in length, 0.05 point is deducted for each second.

Musical Accompaniment

Only one instrument is authorized for floor exercise. This is usually a piano, though any other instrument may be used. A background music is rejected, because the nature of the music should harmonize with the exercise performed. Ideally the music is composed to fit the movement, so that the musical score will enhance the dynamic presentation. The quality of the music should blend with the type of movement and the personality of the gymnast.

If the musical accompaniment is not the regulation one instrument, there is a penalty of 1.00 point. If there is no harmony between the end of the exercise and the music, there is a penalty of 0.50 point. If the music is not adapted to the exercise, a penalty of 0.50 point is deducted. If, in starting the exercise the gymnast fails to begin at the correct time for personal reasons, there is a penalty of 1.00 point.

Execution

There are certain points the gymnast must consider in the execution of the floor exercise. These are: proper rhythm, continuity, sureness, and elegance of execution. The rhythm of the exercise is important because variations of rhythm allow for better execution, and it makes for a more pleasing composition. There is a deduction of 0.20 point for each time during the exercise there is a break in rhythm.

If at the beginning of the exercise the gymnast stops and begins again, she is penalized 1.00 point, unless the incident was due to a technical nature which the jury will evaluate. Frequently in school meets where phonograph recordings or tapes are used, there is a technical problem encountered. If this is not due to the fault of the gymnast, the head judge may determine whether there is a penalty or not.

Should the gymnast forget a part, or repeat a part because it was poorly executed, there is a penalty for repetition of a missed element of 0.50 point. Should the gymnast fall on the floor, which may occur during the execution of some difficult tumbling stunt, the gymnast will be penalized 1.00 point.

At no time may the performer have aid from a coach while performing in the floor exercise area, and it is forbidden for the coach to enter the floor area. If the coach enters the floor area, there is a penalty of 0.50 point; and if the coach signals or speaks to the gymnast, there is a penalty of 0.30 or 0.50 respectively.

Table of Difficulties

The various difficulties will be discussed in general. For specific details the gymnast should review the FIG rule book.

In Chapter 12, the authors have listed skills for beginning, intermediate, and advanced level. The following statements will help in planning for skills which are considered of medium or superior difficulty by FIG. These will be divided into various types of movements as follows:

Jumps and pivots

All leaps and jumps, pivots, or pirouettes with more than one turn and ending in a balance, a walkover, or another element are considered superior difficulty. Two or three leaps with the same amplitude, or leaps with a half turn or pirouette turn into a split, etc., are considered medium difficulty.

Rolls

All type of rolls and combinations with rolls are considered medium difficulty.

Cartwheels, walkovers, tinsicas, and handsprings

All cartwheels, walkovers, tinsicas, and handsprings, whether forward or backward, one or two arm, or whether they are continued with other stunts such as a split, are considered medium difficulty.

Flip-flops

A series of flip-flops on one or two legs; a flip-flop to handstand, or a flip-flop to kip are considered superior difficulty. But round-off one flip-flop is considered as medium difficulty.

Aerials

All aerials are considered as superior difficulty, i.e., aerial cartwheel, aerial walkover, and butterfly.

Somersaults

All somersaults whether forward or backward, tucked or layout, are considered of superior difficulty.

UNEVEN PARALLEL BARS

The uneven parallel bar exercise is primarily swinging, kipping, and circling movements, with releases and regrasps. It is the combination of two movements which may increase the technical value, and the judge must be able to recognize these combinations. There should be a balance of movement from one bar to the other, with elements of suspension and support being used evenly on both bars. No hesitations are allowed, but two preparations for difficult movements including the dismount are permitted. Stops in excess of this are penalized 0.20 each time. The required four elements of medium and two elements of superior difficulty should be dispersed throughout the exercise. The four judges must sit at all four corners of the apparatus so that all possible views of the performance are visible.

Duration of the Exercise

The uneven bar exercise is composed of 12 to 18 movements. This event is not timed. However, should the gymnast fall, she has 30 seconds to remount, and she is penalized 1.00 point for the fall.

Execution

In general, emphasis should be placed on good form in performance rather than only on difficulty. The gymnast should not perform beyond her ability. It is not advisable to have a greater number of difficulties than the prescribed amount because they may necessitate unnecessary preparation breaks in the sequence. The exercise must be a complete whole, with mount and dismount being in harmony with the rest of the exercise.

A Reuther board may be placed on the mat for use in the mount, and a supplementary run is authorized provided the gymnast does not touch the apparatus or pass underneath it. The board may be touched. However, if the bars are touched or the run is underneath the bars, there is a penalty of 1.00 point.

For releasing one hand without supplementary support 0.50 point is deducted, but for releasing one hand with supplementary support, such as a foot on or against the bar or the floor, the penalty is 1.00 point since it is considered as a fall. The movements must be connected with elegance and without additional swing. Extra swings are penalized by 0.50 point.

The dismount must come from a manual support or body support on the bar. There is a 0.5 deduction for the execution of a somersault from a standing position. For a slightly unstable landing in the dismount the penalty is 0.10 point; while for taking steps to gain balance the penalty is 0.50 point. For touching the mat on the dismount the penalty is 0.50 point; while for placing weight on hands or falling on the knees the penalty is 1.00 point.

Though safety of the gymnast is of utmost importance, there are certain rules which the coach must obey, or the gymnast will receive deductions for her execution. If the coach obstructs the view of the judges or steps between the bars, there is a penalty of 0.50 point. If he should touch the rail the penalty is 0.20 point. If the coach speaks to the gymnast the penalty is 0.50, and if he gives signals the penalty is 0.30 point. If the coach aids or touches the gymnast during the exercise or the dismount, the penalty is 1.50 points.

Table of Difficulties

For complete classification of movements, the FIG rule book should be consulted. A review of the combinations and routines found at the end of Chapter 13 will also assist the beginner and intermediate gymnast. The following few examples are given only as guidelines.

Mounts

Medium difficulties: Front hip circle; squat or straddle jump over low bar to catch high bar; glide kip to catch high bar or other combinations.

Superior difficulties: Jump with full twist to front hip circle mount; rear kip, etc.

Movements

Medium difficulties: Glide kip catch high bar; flying hip circle; eagle catch; seat circles; sole circles, etc.

Superior difficulties: Back uprise; front hip circle cast to handstand; stoop circle backward cast pike or straddle catch high bar; front somersault from low bar to catch high bar, etc.

Dismounts

Medium difficulties: Straddle cut-off from high bar; underswing over low bar; Hecht from low bar, etc.

Superior difficulties: Straddle cut-off from high bar over low bar; underswing over low bar with full twist; Hecht from high bar with half or full twist, etc.

VAULTING

The judge should be familiar with the table of values of each vault, and reference should be made to Chapter 14 for values and details of execution.

In both compulsory and optional vaulting, the gymnast has two executions, with the best execution being counted. The gymnast is allowed one supplementary run as long as the apparatus is not touched. If the horse is touched, the attempt shall be considered as completed. The gymnast must announce the vault to be performed and the judges will judge the performance in accordance with the announced vault. If the vault is interrupted by the feet supporting or by sitting on the horse, the vault will be void.

Execution

Run and take-off

As has been mentioned above, one supplementary run is allowed for the vault, providing the horse is not touched. Should the horse be touched on such a supplementary run, the vault is considered completed, and the gymnast should have only one more trial. There is no deduction for a poor run and take-off, but it will manifest in the preflight, the position over the horse, and the after-flight, where penalties will be noted.

Pre-flight

This is the time from the two-foot take-off to the placing of the hands on the horse. Some of the penalties are as follows: For insufficient flight between the board and the horse, up to 1.50 points. If the body is bent during the flight, up to 0.50 is deducted. If the body is bent before the inverted position, or force is used to establish the support, up to 1.00 point is deducted.

Arrival on the horse

If the arms are completely flexed as the hands are placed on the horse, the penalty is 2.50 points.

If there is a stop in the inverted position, there is a penalty of 0.30 to 0.50 point; and if the gymnast fails to pass through the vertical position, there is a penalty of 1.00 point.

If the body is beneath the horizontal on layout vaults at the moment of hand contact on the horse, the penalty is 3.50 points, and if the body is just at the horizontal, the reduction is 2.00 points. If the body is just slightly above the horizontal, the penalty is up to 0.50 point.

After-flight

This is the time from the push-off of the hands while the body is in space until the landing. Should the hands be released too late, the penalty is 0.20 to 0.50 point, and if there is alternate repulsion of the hands, i.e., one pushes off then the other, there is a penalty of up to 0.30 point. If there is insufficient push-off or repulsion for the after-flight, the penalty is from 1.00 to 2.00 points. If the direction of the vault is poor, a penalty up to 0.50 is taken. If the arms, shoulders, and trunk are not in the same line, a penalty of 0.50 is taken.

For failure to get a complete body stretch in squat, stoop, or straddle vaults in the after-flight, the penalty is 2.00 points. Should the horse be slightly touched in these vaults with the feet, there is a penalty of up to 0.50 point.

If there is a turn required in the after-flight, this must be performed with the proper timing and if it lacks continuity, or the turn is completed after the feet are placed on the ground, the penalty is 0.50 point.

Landing

The manner in which the gymnast lands after the flight is of great significance because it shows the extent of body control. The penalties vary according to how much control is lost during this part of the vault. Arriving on the floor heavily and uncertainly or out of balance, is penalized up to 0.30 point. Touching the floor with the hands to regain control is penalized 0.50 point, while a supporting of the hands on the floor is 1.00 point penalty. For a fall on the knees 1.50 points and a fall on the pelvis or hips 2.00 points are deducted. A fall out of balance in which the gymnast's body falls against the horse is penalized 1.50 points.

In competition, the assistance of a coach is heavily penalized as noted below. The spotter may crouch to one side, off the mats, and just be ready should assistance be needed. A student should not be expected to perform a more difficult vault than has been practiced; however, during the excitement of competition mistakes may happen. The coach should be ready, but should not touch the performer except in cases of emergency.

If the coach stands between the board and the horse, a penalty of 1.00 point is made, and if the coach assists the gymnast to perform the vault, the vault is void. If the coach assists the gymnast on landing, the penalty is 2.00 points.

Note: For detailed information of the Olympic events, namely: balance beam, floor exercise, uneven parallel bars, and vaulting, consult the FIG Code of Points for women.

For interpretation of the FIG Code of Points, see C. Bowers, K. Kjeldsen, A. Schmid, and J. Uphues, Judging and Coaching Women's Gymnastics, National Press, Palo Alto, Calif., 1971.

TRAMPOLINE

Trampoline is a special event, and National and World Championships for women have been held since 1964. Much of the women's competition is based on the men's program. Scoring here is, as in all other events, from 0 to 10.0 points.

Duration of the Exercise

For beginners and Junior Olympic competition of under 12 years of age, the compulsory routine shall not exceed 8 bounces. For all others the compulsory routine consists of 10 bounces. The performer may take preliminary bounces to gain height, which are not counted by the counter. The counter shall count aloud the number of landings so that she can be heard by the judges and contestant. She starts counting with each contact of the bed after the first skill or movement of the routine is made. Her count will be from 1 to 10 and OUT. The compulsory routine may be repeated if the competitor indicates her desire to repeat before the scores of the judges are shown. The compulsory exercise may be performed inversely either entirely or in parts.

The optional routine for beginners and under 12 years of age shall be from 8 to 10 bounces. For all others the voluntary routine consists of 10 to 12 bounces. These are likewise counted by the counter who starts at the first skill, counting aloud 1 to 12 and OUT. The voluntary routine may not be repeated.

Position of the Judges

The judges shall be 5 meters (16 feet 4 inches) from the trampoline and to the side so that all judges see the performance from the same angle. If possible, the judges should be in elevated position for better viewing.

Execution – Compulsory Routines

The judging of the compulsory routine shall be based on form, execution, and control. If there is a lack of height, arrangement, and rhythm in the execution, 0.1 to 1.0 point is deducted. If the competitor falls off the trampoline, touches the frame, or is supported by a spotter, her routine terminates and she shall score on the basis of the number of bounces completed at that time. This is determined by the referee. As soon as the counter says OUT, the competitor must stand upright on the trampoline.

The routine must begin a reasonable distance from either end and sides of the trampoline. The performer must wait for signal from the referee to start, and may take as many preliminary bounces as she desires. However, any skills performed after the OUT is called will be penalized from 0.1 to 0.3 point and this is in addition to the prescribed penalty of 0.1 to 1.0 point for the routine as a whole. A lack of form may cause a deduction of 0.1 to 0.5 point for each occurrence.

Execution – Optional Routines

Beginners

The difficulty ratings of the A, B, C, parts as defined in the general rules are disregarded for beginners and AAU competitors below 12 years of age. Instead the following rules for AAU Junior Olympic Trampoline are followed:*

1. Lack of form—deduct not more than 25 percent
2. Lack of execution (height, arrangement, etc.)—deduct not more than 25 percent
3. Lack of control—deduct not more than 25 percent
4. Lack of difficulty—deduct not more than 25 percent

Intermediate and advanced

The voluntary or optional routine shall consist of 10 to 12 movements and must include three to four difficult or "B" rated skills, and at least one superior or "C" combination. The routine should contain both front and back rotating skills with at least two front rotating skills.

Deductions are made as follows:

a. For each part of the routine:
   1. Lack of form—each count deduct 0.1 to 0.5
   2. Lack of difficulty:
      a) Lack of "B" skill or "B" combination, deduct 0.3
      b) Lack of front skills, deduct 0.3
      c) No substitutions will be allowed for prescribed parts except when substitution is of greater difficulty
      d) Any skill performed beyond the 12th bounce will be considered poor execution and penalized 0.1 to 0.3 point per skill. The deduction shall be in addition to the prescribed penalty of 0.1 to 1.0 point for the routine as a whole.
      e) Skills and combinations of higher difficulty may be used in preference to those of lower difficulty with no penalty.
      f) Lack of "C" combination, deduct 0.6 point.

b. For the routine as a whole:
   1. Lack of execution (height, arrangement, rhythm) deduct 0.1 to 1.0 point
   2. Lack of control, deduct 0.1 to 0.5 point

* Information courtesy Mr. Jeff Hennessy, AAU Technical Committee of Federation of International Trampolining, University of Southwestern Louisiana, Lafayette, La. 70501

Table of Difficulties

The following general remarks will give the reader some understanding of superior moves (''C''). Two or more somersaults in succession, either front or back; two or more somersaults with a half twist, either front or back; one 3/4 or more somersault with a full twist backward; a 3/4 to 1-1/2 somersaults with two 1/2 or more twists either front or back; or 1/2 somersault with two half or more twists front or back; a 1/4 somersault with three or more twists front or back; a somersault with three or more twists, front or back.

Samples of ''B'' or ''Difficult'' moves are a 3/4 somersault front or back; two 1/4 somersaults with half twist front or back; a 1-1/2 somersault with one or two twists.

The Intermediate and below stunts or ''A'' stunts are a front or back somersault or barani.

If combinations of skills are made the following difficulty rating is used:

C and C — C

C and B — B

C and A — B

B and B — C

B and A — B

A and A — A

TUMBLING

Tumbling is a special event, and rules for competition are established by the AAU, USGF, and DGWS. The mat is 60 feet long 5 feet wide, and from two to four inches thick. When space permits, additional mats may be used or additional space for preliminary runs.

In compulsory tumbling, each of the trips is allocated a point value, the total of all trips being 10.0 points. In novice and school competition, there is usually a forward trip, a backward trip, and a combination trip, with each of the three trips being given a point designation. If there are four trips, the point value must be split accordingly.

In optional tumbling, the routines must be judged by what is performed on each trip; and each trip must be figured separately and then totaled.

The judges should be in position to see the complete tumbling trip and therefore should be on the sides of the mats a sufficient distance away so that they may have good perspective of the complete trip.

Duration of the Exercise

The maximum of four trips on the mat must be performed in a total of two minutes time, including rests between lengths tumbled. If only three trips are performed, they must be also completed within the two minutes time.

Execution

Only straight tumbling routines should be performed on the mat, and if the contestant touches the floor on either side of the mats, it shall be considered poor form and deductions will be made for form. However, if the contestant wishes to perform the entire exercise without mats on the floor she may elect to do so without penalty.

There is no penalty for a preliminary run either on or off the mats, and the contestant should not be penalized for tumbling off the end of the mats. However, in the later case, deductions may be made for poor form or poor use of the mats if that is the impression given the judges.

Aerial stunts and twisting somersaults are of superior difficulty. Also a series of stunts, such as a series of flip-flops, is considered superior.

The extension of the legs, ankles, and trunk will be considered in the execution, with minor bending of ankles being a 0.10 deduction, and medium bending of ankles or legs 0.20 deduction; whereas a bending of the trunk where not desired is a more severe penalty, and 0.50 will be deducted.

Lightness in landing is of importance, and undue heaviness in landing will be penalized by a 0.20 deduction.

A definite break within the tumbling trip will be penalized from 0.50 to 1.00 point.

Compulsory routines

Inasmuch as compulsory routines have a point value for each trip, the performer must learn to start and stop in good form. The gymnast must learn to judge rest time between each trip so that she may conserve energy for the total two minutes of performance. Connections between the various stunts must be made with ease and in good form. The sequences must be so well learned that there can be no forgetting under the stress of competition.

Optional routines

The gymnast must learn how to place the superior stunts in sequence so that execution is enhanced and energy is conserved. The trips should show variety. Each trip should contain at least one difficult stunt.

Bibliography

Ainsworth, Dorothy S.: The History of Physical Education in College for Women. New York: A. S. Barnes and Co., Inc. 1930

Allison, June: Advanced Gymnastics for Women. London: Stanley Paul and Co., Ltd. 1963

Ambrose, Kay: The Ballet Lover's Pocket Book. New York: Alfred A. Knopf, Inc. 1949

Beaton, Cecil: Ballet. New York: Doubleday and Co., Inc. 1951

Beliakov, Vladimir: Soviet Gymnasts. Translated by David Skvirsky. Foreign Languages Publishing House, 21, Zubovsky Boulevard, Moscow, USSR

Bowers, Carolyn, Kitty Kjeldsen, Andrea Schmid, and Jackie Uphues: Judging and Coaching Women's Gymnastics. Palo Alto, California: The National Press. 1971

Bukh, Niels: Fundamental Gymnastics. New York: E.P. Dutton and Co. 1928

Burns, Ted, and Tyler Micoleau: Tumbling Techniques Illustrated. New York: The Ronald Press. 1957

Carlquist, Maja: Rhythmical Gymnastics. London: Methuen and Co., Ltd. 1955

Cooper, Phyllis: Feminine Gymnastics. Minneapolis, Minn.: Burgess Publishing Co. 1968

Cotteral, Bonnie, and Donnie Cotteral: The Teaching of Stunts and Tumbling. New York: A. S. Barnes and Co., Inc. 1936

Draper, Nancy, and Margaret Atkinson: Ballet for Beginners. New York: Alfred A. Knopf, Inc. 1951

Drury, Blanche: Muscles in Action. Palo Alto, California: The National Press. 1961

Drury, Blanche: Posture and Figure Control Through Physical Education. Palo Alto, California: The National Press. 1961

Fisher, Hugh: The Ballet. New York: Crowell Co. 1953

Frederick, A. Bruce: Women's Gymnastics. Dubuque, Iowa: Wm. C. Brown Co. 1966

Gabriel, John: Ballet School. New York: Pitman Publishing Corp. 1951

Gray, Felicity: Ballet for Beginners. New York: Phoenix House. 1952

Griswold, Laurence: Trampoline Tumbling. New York: A. S. Barnes and Co. 1962

Harris, Rich: Physical Education and Rebound Tumbling. Cedar Rapids, Iowa: Barnes Publishing Co., Inc. 1961

Hayes, Elizabeth: Dance Composition and Production for High School and College. New York: A. S. Barnes and Co., Inc. 1955

Hennessy, Jeff T.: The Trampoline as I See It. Lafayette, La.: International Publishing Co. 1969

Henry, William M.: An Approved History of the Olympic Games. New York: G. P. Putnam's Sons. 1948

Holström, Agne: Swedish Gymnastics Today from Ling to the Lingiad. Stockholm: Sohlmans Förlag. English Version distributed by: Sportshelf, P.O. Box 634, New Rochelle, New York

Horne, Virginia Lee: Stunts and Tumbling for Girls. New York: The Ronald Press. 1943

Keeney, Chuck: Trampolining Illustrated. New York: The Ronald Press. 1961

Keleti, Ágnes, and Éva Kovacs: Muveszitorna (Artistic Gymnastics). Sport Book Publisher, Budapest, Hungary. 1963 (Written in Hungarian.)

Kerezsi, Endre, and Dr. Lájós Sántha, István Sárkany, Gizella Horváth, Ágnes Keleti: Torna Alapismeretek (Basic Gymnastics). Sport Book Publisher, Budapest, Hungary. 1952. (Written in Hungarian.)

Kieran, John, and Arthur Daley: The Story of the Olympic Games, 776 B.C. to 1962 A.D. New York: J. P. Lippincott Co. 1961

Kirstein, Lincoln: Ballet Alphabet. New York: Kamin Publishing Co. 1939

Kirstein, Lincoln, and M. Stewart and C. Dyer: The Classic Ballet. New York: Alfred A. Knopf, Inc. 1962

La Due, Frank: This Is Trampolining. Cedar Rapids, Iowa: Nissen Trampoline Co. 1960

Lawson, Joan: Classical Ballet. London: Adam and Charles Black. 1960

Legat, Nadine: Ballet Education. London: Geoffrey Bles. 1947

Leonard, Fred E.: A Guide to the History of Physical Education. Philadelphia: Lea and Febiger. 1947

Linert, Walter: The Modern Girl Gymnast on the Uneven Parallel Bars. Indianapolis, Indiana: The Author, 233 North Parkview Ave. 1957

Loken, Newton, and Robert J. Willoughby: Complete Book of Gymnastics. Englewood Cliffs, N.J.: Prentice-Hall, Inc. 1959

McClow, Lloyd: Tumbling Illustrated. New York: The Ronald Press Co. 1931

McClow, Lloyd: Play Gymnastics. New York: F. S. Crofts and Co. 1940

Mezó, Dr. Ferenc: The Modern Olympic Games. Pannonia Press, Budapest, Hungary. 1956. Distributed by: Collet's Holdings, Ltd., London

Mosscrop, Alfreda, and Helen Hardenberg, Grace Rockwood: Apparatus Activities for Girls. Minneapolis: Burgess Co. 1952

Munrow, A. D.: Pure and Applied Gymnastics. London: Edward Arnold Pub., Ltd. 1955

Murray, Ruth L.: Dance in Elementary Education. New York: Harper Bros. 1953

Nelms, Henning: A Primer of Stagecraft. New York: Dramatists Play Service, Inc. 1941

Prchal, Mildred: Artistic Gymnastics—Floor Exercise. Berwyn, Ill.: Danny Hoctor Records, Waldwick, N.J. 1964

Ruff, Wesley K.: Gymnastics, Beginner to Competitor. Dubuque, Iowa: William C. Brown. 1959

Ryser, Otto: A Teacher's Manual for Tumbling and Apparatus Stunts. Dubuque, Iowa: William C. Brown. 1951

Skarstrom, William: Gymnastic Teaching. Springfield, Mass.: American Physical Education Association Distributing Agent. 1921

Sjursen, Helen Schiafano: Uneven Bars for Physical Educators and Competitors. Hoctor Dance Records, Waldwick, N.J. 1967

Szypula, George: Tumbling and Balancing for All. Dubuque, Iowa: William C. Brown Co. 1957

Takemoto, Masao: Illustrated Women's Gymnastics. Tokyo, Japan: Ban-Yu Shuppan Co., Ltd. 1958 (Written in Japanese.) Distributor: Frank Endo, 12200 South Berendo Avenue, Los Angeles, California 90044

V-Five Association of America: Gymnastics and Tumbling. Annapolis, Md.: U.S. Naval Institute. 1950

Van Dalen, Deobold, Elmer D. Mitchell, and Bruce Bennett: A World History of Physical Education. New York: Prentice-Hall, Inc. 1955.

West, Wilbur: The Gymnast's Manual. Englewood Cliffs, N.J. : Prentice-Hall, Inc. 1955

Wilson, George B.: A Dictionary of Ballet. Baltimore: Penguin Books. 1957

Yeager, Patrick: A Teacher's Guide for Women's Gymnastics. Statesboro, Georgia: The Author, Southern College, Athletic Dept. 1962

Pamphlets

Amateur Athletic Union of the United States: Gymnastics–Official Rules Guide. Amateur Athletic Union, 233 Broadway, New York. 1963-64

Division of Girls' and Women's Sports: Gymnastic Guide. American Association for Health, Physical Education and Recreation, 1201 - 16th Street, N.W., Washington D.C. 20036

FIG Code of Points—Women's Technical Executive Commission of the FIG, 1968

USGF Interpretations of the International Rules for Women's Gymnastics. USGF, P.O. Box 4699, Tucson, Arizona 85717. 1969

Periodicals

The Modern Gymnast. Sundby Publications, P.O. Box 611, Santa Monica, California 90406

Mademoiselle Gymnast. Sundby Publications, P.O. Box 611, Santa Monica, California 90406

Audio-Visual Aids

Hoctor Dance Records, Inc., Waldwick, New Jersey 07463
    HLP 4010—Volume I, Balls and Ropes
                Volume II, Clubs and Hoops. Blanche Drury and Andrea Bodo Schmid. Adelia Spangenberg Arnette, pianist

    HLP 4011—Floor Exercise for Women. Blanche Drury and Andrea Bodo Schmid. Adelia Spangenberg Arnette, pianist

Index